THE

G-20
SUMMIT
AT
FIVE

THE

G-20
SUMMIT
AT
FIVE

TIME FOR STRATEGIC LEADERSHIP

KEMAL DERVIŞ and PETER DRYSDALE
editors

BROOKINGS INSTITUTION PRESS
Washington, D.C.

Library of Congress Cataloging-in-Publication data
The G-20 summit at five : time for strategic leadership / Kemal Derviş and Peter Drysdale, editors.
      pages   cm
   Includes bibliographical references and index.
   ISBN 978-0-8157-2591-6 (pbk. : alk. paper)
1. Group of Twenty. 2. International economic relations. 3. Economic policy—International cooperation.
4. Group of Twenty countries—Foreign economic relations. 5. Group of Twenty countries—Economic
policy. I. Derviş, Kemal. II. Drysdale, Peter.
 HF1359.G274 2014
   337.1—dc23   2014016991

9 8 7 6 5 4 3 2 1

Printed on acid-free paper

Typeset in Minion

Composition by R. Lynn Rivenbark
Macon, Georgia

Contents

Acknowledgments

The editors would like to gratefully acknowledge the Australian Government's Department of Foreign Affairs and Trade for its support. We thank the authors for their dedication and excellence in research, as well as their collaboration in finalizing the book. We also thank all contributors to the Think Tank 20 series publications (Brookings Institution)—coinciding with G-20 ministerial summits since 2010. Many of the ideas that they contributed over the years have been useful in putting this collection together.

We are especially grateful to Shiro Armstrong, Shane Johnson, Sebastien Willis, and the EABER team of the Crawford School of Public Policy at the Australian National University for their huge input into the organization and success of this project and to Gordon de Brouwer, Heather Smith, and Australian G-20 officials for their advice and comments. We are also grateful to those who have provided invaluable comments in the editing process, including Colin Bradford, Joshua Meltzer, Soumya Chattopadhyay, and Brookings Press staff.

We also thank the participants of the Brookings-ANU workshop in Washington, D.C., on June 10, 2013, and the Brookings-ANU Roundtable and Public Forum in Canberra, on November 14–15, 2013. These events took place with the excellent organizational support of Annick Ducher and Andrea Holcombe in Washington and Shane Johnson, Patrick Williams, and the EABER team in Canberra.

Brookings recognizes that the value it provides is in its absolute commitment to quality, independence, and impact. Activities supported by its donors reflect this commitment, and the analysis and recommendations here are not determined or influenced by any donation. Interpretations or conclusions in all Brookings publications should be understood to be solely those of the authors.

PART I

Principles of Global Governance

KEMAL DERVIŞ AND PETER DRYSDALE

1

G-20 Summit at Five:
Time for Strategic Leadership

The leaders' level G-20 was born at a time of crisis and panic.[1] In early October 2008, when the United States issued the invitation to the G-20 heads of state or government to assemble in Washington, D.C., on November 15, the world was facing the danger of a total collapse of the financial sector in the United States. With global trade and financial links having grown over the decades, particularly after the fall of the Berlin Wall in 1989, a financial collapse in the largest economy—and the financial center—of the world would have brought down the entire world economy.

The United States had to—and did—act to arrest the collapse, through unprecedented intervention in its own banking and insurance sectors. This was quickly followed by equally unprecedented fiscal and monetary expansion and even intervention in the industrial sector, with the government rescuing General Motors at the end of March 2009. These actions contained the crisis but did not prevent a drift toward worldwide recession. It was clear that the financial-sector virus was spreading and that expectations were shattered worldwide. The world was in danger of a steep decline in investment and consumer demand, mass unemployment, and beggar-thy-neighbor protectionist trade policies, triggering a deflationary vicious cycle that the world

We are very grateful to Colin Bradford for his substantial comments on drafts of this chapter and to Homi Kharas, Edith Joachimpillai, and Annick Ducher from Brookings; to Shiro Armstrong, Sebastien Willis, and Shane Johnson from Australian National University; and to Australian G-20 officials for their comments on earlier drafts.

1. Membership in the leaders' Group of Twenty (G-20) is based on the membership in the finance ministers' G-20, which was formed in 1999.

had not gone through since the Great Depression of the 1930s. A floor had to be put under expectations, a sense of resolve had to be projected, fiscal expansion had to be encouraged wherever feasible, and protectionist reflexes had to be countered.

This is how the leaders' level G-20 was born. Previous resistance to including the large emerging countries at the head table, formerly monopolized by the G-7, evaporated. China, India, Brazil, and others were needed for a global psychological and substantive response. The fact that a finance ministers' G-20 already existed allowed the United States to circumvent debate on inclusion. It was easier to simply invite the government leaders of the existing group of twenty than to try to agree on who should be included in or excluded from the November meeting. There was no time for such a debate.

It is not possible to measure exactly the impact of the first (Washington) and second (London) G-20 meetings. We cannot be sure of what would have happened without these meetings. Most observers agree, however, that the combination of decisive action by the U.S. Federal Reserve and U.S. Department of the Treasury, the G-20 commitment at the Washington meeting not to raise trade barriers, and then the signal at the April 2, 2009, London meeting of broadly concerted fiscal expansion and a green light for tripling the "firefighting" capacity of the International Monetary Fund (IMF) did make a critical contribution to turning around expectations and arresting what was threatening to become a global economic free fall.

Five Years Later

Five years after those first two meetings of the leaders' G-20, the key question is whether these summits, which have become an informal institution, can really add ongoing value to global economic governance. At the time of writing, in early 2014, it is anticipated that the Brisbane meeting in November 2014 will take place at the end of a year of overall global recovery, which has not only allowed gradual normalization of monetary policy in the United States but has also seen a tentative recovery in the euro zone.

The recent past is full of examples suggesting that such predictions should always be treated as tentative. A bad surprise cannot be ruled out. A great deal of uncertainty still characterizes the situation in Europe, and question marks have also appeared in China relating to local debt, other possible contingent liabilities of the public sector, and the shadow banking sector. We may yet witness plenty of instability because of the adjustment in the monetary policies of the

United States and other countries (see chapter 5, this volume) or the political consequences of Russia's approach toward Ukraine (see chapter 4). The political tensions in Eastern Europe could still derail the G-20 process in 2014, which would be a great pity and have long-term costs. But apart from this danger, the world will not have been in economic crisis mode in 2014, and G-20 leaders will be meeting at a time when the gathering could demonstrate that it has lasting value for the stability and good health of the world economy.

The absence of an acute crisis could lead the G-20 meetings to become purely ceremonial gatherings, which continue to take place because of the inertia in such processes, leading to cynicism and disappointment all around. Alternatively, the absence of an immediate crisis could be an opportunity for the G-20 to tackle in a sustainable way the major structural medium- and long-term issues that continue to face the world economy. World growth in the past few years has relied on a degree of central bank support that may already be leading to new unsustainable asset bubbles while unemployment remains unacceptably high. The challenge now is to create sustainable world growth based on real investment that stimulates total factor productivity gains and new long-term jobs in the value added chains of the products and services of the future. It is also time to make sure that key economic institutions are robust and able to withstand unexpected shocks if and when they occur.

The Australian National University and the Brookings Institution joined forces and assembled the chapters in this book with the expectation that the leaders will indeed see 2014 as an opportunity to address longer-term challenges and to transform the G-20 from a "crisis committee" into a "steering committee" for the world economy, making it part of a lasting and useful feature of global economic governance.

The G-20 and Global Public Goods

It is possible to group the big issues before the G-20 under six broad headings: macroeconomic interdependence, financial-sector interdependence, trade, energy and climate, development, and economic governance in the global system. The chapters in this book address the issues under all six headings. The emphasis is on interdependence, spillovers, or the global public-good nature of good policies. Scott Barrett, in his excellent book *Why Cooperate? The Incentive to Provide Public Goods* (2007), distinguishes three types of global public goods: those that can be delivered unilaterally (or minilaterally) by the "single best effort" of a country (the invention of a vaccine, for example), those public goods the delivery of which depends on the performance of "the weakest link" country (such as securing fissile material), and those public goods that depend on the combined "aggregate efforts" of all states (reducing the amount of carbon in the atmosphere is an excellent example). The "aggregate efforts" and "weakest link" global public goods generally call for international cooperation, although delivery of the "single best effort" public good may also require international cooperation—because those who can provide the good may hope that some other country can, and it will not want to bear the cost alone.

Fiscal and monetary policies, financial-sector policies and regulations, trade policies, energy and climate policies, and development policies all have associated spillover effects and free rider problems typical of public goods. Major monetary policy decisions in one large country have effects way beyond its borders. If the U.S. Federal Reserve had decided to stop its US$85 billion quantitative easing, asset-buying program overnight, the immediate effects would have been devastating from Rio de Janeiro to Istanbul and Delhi, and this would have triggered negative chain reactions around the globe. If the European Central Bank in mid-2012 had not forcefully declared that it would do "whatever it takes" to preserve the integrity of the euro, the European crisis would no doubt have gotten out of hand. If most G-20 countries had not engaged in large fiscal stimulus programs in 2009, the world economic slowdown could have become a depression. These are all examples of the way in which global macroeconomic interdependence makes appropriate macroeconomic policies into a global public good with both aggregate-effort and weakest-link characteristics.

Trade, financial sector, and climate and energy interdependencies are for the most part of a somewhat long-term nature. In these areas too, there are large spillover effects as well as the go-it-alone temptations inherent in public goods. The collapse of a single large financial global institution, for example, can precipitate a worldwide crisis. Furthermore, robust and well-functioning financial markets are needed to support growth across national boundaries. Thus financial-sector regulation is a global public good with both weakest-link and aggregate-effort characteristics. The weakest-link characteristic is the linking of, for example, the failure of a single bank (Lehman Brothers) or of a single even smallish country (Greece) to massive cross-border effects. It is an *aggregate* effort because each country's financial-sector reforms can contribute to growth worldwide and the strengthening of each country's regulatory system can affect financial stability on a global scale. An international trade system that maintains confidence and prevents beggar-thy-neighbor protectionism is also a global public good. In the energy and climate area, the greenhouse gas emissions of one country or of one city merge in the atmosphere with those of all other parts of the world to create global warming. Each part of the world benefits, therefore, from all efforts—its own and all others'—to mitigate carbon emissions. Limiting climate change is therefore very much an aggregate-effort-type global public good. In the area of climate change, in particular, each country may be tempted to rely on other countries' emission reductions so as to minimize its own costs.

The promotion of economic development and the fight against poverty is also an international public good, in addition to its direct importance for those who have yet to enjoy the benefits of economic, social, and political security that it delivers. The global development and poverty reduction agenda of the G-20 is therefore of interest to the entire global community. In contrast, what small countries do in some areas of policy may not have much effect on others. If Cambodia, Honduras, or Malawi, for example, choose to put up large trade barriers, it would hardly have an effect on the rest of the world, although it would still hurt their own consumers and exporters substantially. But there are circumstances in which what small countries do matters greatly to others. This is the case, for example, with eradicating contagious diseases, combating money laundering or tax evasion, and controlling fissile material. Dealing with these problems requires providing weakest-link-type global public goods. Take the eradication of a disease like polio: if it reappears in a place like Afghanistan, it can spread from there and become, again, a global threat. Thus negative spillovers from very poor or fragile states can be very serious. Small rich states, too, can create negative spillovers, an example being the difficulties experienced by the entire world because of tax havens and small noncooperative jurisdictions facilitating tax fraud, money laundering, crime, and corruption.

While one should not underestimate the importance of weakest-link challenges, in many policy domains, the larger the country, the greater the likelihood of spillover effects from national policies. This provides a rationale for a G-20 grouping of large economies: their decisions are critical for the world as a whole. Yet, as discussed above, small countries can also affect the whole world. For both reasons, therefore, the G-20 must find ways to involve the global community as a whole in its deliberations and work programs.

Fortunately, the possibility of mutual spillover effects increases the chances for cooperative outcomes in groups such as the G-20. There is an incentive to cooperate. A good example is the way the U.S. Federal Reserve defines its mandate and its policy objectives. Its overall policy is based on purely domestic U.S. objectives, as Dennis Lockhart, president of the Atlanta Federal

Reserve Bank, notes: "You have to remember that we are a legal creature of Congress and that we only have a mandate to concern ourselves with the interest of the United States. Other countries simply have to take that as a reality and adjust to us if that's something important for their economies." The effects of U.S. policies on others are not relevant to decisions of the Federal Reserve unless there are feedback effects from other countries *on the American economy.*

Lockhart's straightforward statement—as well as other pronouncements by Federal Reserve officials, including former chair Ben Bernanke himself—make it clear that the Federal Reserve's tapering policies are included in its mandate to consider only effects on the U.S. economy. If the pace of tapering (that is, reducing the size of its bond-buying program) plunges the South African or Turkish economy into recession because of abrupt capital flow reversals, it would be of no concern to the United States, because South Africa and Turkey by themselves are too small to cause significant feedback effects on the U.S. economy. But if the capital flow reversals were more widespread, affecting a large number of emerging market economies, including large countries such as Brazil and India, there would be a nonnegligible negative feedback effect on U.S. exports to these countries, as well as on U.S.-based financial institutions—and therefore on U.S. employment. If the tentative recovery in Europe also were affected, the feedback loop would be even stronger. Moreover, there would be second-round effects: financial markets could suffer globally, and the decline in effective demand in the immediately affected countries would trigger further rounds of demand contractions in their trading partners. This implies that, even with only American interests in mind, the Federal Reserve still has to take into account the impact its actions may have on others. The same can be said for the policies of the European Union, the policies of Japan, and the policies of China—and in fact the policies of all members of the G-20, if these policies would be carried out by a large enough group of countries. Size increases the importance of positive or negative spillovers and strengthens the incentive to cooperate within the G-20.

The G-20 and Global Economic Governance

Size alone does not, however, solve the problem of legitimacy, or the problem of the enforceability of G-20 decisions in some kind of legal or treaty-based framework. Even a "club" representing more than 80 percent of world GDP and more than two-thirds of world population cannot alone resolve the threats coming from weakest-link-type global public goods. G-20 decisions, which really take the form of policy proposals rather than enforceable policy strategies, must in most cases be brought before the governance organs of treaty-based institutions, such as the International Monetary Fund, and be adopted by them on behalf of the global community. For example, consider the decision at the London meeting in 2009 to create almost 200 million units of new special drawing rights. This G-20 proposal was then brought before the IMF executive board and adopted by that board in September 2009. The G-20 cannot decide for others, although the voting power that G-20 members have in most international institutions that have governance systems where votes are weighted by size (however measured) means that the proposals are likely to become decisions. These decisions will then become as binding as decisions of international institutions can be.

The nature of the public global goods and interdependencies involved, as well as the form that global economic governance takes, are the underlying topics that bind together the thematic chapters of this book. The volume also includes a chapter focusing on the role of China, a country that is now clearly the second "giant" on the world scene, as well as a chapter dealing with the role of regional organizations as complements to or competitors of the G-20. Both of these issues are crucial. China in 2014 accounts for about 12 percent of world GDP when measured by market prices and close to 20 percent when measured by purchasing power parity prices. Given that neither the European Union nor the somewhat smaller eurozone yet acts as a single player at the G-20, or in other settings, the United States and China are the two giants on the world scene. China is a newcomer to this role, and how China approaches the G-20, and global economic governance more generally, will have a determining effect on the prospects for international economic cooperation (see chapter 12). In this context, the way the United States approaches China, in turn, will have a great deal of influence on China's own behavior. China's rapid rise and strong growth trajectory mean that it is having a new and large effect on established markets. Although the Chinese economy is not yet as large as that of the United States, the incremental effect of China on the global economy is huge.

Finally, not everything can or should be dealt with in a global context. Regional affinities and strong within-region interdependence make it essential that global economic cooperation is complemented by regional cooperation (see chapter 13). Regional institutions can also play the very valuable role of bridges between the large G-20 member countries and their smaller neighbors. The Chiang Mai Initiative and the Asian Development Bank can complement the IMF and the World Bank. They can, of course, also be regarded as alternatives to these global institutions. In practice, they are both complements and competitors, and they point the way to the interaction among regionally inclusive institutions, globally inclusive institutions, and the G-20. This interaction will determine the nature and the efficacy of global economic governance.

Looking Forward

As the G-20 enters its fifth year, what are the priorities to which it should now turn? In this section we consider mutual assessment and stability, growth and development, infrastructure investment, structural reform, trade, investment, and the agenda for the next G-20.

Now that the troika organizational structure—in which the immediate past, current, and next G-20 hosts cooperate in setting the agenda—is established, the top priorities of the G-20 are avoiding agenda creep, focusing on key issues, and ensuring that there is follow-through. Entrenching the G-20 as an effective institution for shaping global economic governance and for establishing its value requires using the heft of the summits to effect change and set policy direction. In the coming year or two, Russia, Australia, and Turkey make up the troika charged with driving the process.

The macroeconomic prudential systems that have been recommended to buttress macroeconomic policy coordination—and that might assist in ongoing crisis management—are still in the making (see chapter 8). Some important reforms to the governance of international institutions are already agreed upon but are not yet fully implemented. Major gaps exist in global governance, for which leadership is required. As a global economic steering committee, the G-20 could help prioritize issues for the global community—and for international financial institutions in particular. The G-20 can in fact bring focus to the work of these international institutions.

The G-20 was notably effective during the peak of the global financial crisis. Now that the global economy has moved from crisis mode to recovery and the Bretton Woods momentum of 2008–09 has waned (see chapter 2), the group is seen as adopting a stance of lesser urgency. The problems are claimed to be not urgent, the agenda is said to be too broad, and the need and possibility for coordination and cooperation among the diverse countries in the G-20 combine to make the group less relevant than five years ago. These claims have some merit. But the idea that there is insufficient urgency in the current problems to justify strong global leadership is not persuasive.

Can Australia, Turkey, Russia, and successor G-20 presidencies turn around this new normal? Coming out of the crisis into recovery, renewed leadership of the global economy is needed to reassure the world's economic actors that they are in capable hands and that attention is being paid to the principles and institutions that allow for the best governance in this time of enormous change and uncertainty.

There are expectations that the Australian G-20 summit could raise the bar in leadership of the global economy by prioritizing growth within the G-20 framework for strong, sustainable, and balanced economic growth that was established by the Pittsburgh G-20 summit in 2009. Australia has an opportunity during its G-20 presidency to broaden the framework and to reform the Mutual Assessment Process.

Mutual Assessment and Stability

The G-20's 2009 Framework for Strong, Sustainable, and Balanced Growth (G-20 framework) involves a process of mutual scrutiny through peer reviews of medium-term policy trajectories submitted by governments to the IMF, which puts them together into a global outlook. This process can reveal misalignments between countries that can generate dangerous imbalances and inconsistencies that can create damaging spillover effects and risks for the global economy. The G-20 process of review, scrutiny, and peer pressure—the Mutual Assessment Process (MAP)—is facilitated by the IMF but run by the G-20 countries themselves. In the early years, the focus was on global imbalances between the United States and China, when overconsumption and fiscal and trade deficits in the United States were mirrored by oversavings and fiscal and trade surpluses in China. This problem has waned, although the surpluses of the oil-exporting countries and of Germany are still large enough to pose a problem to the world economy. Moreover, the MAP should be viewed not just as a mechanism to cure an illness but also as one to prevent new ones.

The basic critique of the framework and the MAP is that the framework is too narrow and the MAP too weak. The framework is too narrow because it focuses on macroeconomic imbalances, such as those between the United States and China, and ignores the potential of financial markets, institutions, and firms to create systemic risk. The Independent Evaluation Office of the IMF concludes that the IMF, in the run-up to the crisis in 2008, "appropriately stressed the urgency of addressing the persistent and growing global current account imbalances, but it did not look at how these imbalances were linked to the systemic risks that were building up in financial systems."

The Australian presidency has already taken two steps to strengthen the IMF's role in building "the resilience of the world economy." One is to propose a synthesis report within the IMF that will bring together the macroeconomic outlook work on global imbalances with the financial analyses of systemic risk to provide an integrated view of the global economy and the global financial system. The second is to make sure that, once integrated systemic risk assessments are available, they are reviewed at an appropriate policymaking forum, in which judgment calls can be made that mitigate potential upheavals before they occur (see chapter 6).

Hence, broadening the framework to include financial stability as an element of sustainability is moving in the right direction. So too is including financial analyses alongside macroeconomic policy assessment. The MAP has to have a high level of policy accountability and has to permit IMF staff to bring the financial and macroeconomic policy assessments together to strengthen their candor, insight, and pressure on institutional and policy weak points. It would be expected that by the end of the Australian presidency these efforts will bear fruit and that the international arrangements for systemic risk assessment and review will be stronger and more reliable as a result.

Growth and Development

Strong G-20 leadership is important in key areas. With the global recovery under way but still fragile, the G-20 needs to present a credible public message that its members are pulling together to boost economic and job growth. Global growth is still too reliant on unsustainable monetary stimulus, and there still is a sizable output gap, evident in above-average unemployment rates. The need is for high-quality growth driven by private investment. Such investment can benefit from stabilizing expectations about macroeconomic policy, reducing unnecessary bureaucratic burdens on the private sector while making regulation more effective and growth friendly, strengthening the business operating environment, and improving investment in infrastructure, including through private-public partnerships.

The mix of macroeconomic policies supporting the global economy, in some countries with fiscal space, may have overemphasized monetary expansion measures and underutilized fiscal expansion measures. In other countries, monetary policy has been excessively cautious. The composition of fiscal policy packages also matters. A more growth-oriented mix can generate better social outcomes by reducing poverty, inequality, unemployment, and domestic conflict (see chapter 7). This enhances the social sustainability of prudent economic policies, strengthening their trajectory and impact.

The G-20 framework should also be broadened to include sustainable development in all countries, not just developing countries, to ensure that environmental sustainability is integrally connected to mainstream policy decisions and not marginalized to environmental and development ministries (see chapter 3). The G-20 can influence thinking on development issues by aligning its agenda with work over the next two years at the United Nations and in member capitals on the post-2015 development agenda that will follow the era of the Millennium Development Goals (MDGs). This shift would be a strategic move and would raise the profile of development as a universal public concern, embracing core issues for developing countries not represented in the G-20. The G-20 Development Working Group would continue to work through development program issues and coordination challenges that require that international institutions work together in dealing with increasingly cross-sectoral issues.

The MDGs in the end became developing-country ambitions that did not involve advanced economies as partners but as donors, a much more restricted role. Elevating the notion of sustainable growth trajectories in all countries to the status of a universal mobilizer in the post-2015 agenda would move that agenda beyond the MDG focus (see chapter 9).

Affirmation in 2014 of the G-20 as the premier forum for providing strategic guidance on the global economy and on other major global issues is a core objective. Australia, one of the smaller economies, but one with deeply interdependent relationships with the other five Asian G-20 member economies, needs the G-20 to succeed to preserve a measure of influence both in global affairs and in its region.

The focus should be on promoting polices that will support demand while improving longer-term growth and development prospects by implementing reforms already agreed or to be agreed to by G-20 countries. That would help create a climate for investment-led growth—prioritizing increased infrastructure investment and structural (including trade and taxation) reform. Future efforts could build on financial reform measures currently under way to stabilize the global financial system so as to create incentives for long-run investment in directly productive activities and worldwide investment in infrastructure as foundations for private sector growth. These reform measures and systemic incentives need to be completed and the progress on them communicated (see chapter 8).

The February communiqué of the finance ministers' G-20 made it quite clear that the approach was a decentralized one, with each country making an effort to implement growth-enhancing national policies. It was no commitment to some kind of harmonized G-20 policy package. And yet in the work of the IMF, the OECD, and the World Bank on macroeconomic and reform priorities prepared for the February Sydney meeting, the emphasis was on the need for cooperation to ensure more rapid global growth. Effective cooperation would mean that countries with major current account surpluses would boost domestic demand, while countries with large current account deficits would pursue more restrictive macroeconomic policies. Earlier work by the IMF in the context of the mutual assessment process had suggested the importance of globally coordinated macroeconomic policies. For the G-20 to realize its full potential, much greater willingness by the nation-states to coordinate their policies would be desirable.

Growth also crucially depends, of course, on long-term structural reforms on the supply side of individual economies. These structural policies too can have positive spillover effects, as supply side–induced growth can generate greater demand for imports and stimulate world trade. The income growth-lifting strategy of the G-20 will have most traction, especially among emerging member economies, if it encourages G-20 governments to commit to macroeconomic policies and structural reform measures that are mutually complementary as well as growth enhancing. The ambition is for a G-20 leaders' meeting in November 2014 that goes beyond the finance ministers' meeting in encouraging a coordination of macroeconomic policies that connects closely to agendas for structural reform.

Infrastructure Investment and Structural Reform

Financial stability and growth are commonly seen as trade-offs rather than complements. This was especially true when financial stability meant price stability or the absence of inflation. But after 2008 financial stability means stable financial markets and sound financial institutions. In this new context, there is a need to realize that protecting against downside risk in financial markets—by adopting financial regulatory reforms and prudential policy measures intended to reduce leverage, speculation, and volatility—may also provide incentives to engage in long-term investment in productive activities rather than speculative investment in financial instruments disconnected from productive activities. A greater focus on "financial stability for growth" could give a positive turn to these measures, by more directly promoting private sector growth, investment in infrastructure, and sustainable energy systems, which are part of the G-20 Australian growth agenda.

Greater infrastructure investment leading to sustainable economic growth and global economic development can be the central pillar of the G-20 agenda, underscoring a global priority on private sector growth for greater job creation. Increased well-targeted infrastructure investment can be funded through fiscally prudent public spending, greater use of private infrastructure investment funds, and the activation of programs run by multilateral financial institutions.

A special opportunity to mobilize funds and structural reform to facilitate infrastructure investment is through the Chinese-proposed Asian Infrastructure Investment Bank. The reform agenda for Asian infrastructure projects provides a guide to how this could occur. The Asian Development Bank has identified US$8 trillion of national infrastructure projects and more for transborder projects. The Asia-Pacific Economic Cooperation (APEC) forum is leading initiatives to accelerate these projects and ensure that they are delivered. In addition to establishing an Asia Infrastructure Investment Bank, the initiatives include strengthening financial channels and gaining commitments to structural reform. This multipronged approach will generate the needed synergies for greater long-term job growth (see chapter 13).

An outline of how these proposals can be taken forward in Asia would be an important contribution to building a focused, sustainable, growth element into the G-20 agenda.

Trade and Investment

Maintaining open global trade and investment is fundamental not only to the global economic recovery but also to the ongoing strength and dynamism of the global economic system. While the G-20 played some role in limiting the retreat to protectionism during the financial crisis, the World Trade Organization (WTO) has struggled to keep trade liberalization on course, and there is less coherence in other trade and investment liberalization initiatives. Emerging economies also need more open trade and investment regimes if they are to join international production networks and value chains. International trade has been a poor cousin of global macroeconomic and financial reform on the G-20 agenda (see chapter 10). There is no more important priority for the G-20 looking forward than to develop a proposal to renovate the global trading system. While the WTO is the anchor of open trade, it needs to be fixed and a stronger regime for investment put in place.

The G-20 needs to put its weight behind thinking through the improvement that is now needed to reform the global trade and investment regimes. This strongly progrowth agenda for the G-20—implementing financial reforms to enhance investment, and prioritizing infrastructure investment, structural reform, and reform of the global trade and investment regimes—creates synergies among these priorities to generate high-yield outcomes. It should also engage the emerging economies, especially China, Indonesia, India, and Brazil. It is an agenda that matches the current Chinese reform priorities. A strong reform agenda endorsed by China will strengthen the G-20 and align with China's 2014 role as APEC chair.

A model of increasing infrastructure investment and commitment to structural reform can also form the basis of a future sustainable development agenda, with leadership from the G-20 following the close of the UN Millennium Development Goals in 2015.

Climate Change

The G-20 will also be challenged to provide strategic guidance on the climate change agenda. As long as the current international regime is working without a global agreement, it will not meet the targets necessary to limit climate change to only 2 degrees Celsius. With all of the world's major emitters belonging to the G-20, its members can increase their unilateral efforts on climate change and make a significant contribution to "concerted unilateral mitigation." Any such efforts will make every country's mitigation programs less costly and establish leadership through concerted unilateralism on this critical issue (see chapter 11).

Leadership, Focus, and Outreach

Australia's presidency can establish focus and give the G-20 the momentum it needs. Invigorating interactions among G-20 leaders is necessary to assure the global community that these countries are taking responsibility for the world economy and for a stable global financial system.

With the hindsight of five years, it is clear that part of what was lacking before the global financial crisis was that no one was minding the store. There was no effective responsibility for public outcomes in the global economy, because no one country or institution took the initiative. In so far as there was a group in charge, it was the G-7/G-8 leaders, who had been meeting since

1975 as a like-minded group of leaders from industrial economies, all Western except for Japan.

The G-20 brought into the global forum five more Asian economies in addition to Japan: Australia, China, India, Indonesia, and Korea; Saudi Arabia, from the Arab world; Turkey, straddling the East and West; and three Latin American countries: Argentina, Brazil, and Mexico. These, along with South Africa, delivered regional, cultural, and institutional diversity to the high table. Despite its intrinsic limitations, this was a major step forward from the G-7/G-8. But what was less clear in 2008 than it is now is that it ushered in a new style and a new discourse in summitry. Cultural and institutional diversity means that there will be differences of view across a broader range than in a like-minded group of largely Western countries. Agreement may be more difficult, debates more intense, and disagreements more open. In global negotiations it is more important to talk to those with whom reaching agreement is difficult than to those who already agree.

These complexities elevate the importance of having a focused agenda. A corollary is that the G-20 leaders must concentrate on strategic leadership. The proper division of labor is for the finance ministers and central bankers' meetings to deal with the technical detail and for the leaders' meetings to provide strategic guidance on urgent global problems.

Progress has been made on focus in the agenda, which will be key to the centrality and effectiveness of the G-20 going forward. Progress has also been made on outreach, at least in the sense of engaging stakeholder groups across the G-20 community such as business, labor, civil society, youth, and think tanks. Less progress has been made in institutionalizing outreach to countries and organizations beyond the G-20 community. Australia and Turkey, in their respective regions, have particular incentives to change that.

By far the biggest challenge for each G-20 host is the total engagement that must go into providing leadership of the global economy through and beyond the host year. This has to be achieved in a global context that has become politically much more difficult. It would be a great pity if the renewed political cleavages derailed the modest but real progress that has been made on international economic consultation and cooperation. The G-20 should be preserved and strengthened despite the storm waves of politics that hopefully will give way to a greater recognition of common interests and challenges.

PART II

Managing the G-20

PAOLA SUBACCHI

2

Adapting to the New Normal: The G-20 and the Advanced Economies Five Years after Washington

In September 2008, in the aftermath of the collapse of Lehman Brothers that brought the U.S. banking system to the brink of collapse, and the world with it, the president of France, Nicolas Sarkozy, called for collective action to backstop the crisis: "We must rethink the financial system from scratch, as at Bretton Woods." This suggestion was echoed by Britain's Prime Minister Gordon Brown: "We must have a new Bretton Woods, building a new international financial architecture for the years ahead."[1]

Those were the dramatic days when the crisis was spreading to banks in Europe, affecting credit and confidence. As a result the real economy was experiencing a massive contraction in activity across sectors and countries. The sharp decline in demand in developed economies adversely affected economic growth in Asia and other regions of the world. Singapore experienced the biggest fall in exports (around 20 percent year on year), while China recorded a loss in exports of more than 14 percent year on year in January 2009.[2] What started in 2007 as a growing international credit crunch, and what became by September 2008 a global banking crisis, spread quickly into the real economy. International trade, investment, and economic growth were all contracting. A drastic curtailment of credit, collapsing global demand, and a loss of trade finance had a devastating economic effect on both the developed and developing worlds, especially on economies heavily dependent on exports.

1. See Navaro (2012, p. 98).
2. IMF (2009b).

21

The policy response was frantic and patchy, owing to different domestic conditions and governments' different abilities to channel resources into their economies. Interest rates were cut to almost zero in the United States, the United Kingdom, the eurozone, and Japan. In early 2009 the United States and the United Kingdom embraced unconventional monetary policy to stimulate the economy because they could no longer lower interest rates. At the same time, fiscal stimulus packages worth hundreds of billions of dollars were set up, in particular in the United States and China. In February 2009 the new U.S. administration launched a US$787 billion plan to stabilize the financial system. The plan earmarked US$120 billion for infrastructure and science, US$267 billion for direct spending, including increased unemployment benefits, and US$212 billion for tax breaks to individuals and businesses. The U.S. stimulus package followed a scheme similar to the one that China had launched a few weeks earlier to respond to and mitigate the effects of the global slowdown. The US$586 billion stimulus program—the largest that China had ever taken—included a large infrastructure building program (railways, subways, airports) and also aimed to rebuild the communities in southwest China that were devastated by an earthquake in May 2008.

That, however, was not enough. The banking crisis in the United States and then in Europe, notably in the United Kingdom and Ireland, had resulted in a synchronized fall, and countries were going down together. Action was needed, and what better action than gathering the leaders of the world's largest economies?

Using the Group of Twenty central bank governors and finance ministers (the G-20), that had been gathering since 1999, seemed the obvious solution, given the circumstances and the urgency of resolving the crisis. Thus in the autumn of 2008, the G-20 was "upgraded" to include country leaders. U.S. President George W. Bush, by then at the end of his presidency, invited the G-20 heads of state to a summit on financial markets and the world economy in Washington, on November 14–15.[3] This summit was the first formal leaders' G-20 summit. Seven other summits followed between 2009 and 2013— the latest being the summit in St. Petersburg in September 2013—as well as a plethora of communiqués, working group reports, and commitments to action.

This is the genesis of what became the premier forum for global economic and financial affairs. Five years after the Washington summit is an appropri-

---

3. At the time of the G-20 summit in Washington the United States had already elected Barack Obama as the 44th president of the United States.

ate time to assess the work and the impact of the G-20. The crisis, especially its transformation into Europe's sovereign crisis, may still be too recent to allow proper forensic analysis.[4] However, its trigger is now distant enough to offer some conclusive observations. Most of all, five years is long enough to assess whether the expectations around and the commitments of the G-20 have been kept. Has the G-20 managed its transformation from a crisis committee to the premier forum for global economic and financial affairs?

In this chapter I argue that the G-20 has not quite managed to function as a permanent steering committee and has continued to function as a crisis committee. This is partly because the world has been in a permanent state of crisis caused by the contagion from the 2008 financial crisis (2011 and 2012 in Europe) and by the spillovers from the unconventional monetary policy on emerging markets ("currency wars" in 2010 and severe market volatility in 2013). The crisis in Europe's monetary union, in particular, has held the G-20's attention since 2010 because of its potential contagion to other parts of the world. And in 2013, when the euro crisis seemed more subdued, concerns about financial instability in the developing countries on the back of the U.S. Federal Reserve's stance on monetary policy and the emergency in Syria kept the G-20 occupied.

The G-20 has also continued to function as a crisis committee, because the coordination of policy interventions ex post is easier than the implementation of ex ante measures to prevent crises. Governments find policy coordination easier to implement—and easier to explain to their domestic constituencies— during a crisis. Thus responding to the global financial crisis when the world economy was experiencing a synchronized collapse was easier than dealing with the euro crisis, especially when economic recovery was under way in the rest of the world (even though at different paces). It was also easier than managing the spillovers from countries whose financial sectors were considered by the International Monetary Fund as "systemically important" to global financial health.[5]

In this assessment of the G-20 at five, I also suggest that, despite the rhetoric behind the calling of the Washington leaders' summit, there has not been "a Bretton Woods moment."[6] Unlike the Bretton Woods conference in July

---

4. Cooper and Subacchi (2010).

5. Countries with financial systems considered systemically important by the International Monetary Fund are subject to a financial sector assessment every five years and are monitored by the IMF.

6. Helleiner (2010).

1944, the G-20 has not set up a new, rule-based, financial and monetary system, as president Sarkozy and the Chinese monetary authorities had hoped. At best it has mended the existing system, but this is also disputable. The financial and economic crisis did not act as a trigger to rethink the global financial and monetary architecture, and the G-20 did not provide a means of formulating a fundamental restructuring of the international system. However, unlike the Bretton Woods conference that was a single event with the specific objective of creating consensus around a rule-based framework for the governance of the postwar world, the G-20 has become an ongoing forum that ensures continuity in discussing and managing critical issues.

Finally I make the point that functioning as a crisis committee allows the G-20 to ignore its "birth defect"—that is, issues of legitimacy and accountability. Having been selected as the ready-made group that ticked all boxes, including that of the membership of key emerging market economies, especially China, the G-20 did not face the issue of its own governance until 2011, when the French presidency asked the British government to draft a governance review. No significant progress, however, has been achieved in this area, while pressing financial and economic matters have pushed the issue of governance down on the list of priorities. This lack of focus on its own governance is even more striking given that the G-20 has significantly contributed to the reform of the international financial institutions, notably the International Monetary Fund (IMF). Therefore, the G-20 will eventually need to address the issue of governance if the member states want to turn the group into a permanent steering committee.

The chapter is organized as follows. First, I look at the transformation of the G-20 in the aftermath of the global financial and economic crisis and discuss the achievements of the Washington summit. Then I focus on the London summit, arguing that, in terms of coordinated measures and their impact on confidence, it was the event closest to a Bretton Woods moment. Finally I assess the functioning of the G-20 as a crisis committee, discuss the dilemma of efficiency versus legitimacy, and then conclude.

Born as a Crisis Committee

The G-20 prominently held center stage in the frantic weeks that followed the collapse of the U.S. bank Lehman Brothers. When the leaders of the main countries affected by the financial and economic crisis decided to call a meeting to discuss the measures necessary to backstop the emergency, they turned to the existing G-20, whose membership at the time included only finance ministers and central bankers. This group was established in 1999, following the Asian financial crisis in 1997. It was meant to involve "a broad range of countries in discussions on how to adapt the international financial system to the changing global environment."[7] The communiqué that followed the first meeting in Berlin in December 1999 reiterated that "the G-20 was established to provide a new mechanism for informal dialogue in the framework of the Bretton Woods institutional system, to broaden the discussions on key economic and financial policy issues among systemically significant economies and promote cooperation to achieve stable and sustainable world economic growth that benefits all."[8]

At its onset the G-20 grouped the most advanced economies—all G-7 countries are members—some medium-size, advanced economies such as Australia, and the largest developing countries. Altogether the G-20 member states represented about 90 percent of the world's total GDP, with an average per capita income of US$14,000 but with significant differences in income distribution between the rich industrialized countries and the dynamic emerging market economies.[9] Until the 2008 financial crisis, the work of the G-20 had been mostly centered on the international financial architecture, on managing globalization, and on combating the financing of terrorists.[10]

The G-20 summit in Washington was convened with the goal of fixing the financial system. The financial and banking collapse in the United States and its contagiousness for the United Kingdom, Ireland, and Spain—but also to Iceland, Ukraine, Latvia, and Belgium—had brought to the surface systemic shortfalls and the inadequacy of supervision for crisis prevention and of backstops for crisis resolution.

The advanced countries, and in particular the United States and the United Kingdom, were determined to stop the crisis and eventually fix the system. The crisis provided the locus and the objectives for the work of the G-20 in its new format. Even more than at the time of its first appearance, the G-20 came to the scene to stop a crisis and to resolve it. Being a crisis committee is, therefore, one of the group's intrinsic features.

7. In June 1999 the G-7 finance ministers at Cologne announced that they would "work together to establish an informal mechanism for dialogue among systemically important countries within the framework of the Bretton Woods institutional system." Kirton (1999); G-7 (1999).

8. Canada (1999).

9. IMF (1999).

10. Cooper and Thakur (2013); Kharas and Lombardi (2012); Bradford and Linn (2011).

To some extent choosing the G-20 was the easiest option at a very critical time. It was a ready-made group, with an established dialogue and some experience of working together.[11] Moreover, it gathered the key advanced economies, the BRICs (Brazil, Russia, India, and China) and South Africa; large emerging market economies other than the BRICs, such as South Africa and Indonesia, and some developed countries like Australia and South Korea. In terms of its membership, the G-20 went beyond the G-7 and the G-8.

It could not have been otherwise. A mix of governance considerations (developing countries, China in particular, were important components of the global economy) and opportunism (financial backing from the so-called surplus countries, especially China, might be needed) had suggested looking beyond the G-7 and G-8. Moreover, the United Kingdom, and its prime minister Gordon Brown, was keen to use the G-20 to discuss the emergency and to coordinate measures to put the world economy back on track. The United States was happy to avoid a close confrontation with China and to defuse tensions on the issue of currency manipulation—an issue that could have emerged in the IMF's report on China if the Lehman Brothers collapse had not taken the stage.[12] Other countries, however, were less keen. France, for example, was not completely on board—and never seemed to be, even when it chaired the G-20 in 2011—despite President Sarkozy's decisive support for the Washington summit. And Japan, Canada, and Italy were not hugely supportive of the G-20, as they feared a dilution of their influence if the G-20 overtook the G-8. In addition, Japan felt uncomfortable about China's presence at the table.

The spirit of the G-20 as a forum that included developing countries and emerging market economies and the shift in global power was captured in the official photo of the G-20 summit in Washington: the leaders of China and Brazil, Hu Jintao and Luiz Inácio Lula da Silva, were on either side of U.S. President George W. Bush. However, many developing countries, notably China, believed that the crisis was not a problem for these countries but was mainly a problem for the advanced economies. More specifically, they considered it a failure of the Anglo-Saxon model of capitalism.[13] Thus they expected that the advanced economies would work out some solution. For weeks, until the

11. Stronger supervision and regulation of financial institutions and markets, better transparency, and the reform of the IMF and other international financial institutions had been on the agenda for over a decade.

12. See Blustein (2012). For the IMF report, see www.imf.org/external/ country/CHN.

13. Addressing the German Parliament in September 2008, Peer Steinbruck, Germany's finance minister, remarked that "the U.S. will lose its status as the superpower of the world

London summit and after considerable pressure from the U.K. government, China maintained a noncommittal attitude. In September 2008, Chinese Premier Wen Jiabao reportedly stated that "what we can do now is to maintain the steady and fast growth of the national economy, and ensure that no major fluctuations will happen. That will be our greatest contribution to the world economy under the current circumstances."[14] The Chinese leadership implicitly argued that, being a poor country, China could not put its money at risk in order to rescue the world.

Preparing for London

The Washington summit did not deliver much besides the promise of restoring global demand and guarding against protectionism—a pledge that members of the G-20, from the United States to China, Russia, and the European Union, disregarded in the weeks immediately after the summit.[15] But it was decided to hold another meeting in London a few months later. This was necessary to bring aboard President Barack Obama and the new U.S. administration. The weeks leading to the London summit were frantic. There was a genuine belief that the summit would make a difference—perhaps not commensurate with the effort and resources involved, but a difference nevertheless. Many constituencies—from civil society to businesses to think tanks and NGOs—were eager to participate in the G-20 dialogue, as it was deemed to be the new hub of global governance, eclipsing the G-8.

Learning from the G-8 summit in Gleneagles in 2005, the U.K. Cabinet Office and Treasury established a practice that was followed by other chairs.[16] This effort was leveraged by the extensive network of think tanks and NGOs

---

financial system. . . . The financial crisis is above all an American problem. . . . This inadequately regulated system is now collapsing, with far-reaching consequences for the U.S. financial market and contagion effects for the rest of the world." Evans-Pritchard (2008). Giulio Tremonti, Italy's finance minister, suggested abolishing hedge funds, which, in his words, "are absolutely crazy" and "have nothing to do with capitalism." *The Economist* (2008).

14. Morrison (2009).

15. In the weeks immediately after the Washington summit almost all members of the G-20 (especially the largest members, including the United States, China, the European Union, India, and Russia) disregarded the pledge made at the summit to keep open markets. Fifty-five of the seventy-seven enacted trade-restrictive measures (tariffs, subsidies, licensing requirements, restricted entry, and tighter standards). Dadush (2009).

16. Effective outreach depends on how many resources the chair decides to allocate. Countries with a deep and diverse network of think tanks and NGOs tend to fare better in engaging with the various constituencies than countries with limited networks.

that operate in the United Kingdom.[17] Several reports and recommendations were published in the weeks ahead of the summit, possibly the highest number of reports that were produced for any of the subsequent summits.[18] The list of matters that these reports indicated as relevant for the G-20 agenda expanded beyond the crisis into new dimensions, such as a low-carbon economy, energy efficiency, development, and women's rights. As a result, broad long-term issues became entangled with the immediate concern about orderly economic crisis resolution.

Two questions hung over the U.K. chair. The first was how to deal with the G-8, and its Heiligendamm dialogue, which was an ill-conceived attempt to include the G-5 countries (Brazil, China, India, Mexico, and South Africa) in a structured dialogue with the G-8 without formally expanding the latter.[19] The upgrade of the G-20 undermined this plan and, in particular, made the preparations for the G-8 summit, that in 2009 fell on Italy, a difficult task. Who needed the G-8, was the recurrent question, when there was the G-20, in which developing countries were full members rather than invitees? And would the leaders of China, India, Brazil, Mexico, and South Africa be happy to be invited to join the G-8 summit according to a predecided "variable geometry," while the same countries were members of the G-20? How long would it take for the G-8 to be phased out as a relic of the past? At the time of the London summit, then, the fates of the G-20 and the G-8 looked intertwined—as if the survival of the former depended on the abolition of the latter.[20]

The second pending issue was the stance of the new U.S. administration toward the G-20. Although President Obama's support for the G-20 was somehow taken for granted, it was not clear how much the new president was prepared to back up an initiative begun by his predecessor. Things became clearer after Obama's inauguration on January 20, 2009, when the new administration gave its full support to the G-20 in its new format—-and to the London summit.

17. Not only are the think tanks and NGOs engaged with the G-20 chair, they are also involved in monitoring G-20 commitments and its effectiveness in keeping up with those commitments.

18. For example, Brookings published five briefs between February and March 2009. See Linn (2009); Bradford (2009); Prasad and Corkin (2009a, 2009b); Bradford and Linn (2009). Other reports include Chatham House and the Atlantic Council (2009); Oxfam (2009); ODI (2009).

19. This dialogue was established at the G-8 summit in Heiligendamm, Germany, in 2007.

20. In 2009 many experts discussed whether the G-8 would have been abolished in 2011 at the time of France's double presidency of both the G-8 and the G-20. The G-8, however, proved to be resilient.

Even if the world has changed (and many developing economies have significantly expanded their economies and have gained more influence in geopolitics), the United States still plays a critical role in the G-20. In the off-the-record words of officials from various countries who are or have been involved in the G-20, the United States appears to be the most difficult partner around the table. Having U.S. support is therefore critical to any summit. As for the London summit, even if the Obama administration was new and did not have enough standing to call the summit off and reinstate the G-20 as a finance ministers' forum (without diplomatic consequences), it could have been much less supportive and thus have made the London summit a less successful event. Indeed, the U.S. influence was evident when, after the G-8 gathering in Italy in 2009, President Obama, suffering from summit fatigue, asked to reduce the number of meetings. The following year the G-8 and the G-20 meetings were held back-to-back in Canada to avoid having meetings three times a year in three different locations, as had happened in 2009.[21]

The London Summit: The Nearest Thing to a Bretton Woods Moment

When the G-20 leaders gathered in London in April 2009, expectations were high. Assessments of what the G-20 could have achieved and did not tend to be skewed toward the negative. But in early 2009 the London summit was seen as a critical, and almost unique, moment to broker international agreements and solutions and a way to restore confidence in an integrated world economy and in the open-trade regime. "Trade is collapsing and protectionism is on the rise. Time for the G-20 to get going," *The Economist* wrote just before the London summit.[22] The managing director of the IMF, Dominique Strauss-Kahn, warned that developed and developing countries were at a crossroads and that leaders needed to show unity and leadership.[23] The BBC made a comparison between the London summit and the world economic summit that London hosted in June 1933, in the middle of the Great Depression.[24]

---

21. In 2009 the leaders of countries belonging to the G-8 and the G-20 met three times: in London in April; in L'Aquila, Italy, in July for the G-8 summit; and in Pittsburgh in September for the G-20 summit.

22. *The Economist* (2009).

23. IMF (2009).

24. "As delegates gather for the G20 summit in London on 2 April, it is worth looking to the last time London hosted a world economic summit. . . . In June 1933, delegates from 66 countries gathered in London to try and agree on plans to revive the world economy in the midst

From many perspectives, the London 2009 summit was a success. Leaders agreed on fast, coordinated action that helped contain the crisis. Their decisions on an unprecedented fiscal outlay and additional resources for the IMF and development banks helped avoid a global depression, stabilize markets, and restore confidence. The establishment of the Financial Stability Board (FSB) to advance regulatory reform of the financial sector, to initiate reforms of the international financial institutions, and to maintain an open-trade regime against protectionist sentiments are all to the G-20's credit. By fostering a concerted policy response, the G-20 showed that ad hoc policy cooperation was possible in times of crisis.

The work of the G-20 and the discussion at the summit were framed by two key problems: crisis resolution and the strengthening of the international financial and monetary architecture. A number of measures were unveiled to improve the financial regulatory framework and head off future crises. Most of all, the London summit was a critical step toward restoring multilateralism, collective action, and sharing commitments.

The G-20 leaders addressed the immediate crisis in other important ways, notably through their commitment to increase the resources available to the IMF as the key multilateral financial institution with the capacity and the experience to assist member governments to address existing economic challenges. The deterioration of the global economy had put the IMF back in the spotlight, somehow restoring its role after the controversial intervention at the time of the Asian crisis, which had contributed to drying out the fund's lending operations and, therefore, its resources—and also had an adverse impact on its reputation. The global financial crisis propelled the IMF to the forefront of international mechanisms to promote coordination and common assessments of financial policies, reinvigorating its role as a global stabilizer as economies facing acute financial difficulties required intervention.

A substantial increase in IMF resources was announced in London to assist countries in immediate crisis—"to treble resources available to the IMF to US$750 billion, to support a new SDR [special drawing rights] allocation of US$250 billion, to support at least US$100 billion of additional lending by the multilateral development banks, to ensure US$250 billion of support for trade finance, and to use the additional resources from agreed IMF gold sales for concessional finance for the poorest countries." Some countries or regions, such as

of the Great Depression. . . . For those organizing the current G20 summit, the lesson is that boosting confidence by maintaining a united front in the face of the global recession has to be a key objective, whatever the concrete policies that can be agreed." BBC (2009).

Japan and the European Union, committed resources directly to the IMF. Japan had already contributed US$100 billion at the time of the Washington summit. The United States committed the same amount (US$100 billion). Some countries committed to smaller amounts—Canada offered US$10 billion, and India, Brazil, and Russia each committed up to US$10 billion. Others made less firm commitments. China, for instance, declared it was willing to buy US$50 billion in bonds issued by the IMF. In the end the funds raised were only half the amount that the leaders had committed in London. Between April and December 2009 the IMF received approximately US$392 billion.[25]

Increasing the funds available to the IMF was an important step toward reviewing the adequacy of the resources of the IMF, the World Bank Group, and other multilateral development banks, a review that the Washington summit called for during the G-20 meeting in London. At the same time the leaders agreed to create a "flexible credit line" to grant rapid upfront financing in large amounts for "strongly performing economies that needed insurance to protect them from crisis fallout." It was decided that access to this credit line should be restricted to countries that meet strict qualifying criteria. After a credit line was approved, a country could draw on it without having to meet specified policy goals, as is normally the case for IMF loans.

At the London summit it was also agreed to make the IMF's lending and conditionality framework "more flexible and responsive to member countries' needs," with a specific focus on the underlying objectives of a country's structural reform agenda. The new framework was applied to all IMF loan programs. Another important measure was US$250 billion committed over the following two years to support trade finance. Historical experience and awareness of the policy mistakes in the years following the Wall Street crash in 1929 made trade a key concern in London in 2009. G-20 leaders also reaffirmed their commitment to a quick and successful conclusion to the Doha round of trade negotiations, which, according to their communiqué, "could boost the global economy by at least US$150 billion per annum." However, no new deadline was set to complete the Doha round, which had been in discussion for eight years. Doha remained the elephant in the room during all subsequent summits, until 2013, when talks for a proposed Transatlantic Trade and Investment Partnership between the European Union and the United States, and for a free trade agreement between the European Union and Japan, signaled that the world had finally moved on.

25. IMF (2013b).

Furthermore, the G-20 leaders empowered the IMF and the Financial Stability Board with the task of producing guidelines for national authorities "to assess whether a financial institution, market, or an instrument is systemically important" in order for regulation and supervision to be extended to these entities.[26] They also insisted that "these guidelines should focus on what institutions do rather than their legal form." This was an important step as the concept of "systemically important"—institutions as well as countries—came to inform the G-20's subsequent work. Most systemically important countries are developed countries—the United States, the United Kingdom, the eurozone countries, Japan (the fifth one being China)—and most systemically important financial institutions belong to G-7 countries.[27]

Another important achievement in London was the endorsement of detailed proposals to integrate macroeconomic prudential concerns into international financial regulation. Historically, international prudential regulation has focused at the microeconomic level of the soundness of specific institutions and markets rather than larger factors that might contribute to a systemwide buildup of excessive risks. Building on the Washington Action Plan in London, the G-20 leaders backed a number of specific proposals related to bank regulation and accounting practices that emerged from the macroeconomic prudential agenda.[28]

Critical to the success of the London summit was the commitment of Britain's Prime Minister Gordon Brown. A strong believer in international cooperation and multilateral dialogue, Brown also saw the London summit as a way to revive his falling personal ratings and public image in Britain. This might explain the massive media coverage of the event. But besides domestic

---

26. The G-20 transformed the Financial Stability Forum into the Financial Stability Board. The board has pursued a range of financial sector reforms with the backing of the G-20. Since the first leaders' summit in November 2008, financial regulation has been a central agenda item of the G-20, and the topic has retained a prominent place in the communiqués from meetings of G-20 leaders, finance ministers, and central bank governors since then. The Financial Stability Forum was established in 1999 to bring together finance ministries, central banks, and regulators of major financial centers. After the Washington summit, the forum was given a broad oversight role for financial sector reform, and its membership was expanded to include all G-20 countries. The forum received more resources and responsibilities and was renamed the Financial Stability Board at the G-20 London summit in 2009. The board has a broader mandate than the forum, one that clarifies the coordination of institutions responsible for international financial stability.

27. But neither the G-20 nor the G-7 has since addressed the question of whether systemically important countries and institutions should be subject to higher standards and deeper supervision.

28. Subacchi and Heillener (2009).

political considerations, Brown's support proved critical in galvanizing other leaders, policymakers, and civil society and in breaking new ground. The U.K. chair was especially effective at creating consensus, showing how critical committed leaders, especially those holding the G-20 chair, are to driving the whole process forward. For example, much work was done behind the scenes in the weeks before the London summit to persuade China to commit some funds.

Of course the United Kingdom had a special interest in resolving the crisis because it was, together with the United States, the country that had most intensely experienced the impact of the financial crisis. Britain, together with the United States, led the initiative to stop the crisis and create a robust framework of financial regulations. Indeed the London summit went well beyond its remit of crisis resolution and made some decisive steps toward reforming not just the content of the international financial regulatory framework but also its governance. By clearly distinguishing between crisis resolution and crisis prevention, the London summit implicitly set the agenda for the subsequent development of the G-20; the idea was indeed that the G-20 would move on from being a crisis committee to being a permanent steering committee.[29]

Finally, the global financial crisis shaped the context of the London summit and provided the glue that held countries together. At the same time the crisis made the London summit a difficult act to follow. The G-20 summits that followed London never managed to be as successful in reaching out and creating confidence. To some extent the outcome of the London summit has haunted and somehow undermined the chances of success of other summits.

Falling Together, Working Together

The key achievement of the London summit is the strength of the multilateral response to the crisis. The message that came from the summit was that countries were able and willing to work together to stop the crisis and engineer the recovery. As I suggested with some colleagues in a report published before the London summit, the G-20 leaders sent a clear message that they could work constructively together, cooperate, and coordinate their work.[30] This message strengthened confidence, and indeed in the weeks after the London summit both consumer and business confidence recovered. According to a Conference

29. Cooper and Subacchi (2010).
30. See Chatham House and the Atlantic Council (2009), in which a key recommendation is to "show strong leadership and commitment to reforms."

Board survey of consumer confidence in the United States, the index rose to 54.0 in August 2009 from 26.9 in March of the same year.[31] Exports of goods from the G-20 countries were almost 10 percent higher in July 2009 than in April.[32] The stock market also showed significant growth. The FTSE 100 index gained nearly 1,000 points within eight weeks of the meeting of the G-20 finance ministers in early March, from the low of 3,530.73 points. And the S&P 500 index recovered from 683.38 points—its lowest level since 2000—in March 2009 by climbing more than 200 points within three months and rebounding to 1,000 points in August 2009.[33]

Policy coordination has been a recurrent theme of the G-20. What emerged from the London summit was the awareness that policy coordination was necessary, since the impact of the crisis was too large for countries to deal with on their own. It was also necessary to understand and, if necessary, mitigate the impact of bailout plans and stimulus packages on neighboring economies and trading partners. Even if these measures fell within the remit of domestic economic policy, they could have an adverse impact on other countries, triggering protectionist responses and retaliation. The global financial crisis showed that even small countries such as Iceland could be a source of significant spillovers, adversely affecting countries such as the United Kingdom and the Netherlands, where Icelandic banks and investors held significant assets.[34]

Ideally the G-20 should provide a forum for policy coordination to evolve, starting with information sharing (consultation), moving on to consensus building on objectives (cooperation), and then laying out a framework for operational commitments (coordination). In practice, however, the process of policy coordination is never so straightforward. It requires recognition of

31. Conference Board (2009).

32. In March 2009 these exports were 10.7 percent lower than in December of the previous year, implying a 36 percent annual fall if this pace of decline continued. See Council on Foreign Relations (2009); White House (2009).

33. Thomson Reuters (2013).

34. In October 2008, a month after Lehman's collapse, Iceland's banking system collapsed and the foreign exchange market froze up. Its inflation rose above 18 percent, real GDP declined by 12 percent from peak to trough (nominal GDP has declined by about 11 percent since the crisis of October 2008), and unemployment rose to a nearly unprecedented level. Its public sector debt rose from about 30 percent of GDP to over 100 percent in 2011. See IMF (2013a). All three of the country's major privately owned banks—Glitnir, Landsbanki, and Kaupthing—were forced into bankruptcy because of their difficulties in refinancing their short-term debt and a run on deposits in the Netherlands and the United Kingdom. In early October 2008 Prime Minister Geir Haarde said, "There [is] a very real danger . . . that the Icelandic economy, in the worst case, could be sucked with the banks into the whirlpool, and the result could have been national bankruptcy."

countries' growing international economic interdependence and awareness of all trade-offs. And it needs a common analytical framework to identify linkages and spillovers and to measure their impact.[35]

Even at the London summit, when countries were still working together, reaching an agreement on coordinated fiscal measures to boost demand in the main economies proved to be very difficult and risked derailing the meeting. In the weeks before the London summit, the United States and the United Kingdom, on one side, and Germany, on the other, got tangled in an unhelpful discussion about what accounted for additional fiscal stimulus. Should automatic stabilizers, that is, built-in mechanisms such as unemployment benefits that help mitigate the impact of the downturn, be counted? The Germans thought they should be, while the British and the Americans took the view that only additional discretional fiscal measures should be included in the package. The issue was, in the end, resolved, but the fact that in the weeks before the London summit the G-20 countries, in the same coordinated fashion, had provided a total of US$5 trillion in stimulus to the world economy somehow went unnoticed.[36]

By late 2009 the synchronized fall of the world economy had stopped, and the recovery was going to develop along different paths and at different paces, with the developing countries growing at a faster pace than the advanced economies. Consensus among the G-20 member states became more difficult to reach, and this has been the case since. In addition, mechanisms to ensure that national policies are undertaken with external as well as domestic consequences in mind remain inadequate. As a result, dealing with the spillovers from unconventional monetary policy has been a source of frustration among countries, in particular emerging market economies that are at the receiving end of these spillovers.

This is not to say that the G-20 has not been active in promoting the coordination of policies. Since 2009 significant steps have been taken toward strengthening policy coordination—from achieving a common understanding of the global imbalances, and a common framework to deal with them, to the development of the Mutual Assessment Process (MAP). For example, the G-20 established the FSB as the key coordinating mechanism for "translating

---

35. Subacchi and Jenkins (2011).

36. If discretionary fiscal stimulus actions and systemic automatic stabilizer expenditures were combined, the total impact of all G-20 countries would be at an average annual rate of 2.6 percent of 2007 GDP for 2008–10. This was well above the 2 percent of GDP fiscal stimulus target set by the IMF before the London summit. See Bradford and Linn (2010).

political will into concrete agreements on new regulatory measures."[37] In Pittsburgh the leaders agreed on MAP to deal with the global imbalances and broker consensus among the G-20 members on early-warning measures and procedures for crisis prevention and adjustment measures for both surplus countries and deficit countries. The IMF, at the "request of the G-20," provides the technical analysis needed to evaluate how members' policies fit together. However, despite expectations that MAP could become "a useful tool for comprehending structural issues at the basis of macroeconomic imbalances," the reality has proved more difficult and less successful.[38]

Since the G-20 is a heterogeneous group—unlike the G-7—differences in development, income distribution, and pace of economic growth are significant. Thus disagreements about the nature and shape of policy measures to support growth—for instance with regard to austerity packages—could become contentious. Increased multilateralism can lead to increased disagreement. The future of the G-20, and the form of international policy cooperation and coordination that it represents, depends on the ability of member nations to strike a balance between the developed and the developing worlds' interests. Innovative diplomatic practices are necessary for the forum to move forward.

From Crisis to Crisis: The G-20 Remains a Crisis Committee

The G-20 is best at coordinating crisis resolution measures, while coordinating crisis prevention measures is more difficult. While the London summit focused on crisis resolution, the Pittsburgh summit focused on preventing crises and restoring growth, through policy cooperation, surveillance, and peer review. Indeed the framework for "strong, sustainable, and balanced growth" that was launched at the Pittsburgh summit in September 2009 was intended to be a turning point from the emergency of the crisis to the return to normal. In Pittsburgh the IMF was given responsibility for the surveillance process. The implicit assumption was that the economies of developed countries would go back to the precrisis GDP growth path, but this assumption was too optimistic.

The crisis has continued to provide the context, and the glue, for the function of the G-20, and somehow its raison d'être. At the same time, it has constrained the evolution of the group into a steering committee for the management of the global economy. Despite the excellent preparatory work

37. Pickford (2013).
38. Jorgensen (2013).

that both finance ministers and sherpas undertake in the months ahead of each summit, resolving crises, rather than preventing crises, continues to inform, and to drive, the G-20 work and even to define the group's existence.[39] The G-20 has indeed proved effective in dealing with crises, even at the regional level, as with the euro crisis in 2011–12. But intervening ex post is inefficient. Financial crises are very costly in terms of welfare losses and social impact even when the resolution proves successful.

Undoubtedly the constant state of crisis that has gripped the world since September 2008 has diverted attention away from crisis prevention and toward a focus on crisis resolution. Unlike the Asian crisis in 1997—and before that, the financial crises in Latin America, the impacts of which were mainly regional—the 2008 crisis had its epicenter in the developed world. It radiated to the rest of the world, testing the degree to which emerging markets and developing economies in general and the BRICs more specifically were decoupled. In 2010 Greece and Europe's other southern economies were hit by what had become a sovereign debt crisis. In the meantime emerging market economies were experiencing problems in managing capital inflows and the appreciation of their currencies, given the Federal Reserve's unconventional monetary policy. Financial stability became a critical issue for the emerging economies in the G-20, and currency wars derailed the summit in Seoul in November 2010. As a result, the carefully crafted agenda, focused on development (as opposed to aid, which is more typical of the G-8) and on the financial safety net, was pushed aside. With the recovery now seemingly under way, sluggish growth in some advanced economies, notably in Europe, the fragility of the fundamentals in some developing countries, and unresolved questions about the "return to normal"—that is, phasing out the unconventional monetary policy—suggest that the G-20 will continue to function as a crisis committee, at least until the world economy is on firmer footing.

Besides dealing with the long-term effects of the 2008 global financial crisis, and perhaps because of it, the leaders seem happy and willing to stick to the format of the G-20 as a crisis committee. They increasingly use the summits as opportunities to iron out differences and sort out problems, even if these are not part of the official script. This has been the case in all recent summits. In Cannes in 2011 it was the Greek crisis that dominated the discussion as a result of Greek Prime Minister George Papandreou's announced plans to hold a referendum later that year on key aspects of the scheme that European

---

39. Sherpas, in this context, are the "personal representatives of heads of state, who prepare an international summit." See Wikipedia.

leaders had devised to rescue the euro.[40] In Los Cabos in June 2012 it was again the eurozone that dominated the discussion, while in St. Petersburg in September 2013 it was Syria's civil war. It is increasingly the case that the leaders look at the summit as a gathering where they can informally discuss the most urgent matters. In St. Petersburg, for example, some key players were in attendance, notably all five permanent U.N. Security Council members, as well as Turkey and Saudi Arabia.[41] Where else, once a year, could leaders convene around a table for an informal and convivial occasion? Given its relative flexibility and informality, the G-20 has become a shock absorber for the world's tensions and problems.

Legitimacy versus Efficiency?

The continuous functioning as a crisis committee allows the G-20 to overcome its intrinsic birth defect. The group's informal structure allows the necessary flexibility and adaptation for a swift response at the time of crisis, when urgent action is needed to backstop the crisis. But the hurried upgrade has created a governance problem. Members were not chosen on the basis of shared, transparent, objective, and measurable criteria but rather on their membership in the existing G-20. As a result, efficiency prevailed over legitimacy.[42]

The intertwined issues of legitimacy and efficiency—who should be around the table and how the dialogue can be made efficient—have been part of the G-20's environment since the Washington summit. If a vast majority of the world's countries were excluded when the G-20 was just the gathering of finance ministers and central bank governors, this is no longer possible with the emergence of the G-20 at the leaders' level. However, as long as the world remains in a state of constant crisis and the G-20 continues to be the only arena for working toward multilateral and cooperative solutions to the challenge of managing the world economy and the international financial system,

40. "There is no doubt that there is a real sense of urgency in the room and a real sense of urgency from every individual that I have heard. There was also an emphasis on the need for specific actions to come out of our discussion. . . . The eurozone has taken significant decisions." George Osborne, November 3, 2011, at the Cannes G-20 summit.

41. "In the near future we will meet in St. Petersburg. . . . I hope that the president of the United States will be among the participants, and we will certainly have the opportunity to talk in an expanded format, including about the Syrian problem." Russian president Vladimir Putin, September 2013.

42. Subacchi and Pickford (2011).

the need to deal with emergencies takes priority over the issue of governance. In other words, efficiency continues to prevail over legitimacy.[43] If the G-20 gradually descends into irrelevance—or it seems so to a considerable share of the media—then the issue of governance becomes less pressing.[44]

But if the G-20 manages to turn into a full-fledged steering committee with an agenda that reflects that role, then it will have to deal with its own governance. A broader global agenda—a trend and an aspiration that have become evident in recent years—inevitably highlights the G-20's restricted membership and lack of legitimacy and representativeness. For this the G-20 needs to involve other countries and regional organizations to realize a more inclusive membership. It also needs to respond to the increasing demands by nonmembers to be represented in G-20 discussions.

Without greater legitimacy, the G-20 will have difficulty achieving full implementation of any agreement, which would likely be perceived as the decisions of a self-selected group of countries, regardless of how systemically important they may be. Global issues ultimately require global action through fully representative institutions. A working relationship between the G-20 and international, universal-membership organizations is crucial to effectiveness, as was illustrated in recent years by the relationship between the G-20 and the IMF.

While the G-20's governance deficit needs to be addressed in the long run, credibility needs to be improved in the short run. Existing processes need to be streamlined to improve the transparency and accountability of decisionmaking, and the implementation and monitoring of decisions need to be strengthened.[45] Five years after its greatest moment, the G-20 membership is still unable to agree on common objectives, and member states are still unwilling to accept that their domestic policies will be assessed against these objectives.

The paradox, the frustration, and the ambiguity with the G-20 is that it seems unable to address the issue of its own governance despite having driven

---

43. Somehow ironically, the governance review that the G-20 asked the U.K. government to provide for the Cannes summit was one of the agenda items that was ignored because of the crisis in the eurozone. The report prepared by David Cameron, prime minister of the United Kingdom, focuses on "improving existing process and institutions rather than simply reviewing the lineup of countries around the table." See Cameron (2009); see also Subacchi and Pickford (2011).

44. See, for example, Gilles (2012).

45. Subacchi and Pickford (2011).

the reform of international financial institutions, and having kept multilateralism alive. As a process driver, a systemic risk manager, and a bulwark against restrictive forms of unilateralism,[46] the G-20 remains indispensable. However, the emerging system that has the G-20 as its reference point would be more influential with improvements in the group's legitimacy and efficiency.

Conclusion

Five years after the collapse of Lehman Brothers, the world economy remains in a position of instability and faces an array of challenges—from volatile capital flows, to political instability in the United States, to fragile economic recovery in the eurozone, to the eventual phasing out of the unconventional monetary policy, and to geopolitical tensions in Ukraine. Because the world economy remains in a state of flux, the G-20 continues to function as a crisis committee, even though it expanded in the latest summit in St. Petersburg beyond economics and finance.

The G-20 has made some progress toward becoming a permanent steering committee that manages a world economy with deep interdependencies and high potential for spillovers, where short-term domestic policy objectives are often in conflict with longer-term sustainable global growth and the medium-term goal of external stability. A strong, effective, and legitimate governance framework, however, is required to manage the interaction among countries' policies. Mechanisms to coordinate macroeconomic adjustments among countries, especially the systemically important countries, to improve macroeconomic stability and prevent future crises, are also necessary.

The G-20 embodies the tensions in the relationship between international markets and domestic political authorities—and also in the relationship between the advanced economies and the emerging states. Undoubtedly the group has managed to embrace old and new economic powers, to juggle the tension among international financial markets operating within a framework of national rules, and to deliver balanced and sustainable global growth that tries to reconcile different national objectives. But over the last few years it seems to have lost its sense of purpose. It was definitely easier to work together when the emergency was clear to everyone. In addition, since the Washington summit, the original G-20 agenda of long-term financial reform has expanded to address important, but less immediately urgent, questions, such as global

---

46. Subacchi and Pickford (2011).

imbalances, trade, and development, and has become entangled in many other issues, from climate change to the protection of the marine environment. The overcrowded agenda is partly caused by the addition of the sherpa track.[47] This has proved problematic not only because of the legitimacy issue, discussed earlier, but also because of the risk of setting expectations too high and not delivering on commitments.

Moving forward within the framework of the "new normal"—that is, a world economy with lower trend output in the developed countries than in the precrisis years—will require the G-20 to spend a great deal of political capital to spur the most reluctant leaders into action. Leadership and political capital is also needed to communicate clearly to the public about the basis, rationale, and sequencing of their actions to sustain popular support especially if the economic losses from the crisis are not fully restored. When carrying out stabilization and stimulus policies, the G-20 leaders will need to act transparently and be clear about the intentions of domestic policies so that they do not serve as a justification for protectionist retaliation.

Looking back, there was no Bretton Woods moment in late 2008 at the time of the Washington summit or in 2009, and the G-20 has not lived up to the expectations for ambitious reforms. Five years after the most devastating financial and economic crisis in living memory the architectural framework designed at Bretton Woods remains largely in intact—with the exception of the move from the General Agreement on Tariffs and Trade to the World Trade Organization and the entry of Russia into the G-8. Some changes have been made in the governance of the International Monetary Fund, but the old big powers remain reluctant to incorporate new big powers—and these, in turn, seem to resist being incorporated into the existing system. If the G-20 cannot make a decisive mark on reforming global economic governance, it is unlikely to become a permanent full-fledged steering committee for economic and financial affairs.

References

BBC. 2009. "Lesson for G20 from 1933 London Summit." March 23.
Blustein, Paul. 2012. "A Flop and a Debacle: Inside the IMF's Global Rebalancing Acts." Paper 4. Waterloo, Ont.: Centre for International Governance Innovation.
Bradford, Colin I. 2009. "The G Force: Global Governance and the International Economic Crisis." *World Today.* London: Chatham House.

47. The sherpa track focuses on nonfinancial issues such as employment, agriculture, energy, the fight against corruption, and development. Normally the sherpas report directly to the leaders, but the format is not strictly defined. See G-20 (2012).

Bradford, Colin I., and Johannes F. Linn. 2009. "The G-20 Summit—Its Significance for the World and for Turkey." Brookings.

———. 2010. "The April 2009 London G-20 Summit in Retrospect." Brookings.

———. 2011. "A History of G-20 Summits: The Evolving Dynamic of Global Leadership." *Journal of Globalization and Development* 2, no. 2.

Cameron, David. 2011. "Governance for Growth: Building Consensus for the Future." Prime Minister's Office.

Canada, Department of Finance. 1999. "Communiqué of the Finance Ministers and Central Bank Governors Meeting, Berlin, December 15–16."

Chatham House and the Atlantic Council. 2009. *New Ideas for the London Summit: Recommendations for the G20 Leaders.* London: Chatham House.

Conference Board. 2009. "Consumer Confidence Survey." December.

Cooper, Andrew, and Paola Subacchi. 2010. "Global Economic Governance in Transition: Overview." *International Affairs* 86, no. 3: 607–17.

Cooper, Andrew, and Ramesh Thakur. 2013. *The Group of Twenty (G-20).* Oxford: Routledge.

Council on Foreign Relations. 2009. "G-20 Leaders Statement at Pittsburgh Summit: Bold and Coordinated Actions from Crisis to Recovery."

Dadush, Uri. 2009. "Resurgent Protectionism: Risks and Possible Remedies." In *New Ideas for the London Summit: Recommendations for the G20 Leaders.* London: Chatham House.

The Economist. 2008. "The End of the Beginning?"

———. 2009. "The G20 Summit: London Calling."

Evans-Pritchard, Ambrose. 2008. "Financial Crisis: U.S. Will Lose Superpower Status, Claims German Minister." *Telegraph,* September 25.

G-7. 1999. "Report of G-7 Finance Ministers to the Koln Economic Summit, Cologne, June 18–20" (www.G-8.utoronto.ca/finance/fm992509state.htm).

G-20 Information Center. 2012. "Mexico's Presidency of the G20." Discussion paper (www.g20.utoronto.ca/2012/2012-loscabos-disc-en.pdf).

Gilles, Chris. 2012. "G20 Reform: Time to Take Action—or Risk Irrelevance." *Financial Times,* June 18.

Helleiner, Eric. 2010. "A Bretton Woods Moment? The 2007–2008 Crisis and the Future of Global Finance." *International Affairs* 86, no.3: 619–36.

IMF (International Monetary Fund). 1999. *World Economic Outlook.*

———. 2009a. "World Faces Crisis Crossroads at G20 Summit."

———. 2009b. "Sustaining the Recovery."

———. 2013a. "Iceland Article IV Consultation and Third Post-Program Monitoring Discussions."

———. 2013b. "Bolstering the IMF's Lending Capacity."

Jorgensen, Hugh. 2013. "We Must Keep Meeting Like This: Summary of Regional 'Think 20' Seminar." Sydney: Lowy Institute for International Policy.

Kharas, Homi, and Domenico Lombardi. 2012. "The Group of Twenty: Origins, Prospects, and Challenges for Global Governance." Brookings.

Kirton, John. 1999. "What Is the G-20?" G-20 Information Center.

Linn, Johannes F. 2009. "World Bank Reform: Proposals for the Next G-20 Summit." Brookings.

Morrison, Wayne M. 2009. "China and the Global Financial Crisis: Implications for the United States." Congressional Research Service.

Navarro, Armando. 2012. *Global Capitalist Crisis and the Second Great Depression: Egalitarian Systemic Models for Change*. Lanham, Md.: Lexington Books.

ODI (Overseas Development Institute). 2009. "A Development Charter for the G-20" (www.odi.org.uk/sites/odi.org.uk/files/odi-assets/publications-opinion-files/414 4.pdf).

Oxfam. 2009. "What Happened at the G20? Initial Analysis of the London Summit" (www.oxfam.org/en/policy/what-happened-g20).

Pickford, Stephen. 2013. "The G20 and Financial Sector Reforms." Sydney: Lowy Institute for International Policy.

Prasad, Eswar, and Isaac Corkin. 2009a. "Assessing the G-20 Stimulus Plans: A Deeper Look." Brookings.

———. 2009b. "Understanding the G-20 Economic Stimulus Plans." Brookings.

Subacchi, Paola, and Eric Heillener. 2009. "From London to L'Aquila: Building a Bridge between the G20 and the G8." Briefing paper. London: Chatham House.

Subacchi, Paola, and Paul Jenkins. 2011. "Preventing Crises and Promoting Economic Growth: A Framework for International Policy Cooperation." Report. London: Chatham House.

Subacchi, Paola, and Stephen Pickford. 2011. "Legitimacy versus Effectiveness for the G20: A Dynamic Approach to Global Economic Governance." Briefing paper. London: Chatham House.

Thomson Reuters. 2013. "Datastream." New York.

White House. 2009. "The Pittsburgh Summit: Bold and Coordinated Actions from Crisis to Recovery."

CHANGYONG RHEE AND ALOK SHEEL

3

The Role of Emerging Economies in Major G-20 Initiatives

In the five-year perspective of the G-20 experience, the decision to include emerging economies in the dialogue to address the global financial crisis proved beneficial for the world economy. Coordinated expansionary policy action by both advanced and emerging economies limited the global repercussions of a financial and economic crisis emanating from advanced economies. Even as the global economy started faltering in late 2007, emerging G-20 economies continued to post strong positive growth. In fact, during the worst of the global crisis in 2009, when the world economy contracted by 4.2 percent, emerging G-20 economies managed to contribute 1.7 percentage points to global growth while advanced G-20 economies subtracted 1.8 percentage points. Since then, the contribution of G-20 emerging economies to world growth has exceeded 100 percent, implying that the group's resilience has helped offset the weakness in the rest of the world. Hence it can be said that the G-20 emerging economies led the recovery process after the global financial crisis.[1]

1. According to ADB (2011), Asia's strong rebound from the global financial crisis stimulated the global recovery. Indeed, during the global crisis period (from the third quarter of 2008 through the third quarter of 2010), growth of exports from a sample of non-Asian developing countries (Brazil, Mexico, Saudi Arabia, and South Africa) and industrialized countries (France, Germany, Japan, United States) to major Asian countries (PRC, Hong Kong, China, India, Indonesia, Republic of Korea, Malaysia, the Philippines, Singapore, Taipei, China, and Thailand) was higher than the growth of their exports to the rest of the world. Both industrialized countries and developing countries thus benefited from Asia's rapid recovery and consequently healthy appetite for imports.

Financial Regulatory Reform

The ongoing G-20 and Financial Stability Board (FSB) debates on reforming global finance so far have been mostly among advanced economies. Emerging market economies (EMEs) were largely bystanders, possibly because their deposit-and-lending-based financial systems are structurally very different from those in advanced economies. The G-20 has a stream for assessing and monitoring the impact of financial regulatory reform on these emerging market and developing economies. However, instead of simply waiting for new rules to be finalized, implementing them mechanically, and taking corrective action, EMEs need to strengthen their involvement in global financial regulatory discussions.

Over the years, membership in various international forums has expanded to reflect the changing economic power of the EMEs. Unlike the situation of a couple of decades ago, EMEs are now members of international institutions such as the G-20, the Basel Committee on Banking Supervision (BCBS), and the FSB. However, while the EMEs' presence in international discussions is increasingly accepted, they have yet to make an impact on the deliberations. All eleven relevant rule-making institutions are located either in Europe or in the United States.[2] Among the chief executives of those institutions, only one is from Asia, while the rest are from Europe or the United States.[3] This imbalance demonstrates that EMEs are being effectively excluded from important discussions. While this may be because of the relative underdevelopment of their financial markets, it is important for EME voices to be more heard, because the regulatory structure being put in place will also be adopted by their future financial markets.

Financial panics are invariably preceded by escalating leverage. The primary drivers of leverage in advanced market economies (AMEs) and EMEs are, however, strikingly different. The recent galloping leverage in AMEs was meant to increase returns on capital through increased trading of claims on

2. The eleven institutions are the ten members of the Financial Stability Board (the Bank for International Settlements, the Basel Committee on Banking Supervision, the Committee on the Global Financial System, the Committee on Payment and Settlement Systems, the International Association of Insurance Supervisors, the International Accounting Standards Board, the International Organization of Securities Commissions, the Organization for Economic Cooperation and Development, the International Monetary Fund, and the World Bank) plus the Financial Stability Board itself.

3. The Asian executive is Yoshihiro Kawai, head of the International Association of Insurance Supervisors Secretariat.

real economy assets in an environment of low returns. This led to a rapid expansion of financial assets as a proportion of their GDP. High credit growth in EMEs, like the People's Republic of China (PRC) and India, conversely, was primarily meant to finance high rates of investment and growth. Global production has long been migrating to these countries because of rapid productivity shifts. Their economies are consequently far less financialized. Ever since deposit insurance and the central bank discount window were put in place, deposit-based banking has become less susceptible to financial panics and bank runs, as long as capital is calibrated to cover asset deterioration during business downturns. Unsurprisingly, therefore, even as they were affected by sudden stops from abroad, financial intermediation among EMEs held up even as the Western financial system froze.

Financial regulation in a number of EMEs was already more stringent than in AMEs. After the Asian financial crisis in 1997, many Asian economies also tightened their regulations more than the proposed norms. Their central banks paid special attention to asset bubbles. Their "boring" banking could never afford the outsized compensation that encouraged excessive risk taking in AMEs. Banks were tightly regulated and not allowed to become interconnected with shadow banking, and thus regulators did not need to deal with products that were opaque and had complicated structures. EMEs, therefore, found it easy to sign on to the reforms. Indeed, to the extent that the Western financial system became "safer," they stood to gain. Although they are net savers, much EME financial intermediation is routed through the international banking system, where they park their excess savings. A shock in AME financial systems was, therefore, automatically transmitted to EMEs through sudden stops and attendant currency crises, which derailed their economies from time to time. In the past these stops were usually of their own making (through poor macroeconomic management), but this time it was caused by lax financial regulation in AMEs.

The impact of the ongoing financial regulatory reforms on EMEs has been relatively benign so far. Surprisingly, despite the general decline in cross-border claims on financial assets among AMEs, especially in Europe, capital flows to EMEs are back to precrisis highs.[4] Capital flows to EMEs appear to be more affected by monetary policies in AMEs than by their regulatory reforms. In Asia, for example, aggregate inflows to ten large Asian economies fell to 1.7 percent of GDP during the global financial crisis of 2008–09, from an

---

4. McKinsey Global Institute (2013); Cho and Rhee (2013).

average of 8.4 percent in the previous three years. But inflows rebounded sharply in 2010–12 to 7.4 percent of GDP. EMEs' chief concerns about their financial systems remain developmental rather than regulatory: increasing financial savings to accelerate growth and development, notwithstanding the fact that in recent years capital was flowing uphill from EMEs to AMEs. This is arguably a temporary, unsustainable phenomenon and will change as the global economy rebalances. AMEs, on the other hand, need major regulatory changes that inoculate them against the risks their financial systems face. History tells us that the relationship between financial depth and growth is not linear but is more like the Kuznets curve, where high growth is associated with greater financial depth only up to a point, beyond which the association breaks down and the risks increase. AMEs need to roll back their more extreme forms of financialization, which expose them to greater risk without a commensurate impact on growth. They also need to focus more on nonfinancial structural impediments to higher growth, such as falling investment and competitiveness, adjustments to demographic shifts, and rigid labor laws that have contributed to the migration of brick-and-mortar economic activity to EMEs. The priority accorded by the eighth G-20 summit to boosting investment was therefore a step in the right direction.

While financial regulatory reforms are expected to be implemented across all jurisdictions, their immediate impact would mostly be felt in the relatively lightly regulated AMEs rather than in the more tightly regulated EMEs. The impact of the new Basel III banking capital adequacy norms, however, will be almost equal across both AMEs and EMEs.

While the rationale for tightening capital adequacy norms for the banking sector in AMEs, where the recent financial crisis originated, is self-evident; the case for immediately migrating from Basel II to Basel III in EMEs is not. The argument in favor of common norms is to avoid arbitrage. This alone is not very convincing, because any capital migrating to a more regulated environment would incur additional costs because regulation is a proxy tax. Ironically, according to a recent BCBS assessment, G-20 EMEs are actually ahead of AMEs in implementing Basel III.[5] This puts them in the vanguard of Basel III–related financial instruments, which are still little understood by markets, thereby introducing new risks in their financial systems.[6] EMEs need to be better engaged at the rule-making stage and at least raise their voices regarding the phase-in of Basel III, especially since the AMEs are lagging behind them

5. BCBS (2013).
6. "Volcker Rule to Curb Bank Trading" (2013).

in implementation. However, the larger question is, How should EMEs balance a regulatory framework with risks in AME financial systems that could extract a high developmental cost through forgone growth?

There is a danger that scarce savings in EMEs might be pulled away from the investment necessary to sustain current levels of high growth to cover nonexistent risks. Basel III constitutes a double blow for countries like India. It could constrain the rapid credit growth necessary to sustain high growth, on the one hand. One the other hand, it could aggravate the runaway structural fiscal deficit of a government that would need to come up with substantial additional capital by virtue of its large ownership of the banking sector. The cost of capital is already high among EMEs. The enhanced capital requirements of Basel III are almost guaranteed to keep this cost high in the foreseeable future.

What then is the right lesson to learn from the 2008 global financial crisis? After the subprime crisis there was increasing aversion to capital market development, securitization, derivatives, and investment banking. Should EMEs stop proceeding with capital market development and move back to a bank-dominated financial structure? For many Asian economies that have reached middle-income status, a key constraint to graduating to high-income status is the relative underdevelopment of their financial sectors. To avoid falling into a middle-income trap, authorities must ensure that adequate funds are available to finance their economies' sustained growth and development. This entails sharing financial risks more widely as well as allocating funds more efficiently. In other words, greater sophistication of financial markets is still necessary, but it must be accompanied by measures to keep financial vulnerability in check. With relatively stronger regulatory regimes, EMEs in the G-20 have a big strategic stake in raising global financial regulatory standards and in pushing for regulatory reforms in systemically important economies to ensure greater financial stability going forward.

Macroeconomic Policy Cooperation and the G-20 Framework for Strong, Sustainable, and Balanced Growth

Five years on is a good time to take stock of what macroeconomic cooperation within the G-20 has achieved, and what it has not. First, the biggest success is that the strong, coordinated policy response may have averted a second Great Depression. Over the years, however, this stellar achievement has been somewhat tarnished by the fact that the global economic recovery, particularly in advanced economies, has been perhaps the worst in the postwar period. Since it was well known to policymakers that recoveries from financial crises can be painful and protracted because of deleveraging, in retrospect it appears that the G-20 and its Framework for Strong, Sustainable, and Balanced Growth (G-20 framework) dwelt far too much on fiscal and monetary stimulus in the earlier stages and too little on the transmission channels and the structural reforms needed to translate this into a robust recovery.

Second, the major external imbalances that the framework sought to address have indeed been reduced.[7] But external imbalances also reflect internal imbalances. In retrospect, the framework, at least in its earlier stages, dwelt far too much on contentious exchange-rate policies and too little on a coordinated correction of internal imbalances through structural reforms. By and large, deficit countries adjusted to the decline in demand not by increasing investment but by increasing consumption. Likewise, surplus countries adjusted by increasing investment rather than domestic consumption.[8] This has left open the questions of whether the imbalances have been reduced because of lower demand and decline in trade and whether they would return when global growth revives.[9]

Third, although the monetary policies of international reserve issuing currencies result in huge cross-border spillovers, there was relatively little coordination on monetary policies within the G-20.[10] This is surprising, since both central bank governors and finance ministers are part of the G-20 deliberative process. Animated discussions took place on fiscal policies, exchange rate policies, the international monetary system, and capital flows. Finance and central bank deputies spent long hours discussing the trade-offs between austerity and growth. This debate was mostly among advanced economies, as EMEs' growth prospects hinged greatly on the recovery of the AMEs. EMEs were mostly united in their fear that a premature exit from stimulative policies in

---

7. The U.S. current account deficit declined from 5.8 percent of GDP in 2006 to 2.7 percent of GDP in 2012, while the PRC surplus declined from 8.5 percent to 2.3 percent during this period. IMF (2013).

8. Thus investment in the United States declined from 22.3 percent of GDP in 2007 to 19.0 percent in 2012, whereas it rose from 37.4 percent in developing Asia (including the PRC) to 43.3 percent over the same period. IMF (2013).

9. According to IMF (2013), "Policy has played a limited role in narrowing global imbalances." As advanced countries consolidate their public finances, surplus countries may have to live with lower growth if they do not rebalance their economies (p. 13). This seems to be already happening, with the IMF significantly marking down medium-term growth prospects of emerging market economies.

10. Prime Minister of India (2013).

AMES, while private demand remained weak, could choke off their own relatively robust recovery. As concerns over public deficits and debt in advanced economies mounted, however, central banks assumed a growing share of the burden for driving the recovery. The resultant surge in liquidity, and more recently the threat of reversal, made EMEs' exchange rates extremely volatile and threatened their quick recovery from the crisis. G-20 policy coordination in the matter, however, remains extremely weak. The argument that monetary policy is driven by domestic considerations, and thus is less amenable to international policy coordination, applies equally to fiscal policy. Yet it is pertinent to underscore EMEs' ambivalence on quantitative easing. When quantitative easing was first implemented, these countries voiced concern over its cross-border spillovers through a surge in capital inflows and currency appreciation. However, as the tapering of quantitative easing threatened to lead to a sudden stop of such inflows, EMEs made a case for a graduated approach for the same reason: global spillovers. This ambivalence merely reflects the structural weakness of EMEs, which makes them increasingly dependent on international reserve currencies in a globalizing world, a theme addressed in a subsequent section.

Fourth, the G-20 framework has made it difficult for countries to agree on common, enforceable, macroeconomic indicators, rules, or commitments. An attempt to arrive at an agreed threshold for current account balances at Seoul led nowhere. The indicators mandated by the leaders at Seoul to form the basis of country commitments eventually turned out to be no more than each G-20 country's own macroeconomic projections that the International Monetary Fund (IMF) could use for determining the overall consistency of G-20 macroeconomic policies. Countries have also found it difficult to give any forward-looking policy commitments beyond what has already been successfully steered through their own domestic legislative, regulatory, and judicial processes.

It is, therefore, unsurprising that both the Mutual Assessment Process (MAP) and accountability assessments have repeatedly underscored that, while policy coordination has achieved tangible results, the framework outcomes have nevertheless fallen far short of the G-20's objective of strong, sustainable, and balanced growth. However, some degree of caution is warranted in placing unrealistic expectations on the budding G-20 process going forward. In particular, it is important to draw a distinction between coordination and commitment.

In its early stages, the G-20's focus was on coordinating policies—developing a consensus on what needed to be done, with each country contributing what it could, depending on individual country circumstances. The G-20 has been much less successful as it moved toward trying to obtain country commitments. The spirit of cooperation quickly evaporated amid "naming and shaming," which some members of the G-20 had warned against in the early deliberations.

The sovereignty of internal policies of nation-states has been recognized at least since the seventeenth-century Treaty of Westphalia. G-20 leaders have nevertheless incrementally committed themselves to more intrusive policy coordination within a relatively short time. This is in itself a remarkable development, considering the IMF's earlier experience with multilateral surveillance.[11] It is even more remarkable that leaders of the world's biggest developed and developing economies are talking to each other on equal terms and signing common documents on mutually agreed objectives and commitments—in contrast to taking vastly different positions in forums such as the United Nations and Bretton Woods.

The question is, How can the G-20 nudge countries' policies in mutually agreed directions and hold sovereigns accountable for commitments given, especially since these commitments are not legally binding and there is no enforcement mechanism? What gives cause for optimism is that economic interests are becoming increasingly aligned through globalization. Global business cycles and economic interests have begun converging through cross-border trading and financial spillovers. Domestic policy actions in a fast-integrating world, with growing market and policy spillovers, are increasingly linked to global outcomes. Domestic business cycles are becoming more and more globally aligned. If rebalancing does not take place, growth will decline everywhere; but if rebalancing is uncoordinated, the outcomes could be even worse. Policy cooperation—and beyond that policy harmonization or convergence—would be a win-win result. This harmonization is of course the work of specialized multilateral forums like the World Trade Organization (WTO) (trade), the BCBS (financial regulation), United Nations Framework Convention on Climate Change (UNFCCC) (climate policies), and the Global

11. The IMF's Consultative Group on Exchange Rate issues has been evaluating the exchange rates of industrialized countries and, more recently, of major developing countries as well. Its measurements indicate that exchange rate misalignments and current account gaps tend to be persistent even over the medium term. See Abiad, Kannan, and Le (2009).

Forum (tax). However, given its systemic importance, the G-20 could give the decisive push where required if its leaders are firm in their resolve, as they were at the high point of the global financial crisis.

If this resolve weakens as the recovery takes hold, it is because the trust necessary for effective policy coordination will take some time to be on a firm footing. From an EME perspective, this trust is at least partly contingent on the willingness of advanced economies to give them a greater voice and share in global institutions, in which the G-20 has made a good start. Beyond this, agreement on enforceable rules-based policy coordination would run into issues of sovereignty, as it has in the European Union, where the benefits and hazards of such cooperation and harmonization are most clearly manifest. G-20 countries are therefore finding it difficult to make forward-looking commitments beyond what has already occurred in the domestic policymaking space.

The eurozone and the European Union are pushing the envelope of the nation-state, and to a great extent, the challenges facing the G-20 are similar, with economic integration moving far ahead of political integration. At this juncture a new political economy and institutional structure is needed to manage globalization, built on mutual trust, peer pressure, and cooperation. Leaders will no doubt learn how to do so as they go along. Seen from this perspective, the G-20's policy coordination through its Framework for Strong, Sustainable, and Balanced Growth is a brave new experiment in pushing the political boundaries of globalization to harvest this cooperative dividend.

Governance Reform of the World Bank and the International Monetary Fund

While in London in 2009 the enlargement of the resources of such international financial institutions as the IMF was agreed upon relatively easily, given the urgency of the crisis, the consensus on governance reform of these institutions turned out to be much harder to implement. This was to be expected, because this was a zero-sum game, with both the major gainers and losers represented in the G-20.

At the 2009 Pittsburgh summit, G-20 leaders committed to "a shift in IMF quota share to dynamic emerging markets and developing countries of at least 5% from over-represented countries to under-represented countries using the current quota formula as the basis to work from" and "a significant increase of at least 3% of voting power for developing and transition countries" in the

World Bank.[12] The leaders also recognized the need to address other issues, such as the size of IMF quota increases, the size and composition of the IMF executive board as well as enhancing its effectiveness, and the IMF governors' role in the institution's strategic oversight. However, the devil was in the details, and the details were intentionally left ambiguous to allow room for further negotiation. For example, the definitions of "dynamic emerging economies" and "over- and under-representation" can be interpreted differently. It was also well known how difficult it would be for the IMF board to agree on the all-important new quota formulas that would determine winners and losers in this negotiation. The announcement was perhaps an "advance payment" to the emerging economies for their flexibility on issues such as trade policy, exchange rates, climate change, and IMF contributions. In other words, in Pittsburgh the leaders agreed to open the debate, but the really difficult decisions were postponed.

G-20 members endorsed the World Bank reforms in Toronto in 2010, thereby increasing the voting power of developing and transition countries by 4.59 percent (3.13 percent as agreed at the Pittsburgh Summit plus 1.46 percent as agreed during the earlier phase of reforms since 2008). The members also reaffirmed their commitment to secure a dynamic formula to establish equitable voting power for under-represented World Bank members.[13]

In sharp contrast to the IMF, reform at the World Bank made significant progress without much difficulty. This might be because the reform effort was initiated even before the G-20 summits began. It may also have been politically easier for AMEs to reduce their quota at the World Bank, as the fast-growing crisis increased domestic pressures to cut development aid. By contrast, there appears to be greater discord about the proposed IMF governance reforms, perhaps because much more is at stake for AMEs, particularly in terms of members' representation in global macroeconomic policy management and surveillance, with an increasing proportion of IMF assistance going to European countries.

Between the Toronto and Seoul summits, negotiations were held right up to the last minute of finalizing the summit documents. An internal consensus among G-20 members that the deadline should not be missed to maintain the credibility of the summit ramped up peer pressure to end the politically difficult negotiation on time. The problem lay not simply in reflecting political differences between advanced and emerging economies, as opinions differed

12. G-20 Information Center (2009).
13. G-20 Information Center (2010a).

even within the AMEs (the United States and Japan versus Europe), within Europe (large versus small European countries), and even among EMEs.

The most sensitive issue remains the revision of the IMF formula for calculating members' voting power. For example, EMEs take the view that a larger weight should be given to GDP in purchasing power parity (PPP) terms to reflect their greater economic weight, whereas European economies (which have vast intraregional trade flows) and Japan want greater emphasis on openness and past contributions to the fund. The EMEs, which accounted for only 31.0 percent of global output in PPP terms in 1980, increased their share to nearly half—49.6 percent—in 2012. However, in terms of total trade, these economies will continue to lag behind AMEs, having accounted for only 38.1 percent in 2012. Reducing the weight of the openness measure would significantly scale back European countries' power in the IMF, while raising that of the PRC, India, and Brazil.

After serious political haggling at the Seoul summit, agreement was reached to shift more than 6 percent of IMF shares to dynamic EMEs. G-20 leaders also agreed to double IMF quotas. The deadline for the comprehensive review of the quota formula was set for January 2013 and the completion of the next general review of quotas for January 2014. In addition, the leaders also committed to reform the composition of the IMF executive board by reducing the chairs assigned to advanced European economies by two and possibly assigning a second alternate chair for all multicountry constituencies. The board's composition would be reviewed every eight years.[14] At the Cannes and Los Cabos summits, G-20 leaders reiterated their commitments to the deadlines set at the Seoul summit.[15]

However, the deadlines for implementation of the 2010 amendment on quota increases and governance reform (October 2012) and the completion of the comprehensive quota formula review (January 2013) were both missed. The required U.S. approval of the agreement suffered a setback when Congress failed to sign off on the reallocation of its existing $65 billion IMF commitment into a permanent hike in its shareholding.[16] IMF members also continue to disagree on the revised formula for calculating members' voting power. With little agreement within the G-20 on currency, trade, and climate change issues, AMEs may now be of the view that the advance payment has not delivered the grand bargain they had in mind.

14. G-20 Information Center (2010b).
15. G-20 Information Center (2012).
16. Bernes (2013).

At the St. Petersburg summit, no new deadline for implementation of the 2010 IMF quota increase and governance reform was specified, but the target for agreeing on the quota formula was integrated with the January 2014 deadline for the fifteenth General Review of Quotas.[17] Since G-20 countries are also the major shareholders of the IMF, successful completion of these reforms will test the credibility of the forum.

Global Safety Nets, Capital Flows, and the International Monetary System

The global financial crisis of 2008 forced G-20 leaders to reconsider the effectiveness of the existing global crisis management system led by IMF credit-support facilities. This was precipitated by several new important events. First was the realization that financial crises not only affect EMEs but could also wreak havoc in AMEs. As a result, the financial support needed could be extremely large and could test the limits of IMF lending programs. Second, the crisis demonstrated that EMEs could suffer from a serious global liquidity shortage, no matter how sound their macroeconomic management. In fact, ever since the East Asian crisis a decade earlier, EMEs had become aware of the threat of such external spillovers, which, combined with their unhappy experience with IMF programs, provided the incentive to rely increasingly on reserve accumulation as a self-insurance mechanism and on regional safety nets such as the Chiang Mai Initiative. Whether or not reserve accumulation was a conscious self-insurance mechanism, or merely the flip side of a model of export-led growth, it nevertheless helped cushion the sudden stop that followed in the wake of the global financial crisis. At the same time, it became clear that rising global imbalances, and its flip side of excess reserve accumulation, were signs of defiance of the global financial safety-net architecture—signs that needed to be confronted. Otherwise, global imbalances would remain a permanent threat to the stability of the international monetary and financial systems.

In the past sudden capital flow reversals were typically seen as a problem internal to EMEs, such as macroeconomic mismanagement and weak financial systems. For this reason, the IMF and the international community had traditionally advocated structural reforms and sound macroeconomic policies to guard against financial crises in these economies. The 2008 crisis, however, originated in the AMEs, against the backdrop of the U.S. subprime crisis.

17. G-20 Information Center (2013a).

These events resulted in tightened liquidity conditions, initially in the financial centers of AMEs, which were then transmitted to EMEs, causing dramatic reversals of capital flows.

The flip side of sudden stops is sudden surges of capital. This is precisely what followed the sudden stops of the financial crisis, in the wake of the aggressive and unconventional monetary response to the crisis in the AMEs, leading to sharp appreciation in the currencies and asset markets of a number of EMEs. Exchange rates and financial volatility in emerging markets now came to be increasingly associated with the structure of the international monetary system.

To counter these external shocks, several global crisis response mechanisms were proposed to supplement domestic policy measures. The IMF was now willing to contemplate temporary capital controls as a last resort to deal with such surges, which was reflected in "coherent conclusions" arrived at by G-20 countries at the Cannes summit.

Bilateral swap arrangements between the U.S. Federal Reserve and central banks and the IMF's flexible credit line (FCL) were used during the crisis to counteract the impact of sudden stops. While these were important tools, and were put to good use by a number of countries, both mechanisms had significant shortcomings. Bilateral swap arrangements have their limitations as credible and secure sources of foreign currency liquidity because of their temporary, ad hoc, and political nature. The FCL, for its part, has certain advantages over the IMF's other lending facilities, such as the standby arrangement, in that the FCL provides precautionary financing with less stringent conditionality. Nevertheless, since use of the IMF's resources has, until recently, been primarily associated with crisis resolution, a lingering stigma inhibits some countries from accessing the FCL. This points to the need for a mechanism that can break the first-mover problem, in which countries hesitate to approach the IMF for financial support because of a fear of being stigmatized, and therefore penalized, by financial markets.

Perhaps in part because of persistent deficiencies in the existing global financial safety nets, a number of emerging market countries continue to rely on the accumulation of foreign exchange reserves as a form of self-insurance against sudden outflows of international capital. The fact that countries with larger reserves generally fared better in the recent crisis may, in the absence of credible alternatives, further incentivize EMEs to accumulate greater reserves, despite the significant opportunity and operational costs. Not only are the costs of such policies borne by the individual countries holding them, there are also important implications for the global economy. Increasing reserves incentivizes the buildup of global imbalances, and holding excess reserves diverts resources from other productive uses with potentially higher returns, including consumption and investment, which could contribute to global growth. Moreover, as the Republic of Korea painfully learned as it rushed to tie up a bilateral swap with the U.S. Federal Reserve following the collapse of Lehman Brothers, it is difficult to assess what level of reserves is adequate to quell market fears. These observations underscore the imperative for strengthening global financial safety nets.

It is unsurprising therefore that it was under the Korean presidency that the issue of financial safety nets was first brought up within the G-20. While central banks were mostly resistant to the idea of supporting EMEs through bilateral swaps by printing money, it was surprising that these economies were also initially not supportive of the focus on the global issue of financial safety nets in the G-20 amid concerns that such discussions would open the door for criticism of their large accumulation of foreign currency reserves.

The G-20 initiative led to some improvement in the IMF's lending facilities by enhancing its crisis prevention tool kit with the introduction of the multicountry flexible credit line and the precautionary credit line, which was eventually replaced by the precautionary and liquidity line. However, according to the IMF's own assessment, members' use of the new credit lines remains fairly limited because of the stigma associated with their use.[18]

At the Cannes and St. Petersburg summits discussions on strengthening global financial safety nets continued, but the nature of the discussions changed significantly to cooperation between the IMF and regional financing arrangements. The focus on these arrangements gained importance as the European crisis worsened, leading to the establishment of the European Stabilization Mechanism and the European Financial Stability Facility. It may be recalled that when Asian countries raised the possibility of establishing the Asian Monetary Fund and the Chiang Mai Initiative in the immediate aftermath of the Asian financial crisis of 1997, the initial reaction of the international community and the IMF was negative. The international community is finally paying attention to this important topic. Ways to better coordinate the multilateralized Chiang Mai Initiative and the IMF are currently being actively discussed in Asia. The IMF and the G-20 can no longer ignore such regional arrangements, although much work remains to be done to coordinate regional financing arrangements with global institutions.[19]

18. IMF (2011).
19. See Rhee, Sumulong, and Vallée (2013).

Going forward, the G-20 needs to have a fuller and more candid debate on the international monetary system, one that goes beyond financial safety nets, capital flows, expanding the special drawing rights basket, and reviewing the IMF's reserve currency basket, all of which are simply manifestations of the underlying global reserve currency issue.

The Development Agenda

The G-20 development agenda is one of the main agenda items in G-20 summits, together with the G-20 framework. As the first non-G-7 country to host the summit, the Republic of Korea placed development on the G-20 agenda at a time when the global economy appeared to be recovering strongly from the global financial crisis. The objective was to demonstrate the G-20's leadership as a premier forum for international economic cooperation—a leadership that actively engaged all stakeholders in the global economy, not just the members of the G-20.

However, initially the inclusion of the development agenda was not considered favorably by G-20 members, for two main reasons. First, a focus on development would simply duplicate the work of such institutions as the World Bank and the Asian Development Bank. Many G-20 members were of the view that the focus of the G-20 should be limited to those economic and financial issues that the G-20 could address in concrete terms. Second, a focus on development would require expanding overseas development assistance commitments that the AMEs were already struggling to meet. It was therefore decided that the G-20's development discussions should focus on concrete deliverables and otherwise play a steering role in determining the priorities of development policies. At the 2010 Toronto summit, the G-20 established the Development Working Group to create a development agenda. This was followed by the adoption of the Seoul Development Consensus for Shared Growth during the Seoul summit in November 2010.[20]

Though not well recognized, the Seoul Development Consensus introduced new insights into the international development dialogue. It recognized that growth is overwhelmingly the biggest contributor to poverty reduction. It also attempted to ensure the correct emphasis in international development efforts on economic factors—such as infrastructure, private investment, and skills—in achieving poverty reduction through growth. In

20. G-20 Information Center (2013b).

addition, the inclusion in the G-20 of such countries as the Republic of Korea, the PRC, India, and Brazil—that is, countries with varying development models—was a recognition of the fact that there is no single model for growth and development. Further, the development agenda advocated a "client-oriented approach" based on extensive inquiry into what developing countries themselves wanted. The Seoul Consensus thus reflects the view that low-income countries should be equal partners in achieving a resilient and balanced global economy and that addressing bottlenecks in infrastructure investment, and especially bottlenecks to regional infrastructure, is extremely urgent and must be given top priority.

However, once the Development Working Group started to collect G-20 member countries' priorities for the development agenda, it realized that these issues were too diverse and complex to reach consensus. After three months of intensive negotiations under the Korean chair, the G-20 drew up a multiyear action plan, with the following key pillars of development: infrastructure, private investment and job creation, human resource development, trade, financial inclusion, growth with resilience, food security, domestic resource mobilization, and knowledge sharing. Many critics point out that these are too many goals to have meaningful deliverables, but it should be noted that the Development Working Group had to deal with more than a hundred to begin with.

As the G-20 presidency rotated, the importance attached to the nine key pillars varied. The French and Mexican presidencies emphasized infrastructure and food security, but the latter included green growth as part of the agenda. Facing criticism that the development agenda was simply too long and lacked concrete deliverables, G-20 leaders asked the Development Working Group at Los Cabos to establish an assessment and accountability process before the summit in St. Petersburg. The objective was to enhance transparency, identify best practices and lessons learned, draw conclusions, and determine next steps. The first accountability report was released in August 2013. Meanwhile, during the Russian presidency, the G-20 decided to narrow the nine development pillars to four pillars—food security, infrastructure, financial inclusion, and human resource development.

Evaluation of the G-20's development agenda varies. Some see the agenda as enhancing the group's legitimacy, since the development issue is relevant beyond the G-20 and actively engages all stakeholders in the global economy. Ethiopian Prime Minister Meles Zenawi's comment that the Seoul Development Consensus embodies the African consensus is proof that the development agenda has the potential to make the G-20 more inclusive and representative.[21] Conversely, a succession of crises—the global financial crisis, the Europe sovereign debt crisis, and financial market turmoil brought about by talk of tapering U.S. quantitative easing—has constrained the efforts of traditional donors. Also, the initial concern about the expansion of topics is not unfounded: each host has had its own preference for development topics and introduced other ministerial channels beyond the nine pillars identified at the Seoul summit. In this regard, the decision at the St. Petersburg summit to reduce the number of pillars and strengthen the assessment and accountability mechanism is timely. Moving forward, it is important to limit the scope of the development channels and prevent the proliferation of other ministerial channels while strengthening the legitimacy of the remaining development channels through concrete deliverables.

Trade, Climate Change, Energy, Tax Avoidance, and Corruption

The G-20 agenda has expanded since the third summit, in Pittsburgh, where there was a sense that the worst of the crisis was behind us. Climate change, energy, food, fuel subsidies, and illicit outflows were added to the G-20 agenda at this summit. The intention of the G-20 leaders was never to shift international negotiations on these contentious issues to itself but rather to arrive at a broad understanding among systemically important economies about legally binding agreements. This understanding could be reached by implementing what had already been agreed on to arrive at nonbinding agreements.

The G-20's experience in these noncrisis areas has been mixed. The G-20 has spectacularly failed to deliver on two major initiatives to accelerate legally binding agreements in the parent forums, namely the Doha round of trade talks at WTO and climate change negotiations through the UNFCCC. It has, however, enjoyed more success in accelerating implementation of, and building on, what had already been agreed, as in the case of some WTO commitments, anticorruption, and tax evasion. The outcomes in the third area, that is, nonbinding agreements such as phasing out fossil fuel subsidies, are on the whole disappointing because of ambiguities in the formulations, including the measurement of subsidies and the absence of a time line for compliance. On the whole, these initiatives may have distracted the G-20 sherpas from devoting more time to crisis management. At any rate some high-profile failures have raised doubts about the effectiveness and credibility of the G-20

21. *Korea Herald*, July 7, 2011.

forum despite its very substantial achievements in handling the global financial crisis.

The G-20 moved quickly to agree on trade standstills, committing G-20 countries to not roll back existing levels of openness. That international trade has remained largely open, and that protectionist measures have been relatively minor despite a deep recession and a protracted period of tepid global growth, are testimony to the G-20's cooperation in crisis management.[22] This success, however, has been marred by its notable failure to push the Doha round to an early conclusion in the WTO or to prevent the slide toward bilateral, regional, and plurilateral trade agreements.

The spectacle of G-20 leaders resolving to push the Doha round to an early conclusion, summit after summit, and then having trade ministers repeatedly fail to do so at Geneva, severely dented the credibility of the G-20. It could perhaps be argued that the G-20 was too sanguine about the prospects of further liberalizing trade, about which there were already deep divisions between developed and developing countries within the WTO during a severe economic downturn when the natural instinct was to raise rather than lower trade barriers. Leaders could instead have taken credit for preventing the world from retreating behind protective barriers, as it did during the 1930s, arguably tipping a steep recession in economic activity into the Great Depression. The results were there for all to see, for after having initially fallen more steeply than during the Great Depression, global trade bounced back smartly.[23] In retrospect, however, since the G-20 devoted so much of its energy to retrieving the Doha round, the overall perception is that it failed to revive the flagging multilateralism and the movement toward plurilateralism in international trade agreements. Going forward, the big issue at the Brisbane summit could be whether the G-20 will persist with its efforts on Doha or nudge G-20 countries

---

22. While a large number of minor trade restrictive measures have accumulated over time, in the aggregate, they affect only about 3.5 percent of world imports and 4.4 percent of G-20 imports. WTO's measurement of protectionism, however, does not include new forms of protectionism, such as a fiscal stimulus that differentiates between domestic and foreign or nonresident investors, local production requirements, visas and residence permits, financial support to domestic companies, and central bank measures to enhance the functioning of credit markets and the financial system that influence international capital movements in complex ways. As a result, while global exports/GDP ratios have not declined, they have nevertheless stagnated. OECD/WTO/UNCTAD (2012); Evenett (2013a, 2013b); "The Gated Globe" (2013).

23. According to IMF (2013), except for a slight dip during the deep recession in 2009 and early 2010, the ratio of global exports to global GDP (measured at market exchange rates), which had risen sharply during the preceding boom, did not decline.

toward plurilateral agreements, such as the transatlantic and transpacific agreements, being negotiated near Geneva.

The G-20 experience with issues relating to climate change is eerily similar. Climate negotiations have long been stuck in the UNFCCC on the issue of equitable distribution of costs between, on the one hand, developed countries responsible for the existing stock of emissions and, on the other, developing countries whose share in current flows is rising rapidly. Several attempts have been made in various G-20 work streams, including working groups in both the finance and sherpa channels, to arrive at an understanding on reworking the Kyoto Protocol, especially issues relating to the financing of adapting to and mitigating climate change. However, the differences between the positions of the developing economies and those of the advanced economies have proved intractable. Despite several hours of animated deliberations across several summits, the G-20 has very little to show in terms of any breakthrough on climate change negotiations, with developing countries mostly unwilling to engage on the issue because they are wary of undermining the position of their climate change negotiators in the UNFCCC. Developing countries insist on qualifying any statement on climate change issues by reiterating the primacy of UNFCCC principles, in particular the common but differentiated responsibilities of developed and developing countries. Mexico's attempt to tie its priorities for the Los Cabos G-20 summit to a green growth approach generated misgivings among other G-20 developing countries, as this is a contentious issue in UNFCCC climate change negotiations.

The G-20 has enjoyed greater success in persuading member countries to commit to ratifying and implementing international agreements that have already been agreed upon in parent forums, such as those on corruption and tax evasion. The anticorruption initiative, for example, draws on some elements in the Pittsburgh communiqué. The basic idea is to implement and build on such mechanisms as the Financial Action Task Force, the United Nations Convention against Corruption, the Extractive Industries Transparency Initiative, and the OECD Anti-Bribery Convention.

With the relaxation of controls on foreign investment, foreign exchange, and capital flows globally, there has been a surge in cross-border transactions bringing into focus issues of tax evasion and illicit flows that pose serious challenges to the global economy, security, and fiscal management. The G-20 has been a key driving political force to counter tax havens and noncooperative jurisdictions to prevent migration of systemically important financial activities. The threat of naming and shaming, the continuous peer reviews, ratings, and countermeasures, including tax penalties on parties in transactions with tax havens, all appear to be working. The restructuring of OECD's Global Forum on Transparency and Exchange of Information for Tax Purposes to include most financial jurisdictions within its ambit has also helped. It has consequently been effective in pushing countries to enter into bilateral agreements on tax information exchange and, subsequently, to sign the multilateral agreement on automatic exchange.[24] The Financial Stability Board is separately assessing compliance of countries with international standards on cooperation and information exchange among supervisors. However it is still to be seen to what extent this is leading to more effective exchange of information between tax authorities and supervisors.

Conclusions: The G-20 from an EME Perspective

The G-20 is not a simple coalition between the G-8 and the EMEs. Indeed, as the above examples demonstrate, coalitions among G-20 members vary depending on the issues at hand.

While there is no clear evidence that the G-20 reflects non-G-20 members' views better than other international organizations, it is undeniable that the group is a better representation of the reality of the growing economic power of EMEs. Because the latter are equal partners in the forum, they are much more willing to engage with AMEs in a nonconfrontational manner unlike in other multilateral forums where their representation is limited and they have little sense of ownership. The G-20 also appears to be more effective than other larger and more representative multilateral institutions, such as the United Nations, in reaching consensus among its members. Also, since it includes all of the large and systemically important economies, a consensus within the G-20 has the potential to impact global outcomes. This was clearly in evidence in the group's initial stages, when a coordinated policy response by G-20 countries may have averted a second Great Depression. The G-20, therefore, has the potential to become an effective institution for policy coordination to manage the spillovers associated with globalization—or as a global solution to a global problem. However, it needs to expand its outreach to reflect the views of non-G-20 countries as well as to improve its legitimacy.

Overall, there are five important takeaways from the experience of G-20 summits in the past five years:

24. OECD (2013).

First, the G-20 was more effective in the early stages when the global economy was in a deep crisis but less so in coordinating policies during the recovery to get growth back on a sustainable track through structural reforms. There has also been more coordination on fiscal and structural policies than on monetary policies, even though EMEs in particular are the most affected by spillovers.

Second, the finance channel has delivered more concrete outcomes than the sherpa channel, perhaps because the former is involved in readily actionable issues, while the latter is focused on political issues on which consensus cannot easily be reached. Debates in the sherpa channel tend to reflect an impasse in the parent forum, as in the case of climate change finance, the Doha round, and development. The agenda of the finance channel has also not expanded greatly. Most agenda inflation has been through the sherpa channel, but this is largely in response to host countries' preferences. Often, host countries display their leadership by introducing issues on which agreement is hard to secure. A mechanism is needed to prevent such wanton agenda expansion. Nevertheless, the sherpa channel has been effective in accelerating implementation of what has already been agreed to in the parent forum, such as confronting corruption and tax evasion and meeting WTO commitments.

Third, the combination of an expanding agenda and nondelivery risks a credibility problem for the G-20, with most issues being carried forward from summit to summit, along with new additions. These are often couched in ambiguous and excessively long summit documents, which conceal sharp differences among members.

Fourth, while the G-20 has a conscious policy of "outreach" to non-G-20 countries, it needs to reach out more effectively to non-G-20 members to ensure that their voices are heard in global discussions.

Fifth, and finally, the G-20 is more effective when a consensus is reached on what needs to be done collectively but less effective when country-specific commitments are requested and individual countries held accountable. While there is no doubt regarding the need for strengthening the peer pressure mechanism through better monitoring mechanisms to make the G-20 more effective and credible as the premier international steering group on global issues, this mechanism also raises issues of trust and sovereignty that are still unresolved in even more integrated bodies such as the European Union. The G-20 in its new incarnation is a very young organization, and unrealistic expectations should not be placed on it. While its track record may not be stellar, it has nevertheless delivered much more than other multilateral organizations. Its leaders will no doubt improve its effectiveness in reaching consensus.

References

Abiad, Abdul, Prakash Kannan, and Jungjin Le. 2009. "Evaluating Historical CGER Assessments: How Well Have They Predicted Subsequent Exchange Rate Movements?" Working Paper 09/32. Washington: International Monetary Fund.

ADB (Asian Development Bank). 2011. *Asian Development Outlook 2011*. Manila.

BCBS (Basel Committee on Banking Supervision). 2013. "Report to G20 Leaders on Monitoring Implementation of Basel III Regulatory Reforms."

Bernes, Thomas. 2013. "IMF Quota and Governance Reform: Political Impulse Needed for Progress on Reform Process." Ottawa: Centre for International Governance Innovation.

Cho, Dongchul, and Changyong Rhee. 2013. "Effects of Quantitative Easing on Asia: Capital Flows and Financial Markets." Economics Working Paper 350. Manila: Asian Development Bank.

Evenett, Simon J. 2013a. "Protectionism Does Not Have to Leave a Smoking Gun." *Financial Times*, July 19.

———. 2013b. "Protectionism's Quiet Return: The GTA's Pre-G8 Summit Report." *Vox*, June 13.

G-20 Information Center. 2009. "G20 Leaders Statement: The Pittsburgh Summit." October 24–25.

———. 2010a. "The G20 Seoul Summit Leaders' Declaration." November 12.

———. 2010b. "The Seoul Summit Document." November 12.

———. 2012. "G20 Leaders Declaration, Los Cabos, Mexico." June 19.

———. 2013a. St. Petersburg Action Plan. "Annex 4: The St. Petersburg Accountability Assessment and Progress toward Strong, Sustainable, and Balanced Growth."

———. 2013b. "St. Petersburg Accountability Report on G-20 Development Commitments."

IMF (International Monetary Fund). 2011. "Review of the Flexible Credit Line and Precautionary Credit Line." Policy paper. November 1. Washington.

———. 2013. *World Economic Outlook Database. October*. Washington.

McKinsey Global Institute. 2013. "Financial Globalization: Retreat or Reset?" March.

OECD (Organization for Economic Cooperation and Development). 2013. "Progress Report to the G20 Leaders: Global Forum Update on Effectiveness and On-going Monitoring." Global Forum on Transparency and Exchange of Information for Tax Purposes. September.

OECD/WTO/UNCTAD (Organization for Economic Cooperation and Development, World Trade Organization, and United Nations Conference on Trade and Development). 2012. "Reports on G20 Trade and Investment Measures (Mid-May to Mid-October 2012)." October 31.

Prime Minister of India. 2013. "PM's Address at the St. Petersburg G-20 Summit." September 5.

Rhee, Changyong, Lea Sumulong, and Shahin Vallée. 2013. "Global and Regional Financial Safety Nets: Lessons from Europe and Asia." In *Responding to Financial Crisis: Lessons from Asia Then, the United States and Europe Now*, edited by Changyong Rhee and Adam Posen. Washington: Asian Development Bank and Peterson Institute of International Economics.

"Volcker Rule to Curb Bank Trading Proves Hard to Write." 2013. *Wall Street Journal*, September 10.

BRUCE JONES

4

The G-20 in Crisis? Or the G-20 on Crises?

At the time of writing, we are just over five years past the peak of the global financial crisis. Since 2009, substantial progress has been made toward recovery. Yet it is premature to declare an end to the crisis. Slowing global growth, tough transitions in the emerging powers, and the eurozone crisis are the manifest signs of continuing troubles, while credit risks in China and resurgent protectionist sentiment in the major economies are flashing yellow lights about potential deeper troubles ahead. Moreover, by most accounts the regulatory and preventive steps taken after the global financial crisis were only partial in scope and have been only partially implemented. So on the global economy, continued crisis recovery and a watchful eye for new fissures remain the critical challenges for the G-20.

At the same time, though, the geopolitical situation has begun to change, and not for the better. That raises the prospect that crises of a very different type—geopolitical and security—could begin to impact the functions and functioning of the G-20. One form of this is security crises landing on the agenda of the G-20 per se, as happened with the Syria crisis during the Russian G-20 summit in St. Petersburg. The second, more pernicious form would come if a continued deepening of great power tensions in Asia and Europe began to impede whatever economic and financial cooperation has been formed between the established and the emerging—in the financial arena, really the *emerged*—powers.

Bruce Jones is senior fellow and director of the Project on International Order and Strategy, the Brookings Institution; consulting professor, Stanford University Freeman Spogli Institute for International Studies; and chair of the New York University Center on International Cooperation.

There is something of a contrast between these realities and the way G-20 practices have evolved. On the economic side, the dynamism, flexibility, and emphasis on political communication that characterized the first, critically successful, years of the G-20 gave way with surprising speed to routine and to a loss of flexibility in response to events. And the G-20 has resisted tackling security crises, despite repeated warnings it would have to—and was thus ill prepared to do so when that eventuality arose.

Despite premature reports of its demise, the G-20 remains a crucial body for the global economy and for geopolitics more generally. But at an old five years, it needs a tune-up: primarily a greater not lesser focus on the ongoing features of the economic crises—but also some creativity in dealing with security crises in a changing geopolitical landscape.

From Early Success to Early Aging

Poll politicians outside the G-20 (and increasingly within it) and analysts outside the narrow circle of G-20 specialists, and you find a conventional wisdom: the G-20 was important for the global financial crisis, but it rapidly evolved into a talk shop of little impact and little import—a "toothless talk shop," in one analyst's punchy conclusion.[1] Even analysts who had been closely involved in the G-20 in its early years began to argue that the forum needed a serious retooling.[2]

The most trenchant criticisms of the G-20 surely overstep the mark. For one thing, even if the G-20 were disbanded tomorrow, it would still go down in history as one of the most successful international bodies of all time. If its sole claim to fame were that it provided a mechanism to help the major economies limit the impact of the global financial crisis and avoid a great depression, this would stand as one of the most important accomplishments in the history of global governance. What is more, the G-20 has had important continued successes through a mechanism often overlooked in media and punditry commentary.

Much of the criticism of the G-20 has been aimed at summit outcomes, some of that fairly. But there is more to the G-20 than summits; there have been a huge number of interactions between finance and treasury and other economic and state officials of the G-20 in between summits. And important

1. Rafferty (2010). See also Nayyar (2013); "G-20 Summitry and Seoul" (2010); Vestergaard and Wade (2011).
2. Callaghan (2013).

things have happened in these interactions, much for the good. The forging of functionalist relationships between central bankers of the established and the emerging powers is one important outcome, albeit an outcome that is hard to measure.[3] One careful study of this phenomenon uses functionalist concepts to explain the G-20's endorsement of the Organization for Economic Cooperation and Development's (OECD's) international tax transparency agenda.[4] Senior policy officials responsible for the G-20 also point to the interactions between the G-20 and the OECD as evidence of impact—for example, in functionalist pressures on Chinese officials to improve their performance on countercorruption measures.[5]

In addition to the functionalist point, there is an important mechanism at work that elicits little comment. Among policy officials in the rising powers, there is an awareness that the Western economies have a more advanced regulatory and policy infrastructure, something that the rising powers themselves will need to develop if they are to manage the middle-income transition they now confront.[6] Yet issues of sovereignty, of nationalism, of rivalry, even of pride impede the rising powers from simply seeking advice or support from bodies like the OECD—bodies from which they have been excluded, bodies dominated by the Western powers, bodies that symbolize their marginal and often humiliating status in the international system throughout the postwar period. Western analysts often ask why the emerging powers don't simply join the OECD, as the OECD has invited them to—but this question substantially underestimates the psychological and political residue of inequity and arrogance, real and perceived, in relations between the OECD and non-OECD players (some of which continue to the present day in the stalled reform of international financial institutions). It was thus important politically to have a body in which the established and emerging powers were both present at the creation and had equal status.[7] Through that body, confident in their own position, the emerging powers could use the technical knowledge of the OECD without compromising their status.

---

3. Notes, Brookings/Australian National University workshop on the G-20 at Five, Canberra, November 14, 2013.

4. Eccleston, Kellow, and Carroll (forthcoming).

5. Senior policy officials, author interview, White House, January 2010.

6. On the challenges of the middle-income transition, see Sharma (2012); on its dynamics, see Kharas (2010).

7. For an OECD perspective on these interactions, see Angel Gurria, "The OECD and the G-20—An Evolving Relationship," remarks made at the Institute of International European Affairs, Dublin, November 4, 2009.

Finally, and of some importance, the G-20 has continued to resist protectionist pressures. This was true in Mexico City, and it was true again in St. Petersburg.[8] But while there was a modest degree of press reporting about these outcomes, it is a story that has been largely left out of the broader narrative of the G-20.

Perhaps it was left out partly because of a diminishing emphasis on political communications. The early days of the G-20 were characterized by top-level attention to political communication. This was not just to satisfy media pressure. It was a recognition of the fact that the global economy is not run by governments alone, or even primarily by governments. Confidence of the publics and of the private sector is a crucial ingredient in the global economy. Because this confidence was badly shaken by the failures that led up to the global financial crisis, restoring public and private sector confidence was a central objective of the Washington, London, and Pittsburgh summits—that trifecta of G-20 summits that should, in retrospect, be viewed in essence as a single global action (under joint U.S. and U.K. leadership) to forestall a global depression.

Since that time, political communication has waned. As Colin Bradford notes, there has been a growing political focus on satisfying narrow domestic constituencies, and leaders have adopted not the posture of "We're working together to forestall a shared crisis" but rather "I'm here to defend my nation's interests."[9] The more leaders posture that way, the harder it is to forge cooperative outcomes.

Of course, there's always been some of this in global summitry. One former head of state, who participated in many international summits, has reflected on this issue.[10] During the American G-8 summit in Denver, he recalls, there were, inside the room, close and intimate discussions among the leaders about common challenges. Behind closed doors, U.S. President Bill Clinton, in particular, was a globalist par excellence. But when the summit ended, and it was time for photographs and messages to the press, Clinton made a clear and deliberate gesture: all but turning his back to the assembled world leaders, Clinton had a hearty handshake for the cameras with the mayor of Denver. The message to the assembled American media: This isn't about international politics; this is about American jobs. Clinton was not only addressing his

8. See "G-20 Summit" (2012); "G-20 Extends Its Commitment" (2013).
9. Bradford (2013).
10. Brookings workshop, Project on Managing Global Order, March 2008.

domestic audience but also his peers. The message was: Remember, whatever I said in the room, I'm first and foremost a *domestic* political actor.

Nor is it surprising that there would be a rebalancing between collective messaging and domestic politics as we move farther out from the peak of the crisis. As the acute waves of a crisis recede, it is harder and harder to sustain press attention or to communicate in simple terms. The overwhelming pressure to act in the face of acute systemic crisis made it feasible for leaders to talk in a collective voice. The farther the crisis recedes, the more difficult that becomes.

And yet, as Bradford argues, "Leaders must still lead and be perceived to lead."[11] The challenge, as he puts it, is that "there is a great need . . . for leaders to not only embrace the anxieties of their publics but also provide them with a vision of a better future within a realistic understanding of the global context." He concludes that "more deliberate efforts by leaders to lead and to communicate their leadership more clearly will help guide their people to define their future in a complex global economy in which there are opportunities as well as challenges."[12]

By this metric, there is little doubt that successive G-20 presidencies have fallen short. There is always a healthy dose of ego and nationalism in summitry, but the balance between constructive national agendas and vanity projects matters, as does the willingness of a host country to balance the focus between pet projects with critical shared concerns and the meat and potatoes of a steady agenda. Looking back over five years, we can say that, after the U.S.-U.K. trifecta, Korea managed this balance exceedingly well and should be given substantial credit for keeping global development issues on the agenda at a time when continuing global economic frailty could easily have pushed them off. But the French, Canadian, and Mexican G-20 presidencies did far less well.

Many of the weaknesses of those G-20 processes have been widely documented and do not need to be revisited here. But one strand of concern that does require further comment is the theme suggested above: the growing disjuncture between the steady, paced modalities of the G-20 (or more rudely, the rapid bureaucratization of the G-20) and the still-unfolding waves of the global financial crisis.

11. Bradford (2013).
12. Bradford (2013).

This contrast was particularly manifest during the Mexican G-20 presidency. Throughout that year, there was a palpable gap between two realities: the eurozone crisis, which was unfolding and deepening throughout the course of the Mexican presidency, and the lack of high-level G-20 action on that crisis. In fact, an earlier opportunity was missed as well, during the French presidency, when the contours of the Greek financial crisis were becoming clear. The crisis deepened during the Mexican presidency. There was a striking, and frankly quite worrying, divergence between the two processes. On the one hand, the progressive buildup of the eurozone crisis was replete with endless eurozone summits, special sessions of the International Monetary Fund (IMF), and emergency meetings of just about every institution and government in the world except the G-20. Meanwhile, the G-20 was preparing for the 2012 Cancun summit in June. The obvious alternative was to convene a special G-20 summit in late 2011 or early 2012 to deal with the crisis. Of course, the eurozone crisis was a topic for officials engaged in the G-20 preparation, and the discussions of the eurozone crisis dominated the Los Cabos summit in June 2012. But by then the eurozone crisis had been unfolding for a year. It does seem to be the case that political and media encounters with European officials at Los Cabos added to their sense of pressure to act, and in this the G-20 had some influence. But throughout, the G-20 certainly looked, and arguably was, essentially irrelevant to the largest economic crisis of the moment—and one with global ramifications.

Of course, the correct locus of action for the eurozone crisis was in Europe itself; no one would have expected the G-20 to act in the absence of European action. But as European leaders dragged their feet, the G-20 did little or nothing to spur decisive action. That role was eventually played by a combination of the IMF and the European Central Bank (ECB). The G-20 members were important to the IMF and ECB response, but the G-20 as a mechanism was not.[13]

There is a counterargument here, which says, in effect, Look, this is your problem. It says, that is, that it was right for the G-20 to let Europe handle its own crisis. This argument has an important flaw. The eurozone crisis was a crisis of a scale that, if not handled correctly, threatened the entire global financial system and the global economy—precisely the kind of issue that should be squarely on the G-20's agenda. And in the end it was not only Europe that was involved in the response. At the IMF a rescue fund, or fail-safe fund, was established, with contributions from, among others, Russia, China,

---

13. For a similarly critical account of the G-20's effort on the eurozone crisis, see Kirkegaard (2012).

Brazil, India, and Europe.[14] The political event at which the non-European powers made their contributions was the Mexican G-20 summit in Los Cabos; in this sense, the gathering provided an opportunity for high-level political action involving this wider set of powers.[15] But most of the work had been done by the IMF long before the G-20 summit. Of course, I could argue that, since the IMF was working, there was no need for the G-20 to step in, and there is some merit to that argument. But the IMF cannot do two things that the G-20 leaders' level can do—put pressure on top leaders and send a powerful political signal of reassurance. Throughout this period, the lack of a G-20 summit meeting specifically on the eurozone crisis meant that the European leaders most involved in the response were not subject to the kind of collective pressure for action that the G-20 can arguably produce. So while Chancellor Angela Merkel was visited by U.S. Treasury officials, and President Barack Obama made phone calls to her as did other world leaders, the German chancellor was not compelled to sit before eighteen of her peers, the most powerful of which strongly disagreed with her approach to the crisis, and explain herself and German policy.

Perhaps a G-20 summit focused on the eurozone crisis would not have succeeded in shifting Merkel to a more expansive position, but the fact that it was not even tried did appear to reinforce the conventional wisdom about the toothlessness of the G-20. Certainly seen through the lens of political communication with the private sector and the publics, the fact that the G-20 was not responsive—or at the very least was not seen as responsive—to the eurozone crisis damaged its credibility and its ability, over the long term, to maximize its impact on global economic recovery and the forestalling of new financial crises with global impact.

Following Mexico, there were very low expectations for the Russian presidency. One observer quipped that in the course of two years the Russians had the opportunity to break three important international bodies—the G-20, the Olympics, and the G-8.[16] In fact, the Russian presidency exceeded expectations. There were important, if highly technical, outcomes on aligning taxation and on priming the pump for infrastructure spending. G-20 members continued to focus on the steps needed to deepen implementation of the G-20's continuing focus on "strong, balanced, and sustainable" growth. It was an unsexy set of outcomes but no less important for that fact. Indeed, the

14. "Europe Eyes IMF Channel" (2011).
15. Lagarde (2012); Rastello (2012).
16. British G-20 official, private communication, May 2012.

success of the Russian G-20 can be taken as an important piece of evidence in support of the theory that core participation in and leadership of global institutions tend to generate relatively responsible behavior.[17]

But Russia's credible economic stewardship was overshadowed by a different kind of crisis.

The G-20 and Security Issues: Syria Intrudes

The story line of the Mexican G-20 presidency skips one important initiative: the decision to host a foreign ministers' meeting of the G-20. This was a gutsy decision—and from my perspective, a welcome one. I wrote in support of it at the time, as did many others.[18] The argument was simple: because the G-20 has succeeded in forging effective ties between the established and emerging powers in the economic realm, it would be helpful for it to build similar relations between these powers in the foreign policy and security domain.

Moreover, it was starting to be problematic that, in the international architecture as a whole, events had produced a very odd net outcome. Assume that, in the period ahead, some form of interaction between the established and the emerging powers on diplomatic and foreign policy issues and security crises is going to be necessary for crisis management. Unless those interactions are to be confined purely to the bilateral level, some form of international architecture will be needed to structure them. Before the global financial crisis, there was some movement—albeit slowly—in that direction, in the Heilingendamm process— that is, the outreach process whereby the G-8 engaged five of the emerging powers (China, India, Brazil, Mexico, and South Africa) in their preparations and summits. (Russia of course was already in the G-8.) Although the bulk of this interaction was around economic issues, the fact that the G-8 has had an agenda that reaches beyond the narrow economic and financial realm meant that there was a prospect for interactions on foreign and security policy between the established and the rising powers. When the G-8 outreach process began to flag, the emerging power members began to caucus on their own—arguably the precursor to the BRICS' summit mechanism, which has continued to this day. Russia and China, of course, are also on the UN Security Council (UNSC). For a brief moment in the mid-2000s, there was some momentum for a partial reform of the UNSC that could have brought India, Brazil, Japan, and others into it, at

17. On the political impetus for the Russians to succeed in the management of the G-20, see Smith (2013). For an overall comment on the Russian G-20, see Kirton (2013).
18. See, for example, Patrick (2012); Jones and others (2012).

least on a long-term if not initially a permanent basis.[19] But that momentum stalled, and when the global financial crisis hit, the focus shifted—understandably—to financial issues and the international financial architecture.

All of this was sensible, but it produced an odd outcome. Until the Ukrainian crisis, Russia remained in the G-8 despite deepening divides between Russia and the West on foreign policy matters: during the U.K. G-8 in 2013 the Canadian prime minister, Stephen Harper, voiced what many were thinking, referring to the session as a meeting of the G7+1.[20] In the USNC the established powers have the opportunity to interact with the two rising powers least likely to cooperate with them on the most divisive issues: Russia and China. But in no major forum could the Western powers have a sustained interaction on foreign policy and security issues with India, Brazil, Indonesia, and Mexico. (Turkey, of course, is in NATO.) And there is one power, and only one, that sits in all top-level bodies (IMF, G-20, UN Security Council, BRICS)—Russia. A very odd architecture indeed and one hardly geared to channeling collective action by the world's new suite of top players—or to managing conflicts among them.

So there was a solid case for the Mexicans to innovate with a foreign minister's track for the G-20. There was controversy here, of course; Russia and China signaled that they were unhappy about the idea, and within Western capitals a number of sherpas and financial ministers were displeased. For a while it was unclear whether the meeting would proceed. But the then U.S. secretary of state, Hillary Clinton, seized the opportunity she had so far been denied—of participating in the G-20—and announced that she would attend.

Indeed, from the earliest days of the G-20 there have been two schools of thought about the relationship between the G-20 and hard security issues. The dominant school has been what we might call the financial purists, who argue to keep security issues well away from the G-20—to keep it narrowly focused on financial and economic questions. This argument is based on principle and buttressed by turf. This argument is important. It is that economic issues occupy a space characterized—at least in broad terms—by functionalist relations, a substantial degree of shared interests, and thus an important degree of comparatively uncontroversial cooperation. Not that there aren't huge interests at stake or important divergences in positions among members. This point reinforces the argument of principle: while the global economy was in a very delicate state, high levels of global cooperation were needed to right the

19. For an account of the back and forth on UNSC reform, see inter alia Trachsler (2010). The BRICS are Brazil, Russia, India, China, and South Africa.
20. "Canada's PM Harper" (2013).

ship, and there was a genuine fear of introducing into the body charged with that task issues that risked upsetting relations or driving wedges between the players.[21] Turf issues were never far away, though, as senior economic managers aimed to keep foreign policy players away from "their" forum.[22]

Then there is the "stuff happens" school of thought, which argues that, at some point in time, a security crisis with geopolitical consequences is going to break at the same time as the summit, and inevitably the leaders will want to discuss it; that, in other words, it will force itself onto the agenda. So there is no point in worrying about security issues until then. The argument is a simple and a practical one: When leaders get together, they will talk about whatever is foremost on their minds, or foremost in the news, irrespective of what their sherpas or officials would prefer.[23] The problem with this line of argument is that, in the absence of a preparatory mechanism, simply having leaders talk about an issue that is on their minds or in the news (which may amount to pretty much the same thing) is unlikely to lead to a constructive outcome. So, again, there is logic in a foreign ministers' track.

Unfortunately, the Mexican foreign ministers' meeting was poorly managed. In particular, the agenda for the session was poorly conceived; rather than providing a format to discuss new issues, or transnational threats that sit uncomfortably in the United Nations, the agenda was a banal sampling of routine foreign policy issues typical of a second-tier UN meeting. The Mexican presidency argues that what doomed the meeting was not the agenda but rather Russian and Chinese recalcitrance about having the G-20 discuss foreign policy issues at all, and there is some merit to that argument, as there is to the fact that India and Brazil's G-20 teams went too easily along with the coordinated Russian and Chinese position. But there was nothing about the presentation of the meeting or the agenda that gave substance or logic to the proposal or grounds for those in favor of the idea to defend it. Participating foreign ministries saw the meeting as having fallen flat, so it was no surprise when the Russians chose not to repeat the exercise.

And yet, it was, of course, during the Russian presidency that foreign policy and security issues forced themselves onto the G-20 agenda. The issue was the Syrian crisis and, more specifically, the August 21 chemical weapons attack, reportedly and presumably by Syrian President Bashar al-Assad's military.

21. For example, see Roberts and Olson (2013).
22. Author interviews, Washington, Ottawa, Tokyo.
23. Smith (2012); Patrick (2012).

In fact, St. Petersburg was not the first time that Syria caused the membership boundaries of global bodies to be blurred. In 2012, during preparations for the Camp David summit of the G-8, Turkey was invited to address a meeting of that group's foreign ministers (albeit by video). It was a reminder of two things: that many of the world's global forums have not adapted their membership to the new realities; and that the G-20 still faces competition in terms of high-level tools that can be used to manage global issues. But the St. Petersburg G-20 discussion on Syria marks an important break in the G-20's pattern. This was the first time that its leaders took on a foreign policy and security issue—and one at the very top of the geopolitical agenda at that.

Some participants in the St. Petersburg G-20 summit argue that the discussion on Syria was substantive and mature.[24] Noted G-8 and G-20 watchers, like John Kirton, agree.[25] Fair enough, but the fact that the agenda item was added more or less at the last minute meant that there was little preparation for the discussions; further, there was no concrete outcome. The Syria discussion happened very much the way the "stuff happens" school of thought predicts—and with a predictably limited effect. The discussion of the Syria crisis added nothing to other discussions (financial, economic, food, and energy) or to the summit's report. Nor did it contribute meaningfully to the resolution of the Syria crisis.

That no outcome was achieved could be chalked up to the difficulty of the issue, but the fact of the matter is that, mere weeks later, the United States and Russia did forge an agreement on removing chemical weapons from Syria, a deal subsequently endorsed by the UN Security Council. However, the process by which that deal was forged was chaotic and did little to provide reassurance or to damp down geopolitical tensions. Quite the opposite. On the American side, the episode was characterized first by a surprising degree of confusion about whether or not there would be domestic consent for military action in response to the chemical weapons attack, the scale of that action, what effect it might have, or what American policy would be in the aftermath. When, some days later, the U.S.-Russia deal to remove the chemical weapons was done, President Obama would note that he had originally floated the idea with Putin at the G-20 meeting, but in public, at least, the deal emerged when U.S. Secretary of State John Kerry floated the idea at a press conference with Russian Foreign Minister Sergey Lavrov. (He then immediately distanced himself from it.)

24. Notes, Brookings/Australian National University workshop on the G-20 at Five, Canberra, November 14, 2013. See also Joint Statement on Syria (2013).
25. Kirton (2013).

The White House also distanced itself from the proposal in a statement the following day. Then, apparently to American surprise, Putin endorsed the proposal and drove it forward. The process allowed Putin to take credit for it, and he seized the opportunity to lambaste the Americans, penning an arrogant and aggressive op-ed in the *New York Times*.[26] It was a process that did little to give confidence in U.S. leadership but, at the same time, did little to bolster American confidence in the UN Security Council. Only Russia gained diplomatically.[27]

Now, imagine a counterfactual. A foreign ministers' track, or something with a similar function, was established by the Mexican presidency. Obama signals to Putin, after the chemical weapons attack, that he wants to grapple with Syria at the St. Petersburg summit. Putin needs St. Petersburg to be a success. The foreign ministers' track gets to work, and by the time Obama arrives at St. Petersburg the homework has been done on a plan to remove the chemical weapons from Syria. The deal is finalized in St. Petersburg, announced in a joint press conference by Putin and Obama, and referred to the UN Security Council for voting and implementation. There is no guarantee, of course, that this would have been the outcome; an effort at a deal might have fallen short in St. Petersburg. But there is a precedent in the way Russia and the United States used the G-8 in 1999 to finally resolve their differences over Kosovo (in that case, after American and NATO military action). And the odds of a managed process would have been greater had there been a preparatory process or channel, and the effect would have been salutary—an important piece of evidence that the great powers are still capable of cooperating to prevent the worst outcomes in serious crises. Substantively, it is the same outcome—but diplomatically and geopolitically, a significantly better one.[28]

Opposition to the G-20 expanding into foreign and security policy issues comes from this line of argument as well: that the G-20 taking this on would weaken the authority of the United Nations. But there is no realistic scenario in which the G-20 takes on the kind of operational roles that the UNSC man-

26. Putin (2013).

27. All this being said, media stories and punditry that the Putin-Obama deal had reasserted Russia's position as a Middle East player or even as a global power were seriously overwrought. Russia has no new allies, no new assets, and no new capabilities as a result of the deal, and whatever soft power gains Putin made were temporary and quickly washed away by Putin's excesses over gay rights and the controversy over the way gay rights would play out at the Sochi Olympics.

28. It is worth noting, parenthetically, that such an outcome—like the G-8 deal on Kosovo—would do nothing to undermine the UN Security Council's position as the preeminent mechanism for managing international peace and security issues.

ages; at most, the G-20 can be a forum for political prenegotiation and deal making between top powers, which would then move their protoagreements to the UN Security Council for formal decisionmaking and action.

So the question arises: Should we move toward a standing capacity for the G-20 to handle foreign policy and security crises? The answer depends in part on an assessment of the geopolitical landscape ahead.

Changing Geopolitics and the Case for G-20 Action

Are we—as the French foreign minister, Laurent Fabius, argues—in an apolar or a zero-polar world?[29] Have we entered what Ian Bremmer and David Gordon as early as 2011 described as a G-zero world, where neither U.S. unilateral leadership nor collective action is possible?[30] If we have—that is, if we have entered a moment wherein geopolitical tensions are certain to block the great powers' cooperation—then there is a serious risk in moving the G-20 into the foreign and security policy terrain. Divisions among the powers would impede effective agreements by the G-20 and risk undermining their cooperation on economic and financial matters. Fortunately, we are as yet a long way away from a G-zero world or from the breakdown of cooperation between the great powers.

The argument that this is so warrants greater discussion than is possible here, but the essential points can be summarized.[31] First, reports of the death of American power have been greatly exaggerated. The United States remains not just the largest economy in the world but also the most influential—a position of strength that it is likely to retain even after China overtakes it in terms of GDP. China will in the not too distant future become the largest economy in the world in sheer size, but it will still have a far lower per capita GDP than the United States, with less influence in global markets and with far fewer shares of global profits in most key industries.[32] The United States retains the largest military in the world and is the only state with a genuine capacity to deploy force globally. It has unparalleled political relations, diplomatic capability, intelligence assets, and higher education establishments. And most of all, it has a suite of allies—at least a dozen of the world's top economies are U.S. allies or close partners. And of the rest, most are closer geopolitically to the United States than they are to China or any other putative U.S. rival.

29. Fabius (2013).
30. Bremmer and Gordon (2011).
31. I make this argument in greater length and with greater evidence in Jones (2014.)
32. Starrs (2013).

The challenge posed to the United States from the BRICS is less than meets the eye, for two reasons. First, separately, each of the BRICS faces substantial challenges domestically, both on the economic front and in related political transition.[33] This is captured by the concept of the middle-income transition and the complex set of reforms that must accompany the shift from economic production oriented around low-cost labor and the export of cheap goods to one based on greater innovation and technological sophistication. Second, while the BRICS' summit maintains a façade of unity around key questions in the international financial order (including international financial institutions' reform), the reality is serious tension conflicting with possible deeper economic ties. More to the point, the most important BRICS share important interests with the United States and the Western powers—or at the very least, their interests overlap to a substantial degree.

The dynamic that most resembles this breakdown is U.S.-Russian relations following the Ukraine crisis and Russia's move to annex Crimea. At the time of writing, two things remain unclear: how long the crisis will endure, and how wide the spillover will be. We've seen new tensions rise in some theaters (North Korea), but cooperation continues in others (Africa, Afghanistan). What is less in doubt is the serious deterioration in the relationship between the United States and Russia.

All this means that there is more scope for problem solving than the zero-polarity argument would suggest. Two facts supporting the G-zero theory are the failure of the international system to deal with Syria and deadlock in UN negotiations on climate change. But there are also important counterarguments. At the unquestioned height of American power, in the late 1990s, the international system was deeply divided over first Bosnia and then Kosovo. In the first of those crises, as many people died before America acted as have died so far in Syria; yet American leadership was not thought to be in decline. In Kosovo, geopolitical differences between Russia and the United States deadlocked the UN Security Council until NATO eventually launched military action; yet there were no claims of an apolar world. In fact, the major powers were cooperating in the Security Council and in many other settings, including in crises that involved force.

Two points on climate: the notion that something as extraordinarily complex as a shift from high-carbon energy to a low-carbon energy mix was going to be negotiated in a set of inclusive UN summits was surely always a false expectation. Even as the UN conference of parties limps along, progress has

33. Sharma (2012).

been made on interim measures through bilateral agreements between the United States and China and between the United States and India.[34] And there is ample evidence of cooperation on various aspects of the global economy, on transnational threats, on development, on fragile states—the list goes on.

All this being said, there is no question that we have entered a phase of mounting geopolitical tensions. These tensions are most important in three regions, each with very different dynamics.

First, there is the Middle East, with its violent revolutions and counterrevolutions. The giddy first days of the overthrow of Tunisia's President Zine El Abidine Ben Ali and the resignation of Egyptian President Hosni Mubarak in the face of sustained demonstrations in Tahrir Square and beyond seem long behind us. In those first days, regional activists and Western commentators alike rushed to welcome the outbreak of democracy. The history of revolutions and transitions from authoritarian rule gave cause for more caution—the history of these transitions is one of long, tortured, often violent, and frequently unsuccessful change.[35] Even if we assume ultimate success for democratic forces—and there is no solid historical basis for that assumption—there is every reason to believe that we are still in the early phases of turbulent transitions. The Middle East looks likely to be in a combination of political and violent crises for at least another half decade, possibly longer.

It would be a mistake, though, to imagine that every aspect of this turmoil will divide the major powers. The crisis in Syria, the Arab Spring's most violent to date, has of course divided Russia and the United States and, to a certain extent, has also created tensions between the United States and China and India. But even there, as the crisis has evolved, important points of alignment exist, especially around a desire not to see al Qaeda emerge as a major force in Syria. That speaks to a common theme: whatever the differences between the major outside powers over their preferred constellation of power in the various Arab capitals, none has an interest in all-out chaos, and all share an interest in forestalling a resurgence of al Qaeda or related brands of Islamic fascism. They share a profound interest, too, in the stability of energy flows from the Persian Gulf. That the United States and Russia and China have been able to work together on sanctions on Iran speaks to the potential for cooperation—or at the very least reducing conflicts of interest in the Middle East and the Persian Gulf.

34. Most important, arguably, is a U.S.-China agreement on hydrofluorocarbons; see "United States and China Reach Agreement" (2013).

35. Huntington (1968); Fukuyama (2011); Diamond (2011).

Second, and arguably more complicated, are the geopolitical tensions in Asia. These are newly prominent but have been growing for more than a decade. At play are several reinforcing dynamics. One dynamic is the competing claims on the substantial energy reserves in the South and East China Seas. (The seas are also major fishing grounds, an added source of competition.) A second dynamic is that these claims overlap two sets of contested territories—claims that arise from China's bold (some would say reckless) claim to sovereignty within the infamous nine-dash line; and more dangerously, claims that linger from unresolved boundaries at the end of World War II. A third dynamic is that these unresolved tensions linger on in the relations between Asian powers and are frequently stoked by nationalist politicians in Japan, China, and Korea. Finally, China's economic rise appears to be unleashing pent-up competitive sentiments; some observers argue that there is a strong sentiment in the Chinese military for a confrontation with Japan, to right what the Chinese see as historical wrongs dating from World War II. Relations between the world's second- and third-largest economies are shockingly bad; a 2013 poll shows that positive sentiments about China were held by only 5 percent of Japan's population.[36] The result has been tension between Japanese and Chinese navies and air forces and even intermittent near clashes. Nor is the United States isolated from these dynamics, as the standoff between a Chinese warship and the U.S.S. *Cowpens*, in December 2013, illustrates.

Geopolitical tensions in Asia are most likely, over time, to undermine the G-20. Already, Japan-China tensions have led to a weakening of trade between these two giant economies. That is bad enough, but if geopolitical tensions mount further, or if there are active clashes, even if limited in scale, the effect on global confidence could be substantial. Deteriorating geopolitical relations could undermine the ability of some G-20 members to cooperate within international forums. Sharp exchanges between Japan and China have already occurred in multilateral meetings—for example, in the Warsaw Conference of Parties of the UN Framework Convention on Climate Change, where the Chinese condemned Japan for its decision to temporarily suspend its Kyoto Protocol commitments.[37] And naval and maritime tensions in Asia's waters could complicate what is otherwise a critically important economic, energy, and climate agenda—

---

36. "Global Image of the United States and China" (2013).

37. In point of fact, many other countries condemned Japan as well—rather unfairly, in my view, given what Japan had gone through as a consequence of the 2011 tsunami and the Fukushima disaster. Also see Miao, Han, and Gao (2013).

namely, investments in Asia's trading infrastructure and energy infrastructure, both to boost global spending and to lay the energy pathway (it is hoped, a greener rather than a grayer one) for the next phase of Asian growth. This issue may be of particular concern to the Australian G-20 summit, given the likelihood that it will want to focus in substantial part on infrastructure in Asia.

Third, and most acute, the EU-Russia political struggle over Ukraine, the collapse of the Yanukovych government in spring 2014, and the subsequent Russian intervention into and then annexation of the Crimean peninsula have recast relations between Russia and the West. While these strategic events in Europe need not connect to the G-20, media reports that the Australian foreign minister, Julia Bishop, had floated the idea of excluding Russia from troika preparations for the Brisbane summit caused the BRICS to band together in response, stressing that no one owned the G-20 and that it was no one's business to kick anyone out—not that that had been proposed. While the course of developments between the Crimea annexation and the Brisbane summit is (at the time of writing) unpredictable, the likelihood of significant U.S.-Russia or EU-Russia tensions infecting the Brisbane summit is high.

Quite apart from these regional security dynamics, internal and geopolitical, there are tensions as well in a series of policy domains where governance mechanisms are comparatively weak. These include cybersecurity, the broader domain of Internet governance, maritime security, and energy security. In the latter there is as much shared interest as there is competition, and it is one area where the emerging powers might actually be ready to shift toward more engaged cooperation with the International Energy Agency.

All of this suggests, at the very least, an active agenda for managing geopolitical tensions. Is that a job for the G-20? If the answer is no, the question is, Then who? The UN Security Council does not have all the players in it and is far better suited to operational crisis management than to processes that can lower geopolitical tensions. And the G-8 is too narrow. The G-20 may not be the best possible answer to the question of where to apply to try to lower geopolitical tensions, but for now it is the only answer we have.

Crisis Management and Brisbane

There is a more prosaic way of approaching this set of issues. Put yourself in the shoes of one of Australia's G-20 managers, preparing for the Brisbane summit in November 2014. Now, scan the world agenda, and in particular the evolving situations in North Korea, Syria, Iran, Egypt, and the East and South China Seas. Now ask this question: What are the odds that one of these situations breaks into crisis mode at the moment of the Brisbane summit? It is hard to say what the odds are of any one of these situations being in crisis mode at that juncture, but take them all together and the odds are surely low that none of them is.[38] In other words, Australia's G-20 managers—and Turkey's, when we look ahead to 2015—would be wise to plan on the likelihood of a security crisis dominating the headlines and the leaders' attention when they meet in Brisbane.

That is not to say that security crises are the only issues that will require acute and careful management by the G-20. No. To return to the opening theme of this chapter, there are still important residual effects of the global financial crisis, including the continuing saga of the eurozone crisis. Moreover, early signs of a wider global slowdown should be a cause for serious worry.

The core agenda of the Australian G-20 must surely be a continued focus on economic recovery, and indeed the Australian leadership correctly shows every sign of focusing on economic issues. But the G-20 is now mature enough to walk and chew gum at the same time, to use the American colloquial expression. In other words, the Australian G-20 summit can concentrate on financial issues while at the same time addressing foreign and security policy questions so as to lower geopolitical tensions and manage geopolitical crises.

It is surely the core point of the G-20, beyond specific financial or economic outcomes, to pull both the established and the emerging powers into joint management of the international agenda. By doing so it helps forge networks, build relationships, and foster joint action where necessary to keep the global economy on course. One productive consequence is functional ties among the members of the G-20 on core economic and financial issues. It is obviously crucial that the core economic agenda not be derailed, especially now, with the global recovery still fragile and signs of downturns in every one of the major emerging economies—and in several of the advanced economies as well. But ultimately, it is naïve to believe that the period ahead is not going to involve mounting tensions on a range of security issues in which the established and emerging powers will be entangled. Some of those tensions divide the powers, some unify them. At present the international architecture is not robust

---

38. There is a far wider set of crises, of course, from South Sudan to Chad to the Ivory Coast, but these are less likely—short of imminent outbreak of genocide—to rise to the strategic level that would warrant the combined attention of the world's top leaders.

enough to do either one of two necessary things: to channel collective action by the wider suite of players or to defuse geopolitical tensions among them. What would surely help is to establish a mechanism that would build a network of ties among senior officials in the security sphere.

How can this mechanism be built? There are two options: the G-20 could establish a foreign ministers' track, or it could explore more innovative, less formal options. Specifically, for Brisbane, I recommend that the Australian government take the following approach:

—Ask the leaders to bring with them to Brisbane a senior national security official.

—Leave it to individual leaders to decide whom to bring—their foreign minister, their national security adviser, or their diplomatic adviser. The decision should be theirs, but perhaps influenced by the agenda (see below).

—Host an informal side event for these officials, chaired by either Australia's national security adviser or its foreign minister.

—Leave the outcome open. At the time of inviting, the meeting should have no planned outcome—no statement, no communiqué; it should be an informal session.

—Communicate to the G-20 members, not in the formal invitation but through channels, that the informal session will be available should a major crisis demand G-20 leaders' attention, the way the Syria crisis did.

This approach does not forestall a discussion in the leaders' summit itself on a germane issue, should a situation arise that demands it; but it creates a built-in preparatory mechanism if one is needed.

What would the agenda of such a session be? Certainly it should avoid repeating the mistake of the Mexican foreign ministers' meeting and take up issues that would cause it resemble a mini General Assembly; there is no surer way to ensure that serious national security players would avoid it. There are three options here, each with pros and cons:

—Focus on a specific, first-tier crisis in which geopolitical tensions are complicating the response. This could be Syria, or the East China Sea, or North Korea, perhaps others. The upside of this: by definition it would be an agenda item already on leaders' radar and would command attention from their most senior and trusted national security officials—precisely the people who would be important to engage. The downside: by definition, this would be a topic that would risk resulting in no action or acrimony, and unless it proves surprisingly successful, would not contribute to building confidence or functionalist ties among national security officials.

—Focus on a specific, but second-tier crisis that affects all countries. An example would be Libya. The first phase of the Security Council's response in Libya was strongly unified, then it was somewhat divided, then it became tense. But as post-Qaddafi Libya has struggled with stability and rising radicalism, great-power perspectives have converged. The United States has taken new steps regarding building the Libyan army, and many within the United States (and the United Kingdom and France) are ruing their decisions to weigh in against the deployment of a stabilization force after the fall of Libyan leader Muammar Qaddafi. There is a UN and a World Bank presence on the ground, but both could use a boost. There are clear, shared, great-power interests in halting the deterioration of the security situation and clear, shared, great-power interests in ensuring the stability of Libya's oil infrastructure and ability to continue to produce. An informal session of the G-20's national security officials could give a political boost to international efforts to stabilize Libya (efforts by the UN, for example, or the World Bank).

—Focus on a thematic question, like energy transit security, or piracy, where there are strong, shared great-power interests but as yet no multilateral mechanism to foster joint action. This could build on such matters as the ongoing efforts on counterpiracy in Somalia and the Caribbean, the international response to the attack on oil installations in Algeria and the killing of Western oil workers there, and the counternarcotics and countersmuggling efforts in the Gulf of Guinea. Here, the G-20 could even go beyond merely trying to build up political support for deeper, joint efforts; it could explore institutional innovations. Consider the way that the G-8, in its later years, often sparked institutional innovations that would be housed outside the G-8, on issues of shared concern—like the Financial Action Task Force, which tackled terrorist financing, and the Proliferation Security Initiative. This approach may be complicated if there is a sustained deterioration in U.S.-Russia relations; but it could also provide an occasion for a return to cooperation if tensions have eased somewhat.

Of course, should a major situation break into crisis mode, the proposed agenda could be left aside in favor of focusing on that specific crisis, and preparing a leaders' discussion should one be required.

Although any variant on this approach would have costs for the Australian presidency, and some risks, it would have one very substantial upside: it would create a safety valve that would allow the Brisbane summit to stay focused on the economic and financial issues necessarily still at the core of its agenda, even in the face of a brewing crisis. Given how important the Australian G-20 summit is both to the real agenda of the global economy and to the political agenda of restoring public and private sector confidence in the G-20, the costs and the risks seem manageable.

A Time to Lead

There are pros and cons to this overall approach and pros and cons to any potential agenda item. If the Australian government does decide to adopt something like this approach, a decision on the agenda should be discussed in advance with core G-20 members, including not only the United States but also those members, especially Russia and China, that were leery about the Mexican foreign ministers' track. But the G-20 presidency has its prerogatives, and Australia has the deep relationships with all the critical players to be able to weather some criticism should some members be uncomfortable with this approach. There will be no advances in the management of geopolitical tensions without innovation and risk taking, and the history of effective multilateralism tells us that middle powers with close ties to the top powers are best placed to play this role.

On the financial and economic issues that remain at the core of the G-20's agenda, the basic message of this chapter is a simple and obvious one, but one that has been lost in the calcification of the G-20's routines: whichever country holds the G-20 presidency has to be prepared for the possibility that there will be a financial or economic crisis over the course of their year. At the time of writing, the situation that looks like it has the most potential to play that role is the French economy, but other issues could move from flashing yellow to red during the course of 2014. Should that happen, the credibility of the G-20 would be enhanced by responsiveness. Australia could take the following actions, as appropriate: change the timing of the summit, hold a special summit, or convene G-20 leaders (or the majority of them) in side events of other international gatherings (for example, the Asia Pacific Economic Cooperation forum and the UN General Assembly).

It is past time for the G-20 to innovate in the foreign policy and security domain and to find creative ways to contribute on the geopolitical side of things. The G-20 may not be the perfect vehicle for that function, but for now it is the only one available. If the tools necessary to manage rising geopolitical tensions are not forged in this body, there is a danger that the underlying relationships, which allow the G-20 to perform as it has—criticisms aside— on financial and economic issues, will begin to erode, putting the group's core functions in jeopardy. It is not too late to manage rising geopolitical tensions and maintain a degree of stability in great-power relations. And the G-20 has an opportunity to play this important role. But there is no time to lose.

References

Bradford, Colin. 2013. "Political Leadership Changes and the Future of the Global Economic Order." Paper prepared for the 20th Anniversary Conference of the Institute for Global Economics. Seoul. October 13.

Bremmer, Ian, and David Gordon. 2011. "G-Zero," ForeignPolicy.com, January 26 (blog.foreignpolicy.com/posts/2011/01/07/g_zero).

Callaghan, Mike. 2013. "The G-20: In Need of a Reboot." *Diplomat*, January 31.

"Canada's PM Harper Dubs Summit 'G7+1' as Russia Only One Not to Side with Syrian Rebels." *RT*, June 17, 2013.

Diamond, Larry. 2011. "A Fourth Wave or False Start? Democracy after the Arab Spring." *Foreign Affairs*, online, May 22 (www.foreignaffairs.com/articles/67862/larry-diamond/a-fourth-wave-or-false-start).

Eccleston, Richard, Aysnley Kellow, and Peter Carroll. Forthcoming. "G-20 Endorsement in Post-Crisis Global Governance: More than a Toothless Talking Shop?" *British Journal of Politics & International Relations*.

"Europe Eyes IMF Channel for Bailout Fund as China Considers Contribution." 2011. *Bloomberg News*, October 28.

Fabius, Laurent. 2013. Speech. 40th Anniversary of the French Policy Planning Staff (CAPS). National Library of France, November 13.

Fukuyama, Francis. 2011. *The Origins of Political Order: From Prehuman Times to the French Revolution*. New York: Farrar, Straus, and Giroux.

"G-20 Extends Its Commitment against Protectionism till 2016." 2013. *The Hindu*, September 7.

"G-20 Summit: Nations Agree to Delay Trade Barriers Amid Protectionism Panic." 2012. Reuters, June 19.

"G-20 Summitry and Seoul: Policy Powerhouse or Multilateral Talk Shop?" 2010. Discussion. Friedrich Ebert Stiftung and the Century Foundation, October 27.

"Global Image of the United States and China." 2013. Pew Global Attitudes Project, July 18.

Huntington, Samuel P. 1968. *Political Order in Changing Societies.* Yale University Press.

Joint Statement on Syria at the G-20 Summit in Russia. 2013. Office of the Press Secretary. White House, September 6.

Jones, Bruce. 2014. *Still Ours to Lead: America, Rising Powers, and the Tension between Rivalry and Restraint*. Brookings.

Jones, Bruce, and others. 2012. "Perspectives on the G-20 Foreign Ministers' Meeting." Brookings.

Kharas, Homi. 2010. "The Emerging Middle Class in Developing Countries." Working Paper 285. OECD Development Center.

Kirkegaard, Jacob. 2012. "Did the G20 Help the Eurozone." Interview by Christopher Alessia. New York: Council on Foreign Relations.

Kirton, John. 2013. "A Summit of Substantial Success: Prospects for St. Petersburg 2013." G-20 Information Center.

Lagarde, Christine. 2012. "IMF Managing Director Christine Lagarde Welcomes Additional Pledges to Increase IMF Resources, Bringing Total Commitments to US$465 Billion." Press Release 12/231, June 19. Washington: International Monetary Fund.

Maio Xiajuan, Han Mei, and Gao Fan. 2013. "Japan's New Emission Target Condemned at UN Climate Talks." *CRI English*, November 16.

Nayyar, Dhiraj. 2013. "Dear PM: G-20 Is Irrelevant, Is That Why You're There?" *Firstpost*, September 6.

Patrick, Stewart M. 2012. "Viva México! The G-20's New Political and Security Agenda." The Internationalist (blog). Council on Foreign Relations, February.

Putin, Vladimir V. 2013. "A Plea for Caution from Russia: What Putin Has to Say to Americans about Syria." *New York Times*, September 11.

Rafferty, Kevin. 2010. "The G-20 Is a Toothless Talk Shop." *Real Clear World*, November 19.

Rastello, Sandrine. 2012. "China Leads Nations Boosting IMF's Firewall to $456 Billion." *Bloomberg News*, June 19.

Roberts, James M., and Ryan Olson. 2013. "G-20 Leaders Should Address Economic Growth." Issue Brief 4035 on Economy. Washington: Heritage Foundation.

Sharma, Ruchir. 2012. *Breakout Nations: In Pursuit of the Next Economic Miracles.* New York: Norton.

Smith, Gordon. 2012a. "The Evolving Role of the G-20." Perspectives on the G-20: The Los Cabos Summit. Waterloo, Ont.: Centre for International Governance Innovation.

———. 2013b. "Political Dimensions of Russian G-20 Presidency Deserve a Closer Look." Priorities for the G-20: The St. Petersburg Summit and Beyond. Waterloo, Ont.: Centre for International Governance Innovation.

Starrs, Sean. 2013. "American Economic Power Hasn't Declined—It Globalized! Summoning the Data and Taking Globalization Seriously." *International Studies Quarterly*, April.

Trachsler, Daniel. 2010. "UN Security Council Reform: A Gordian Knot?" Analysis in Security Policy 72. Zurich: Center for Security Studies.

"United States and China Reach Agreement on Phase Down of HFCs." 2013. Office of the Press Secretary. The White House, September 6.

Vestergaard, Jakob, and Robert Wade. 2011. "The G-20 Has Served Its Purpose and Should Be Replaced." Policy brief. Copenhagen: Danish Institute for International Studies.

PART III

The Core G-20 Economic Agenda

RAKESH MOHAN AND MUNEESH KAPUR

5

Monetary Policy Coordination: The Role of Central Banks

Since the onset of the North Atlantic financial crisis in 2008, central banks in the United States and the other major advanced economies have pursued extraordinarily accommodative monetary policies through unconventional policy actions. Accordingly, policy rates have been near zero in these economies for almost five years, and both short-term and long-term interest rates have touched historic lows. These low interest rates encouraged the search for yield, and consequently, large amounts of capital flowed out from these reserve-currency economies to the still relatively fast-growing emerging market economies (EMEs), complicating their macroeconomic management.

Capital flows to the EMEs are known for their volatility. This volatility was again in evidence during May through August 2013, when the U.S. Federal Reserve first hinted at possible tapering from its unconventional monetary policy. The mere announcement of tapering led to large capital outflows from the major EMEs, resulting in sudden and large currency depreciations; it ignited fears of a return of the type of crises experienced in the 1980s and 1990s. However, stronger macroeconomic and financial policies pursued by the EMEs, and the buffers they had built over the past decade, helped them avoid a full-blown financial crisis. Nonetheless, the tapering episode has hurt their near-term growth prospects significantly while also illustrating the potential underlying vulnerabilities in the international monetary system.

Developments since 2008 have put a spotlight on the key role that monetary policy in the reserve currency countries has on the global economy. Given

Comments by Colin Bradford on a draft of this chapter are gratefully acknowledged.

these spillovers, there is a renewed debate on the merits of coordination of monetary policy among the major central banks. The conventional wisdom is that there are no significant benefits from international coordination of monetary policies. In this view, the global economy is best served by central banks focusing on fulfilling domestic inflation and output objectives, with central banks being one-objective, one-instrument institutions (focusing on price stability and with short-term interest as the only policy instrument). Financial regulation is best kept outside the central banks. This view is analogous to the precrisis dominant orthodoxy with regard to domestic financial regulation: that effective microeconomic prudential regulation of individual institutions ensures the systemic stability of the overall financial system. But this perspective and orthodoxy stands challenged by the 2008 crisis. There is now a greater recognition of synergies among the central banks. They are being entrusted with monetary policy as well as prudent microeconomic and macroeconomic financial regulation so that financial stability can be fostered. The central banks' institutional setup is being redesigned accordingly—for example, in the Bank of England, the European Central Bank, and the Federal Reserve.

The banking sector regulatory architecture has been characterized by international cooperation for a number of decades now: the Basel I, II, and III standards are the well-known outcomes of this approach.[1] The North Atlantic financial crisis provided an impetus to international economic and financial coordination, especially regulatory coordination and unprecedented and concerted fiscal expansion. Against the background of deteriorating economic conditions worldwide in the aftermath of the Lehman Brothers collapse in October 2008, the G-20 leaders at their Washington summit (November 15, 2008) agreed that "a broader policy response is needed, based on closer macroeconomic cooperation, to restore growth, avoid negative spillovers and support emerging market economies and developing countries." At the direction of the leaders, the G-20 constituted four working groups, and these were tasked with the objectives of enhancing sound regulation and strengthening transparency, reinforcing international cooperation, promoting integrity in financial markets, reforming the International Monetary Fund (IMF), and reforming the World Bank and other multilateral development banks.

The G-20 leaders' initiatives led to a significant strengthening of financial-sector regulations and the regulatory architecture, including the establish-

---

1. See Caruana (2012a); chapter 8, this volume.

ment of the Financial Stability Board (FSB) in April 2009. The FSB was a response to the November 2008 call from the leaders of the G-20 for a larger membership of the erstwhile Financial Stability Forum. The FSB coordinates the work of national financial authorities and international standard-setting bodies in order to develop and promote the implementation of effective regulatory, supervisory, and other financial-sector policies. At their Pittsburgh summit (September 2009), the G-20 leaders pledged to work together to ensure a lasting recovery and strong and sustainable growth over the medium term. To meet this goal, they launched the Framework for Strong, Sustainable, and Balanced Growth.

The G-20 initiatives also led to a noteworthy increase in the resources and lending capacity of the IMF in 2009 and again in 2012, which was a critical step in restoring global financial stability. At the G-20 London summit (April 2009), the leaders agreed to treble the resources available to the IMF to US$750 billion, to support a new special drawing rights allocation of US$250 billion, to grant at least US$100 billion of additional lending capacity to the multilateral development banks, and to ensure US$250 billion of support for trade finance. The G-20 initiatives led to an additional US$450 billion of resources for the IMF through bilateral borrowings in 2012. However, the delay in ratification of the 2010 quota and governance reforms has steered the IMF away from being a quota-based institution to depending increasingly upon borrowed resources. As a result, quota and voting shares of many dynamic EMEs are lower than their relative economic weights in the global economy, raising serious issues of governance and potential implications for effective IMF surveillance and advice. Overall, there have been welcome G-20-led initiatives at improving international economic and financial coordination since the onset of the North Atlantic financial crisis, and these have played a critical role in providing some stability to the global economy while avoiding a repeat of the 1930s Great Depression.

Domestically oriented monetary policy, rather than international coordination, is still seen as the optimal arrangement, although there are calls for a reassessment.[2] In Saint Petersburg in September 2013, the G-20 leaders echoed the conventional view: "Monetary policy will continue to be directed toward domestic price stability and supporting the economic recovery according to the respective mandates of central banks," although being "mindful of the risks and unintended negative side effects of extended periods of monetary easing. We

---

2. Eichengreen and others (2011).

recognize that strengthened and sustained growth will be accompanied by an eventual transition toward the normalization of monetary policies. Our central banks have committed that future changes to monetary policy settings will continue to be carefully calibrated and clearly communicated."[3]

It is, however, not the case that there has been no coordination at all. In the aftermath of the North Atlantic financial crisis, the activation of swap lines by the U.S. Federal Reserve with central banks in major advanced economies and a few select emerging markets is an example of some coordination. But this coordination appears to have been motivated by the fear, on the part of these advanced economies, of an adverse impact on themselves of the sudden drying up of liquidity. Thus this coordination does not appear to have been motivated by the likely impact of their monetary policies on the EMEs, an issue that is the focus of this chapter. Similarly, the Plaza and the Louvre accords of 1985 and 1987 are well-known illustrations of international monetary coordination, on the currency front, wherein the major industrial countries agreed to depreciate the U.S. dollar by engaging in coordinated interventions in the foreign exchange markets.[4]

Although there is no regular coordination among the major central banks on monetary policy actions, a great deal of discussion does occur among leading central banks at various international forums. The major forum for such discussions has been the bimonthly Bank for International Settlements (BIS) meetings of central bank governors, supplemented by periodic meetings of deputy governors. The G-20 and the G-7 are the other major international forums. Various conferences held by major central banks—for instance, the annual conferences at Jackson Hole, Wyoming—provide other opportunities for central bankers to exchange views. But these conferences focus mostly on analytical issues for monetary and other economic policies. Arguably, monetary policymakers share a more elaborate intellectual framework than their counterparts in financial regulation, which is well illustrated by the dominant consensus in favor of inflation-targeting monetary policy frameworks in the precrisis period. But such a consensus has its pitfalls, as was revealed by the North Atlantic financial crisis itself.

Against this backdrop, this chapter discusses the scope for international monetary policy coordination. We begin with a review of the monetary policies in the major advanced economies since 2007 and assess the extent of coordination among the major central banks. The following section then

3. G-20 leaders (2013).
4. Frieden and Broz (2013).

addresses the spillovers of monetary policies in the advanced economies toward the EMEs and focuses on the key channels (capital flows and exchange rates) of these spillovers and their implications for the EMEs. The next two sections critically assess the scope and feasibility for international monetary coordination and discuss options for the EMEs to manage the spillovers. Concluding observations end the chapter.

Monetary Policy in the Postcrisis Period: Continued Domestic Orientation and Large Spillovers

Beginning in September 2007, after the onset of the subprime crisis in August, the U.S. Federal Reserve switched its monetary policy stance toward an easing mode. It cut its policy rate from 5.25 percent in August to 2.00 percent by April 2008 and reached the zero bound by December 2008; it remains at that level five years later. The monetary response of the Bank of England and the Bank of Canada broadly tracked that of the Federal Reserve. The European Central Bank initially paused, until mid-2008, then tightened a little bit and went into easing mode only in October 2008, following the collapse of Lehman Brothers; this central bank reached its lowest rate of 0.25 percent only in November 2013. Other central banks displayed a more varied two-way response.

Conventional Monetary Actions: Uncoordinated

Since the summer of 2007 the conventional interest rate actions of the various central banks were in response to their respective domestic situations, even though they were heavily influenced by developments in the United States, too. However, on one occasion (October 8, 2008), in the immediate aftermath of the Lehman collapse, there was a coordinated reduction of 25–50 basis points in the policy interest rates by the central banks of six advanced economies to ease "global monetary conditions."[5] The Federal Open Market Committee of the Federal Reserve welcomed the opportunity to coordinate this policy action with similar measures by other central banks: "By showing that policymakers around the globe were working closely together, had a similar

---

5. Board of Governors of the Federal Reserve System, 2008a; Eichengreen (2013b). The six central banks were Bank of Canada, Bank of England, European Central Bank, the Federal Reserve, Sveriges Riksbank, and Swiss National Bank. An earlier occasion of coordinated interest cut and liquidity provision was by the G-7 in response to the 1987 stock market crash in the Unites States. See Ostry and Ghosh (2013).

view of global economic conditions, and were willing to take strong actions to address those conditions, coordinated action could help to bolster consumer and business confidence and so yield greater economic benefits than unilateral action."[6]

The G-20 meetings were relatively more forthright on the need for a coordinated fiscal stimulus but less so in the case of monetary stimulus. This apparently divergent G-20 approach perhaps reflected the precrisis consensus that monetary policy, and not fiscal policy, is better suited for macroeconomic stabilization. As documented above, almost all central banks had started monetary easing by October 2008 (with the United States taking the lead and almost in the vicinity of the zero bound by that time). With regard to fiscal policy, the precrisis orthodoxy typically viewed fiscal multipliers as low, and hence limited gains were seen from fiscal policy in many quarters. And since monetary policy actions had already been taken beginning in October 2008, this might have also made fiscal authorities somewhat hesitant to loosen fiscal policy.

Liquidity Swap Facilities: Coordinated

In contrast to the conventional monetary policy actions (policy interest rates), there has been a higher degree of coordination among the major central banks on the provision of liquidity through swap facilities, although the use of these facilities has been a one-way operation (from the Federal Reserve to other select central banks). In the aftermath of the subprime crisis, concerns about credit risk and higher demand for liquidity placed extraordinary strains on the global market for interbank funding in U.S. dollars. Accordingly, the Federal Reserve entered into U.S.-dollar liquidity lines, beginning in December 2007, with the European Central Bank and the Swiss National Bank. These facilities were extended to another twelve central banks during September and October 2008.[7] These swap facilities have been renewed at times, and as of October 2013 these arrangements exist with five central banks.[8] The Federal Reserve boosted the available liquidity under these swap lines from US$67 billion in December 2007 to US$620 billion in early October 2008. In view of the

6. Board of Governors of the Federal Reserve System (2008b).

7. These additional central banks were Reserve Bank of Australia, Banco Central do Brasil, Bank of Canada, Danmarks Nationalbank, Bank of England, Bank of Japan, Bank of Korea, Banco de Mexico, Reserve Bank of New Zealand, Norges Bank, Monetary Authority of Singapore, and Sveriges Riksbank.

8. The central banks were Bank of Canada, Bank of England, European Central Bank, Bank of Japan, and Swiss National Bank.

deteriorating market conditions, the Federal Reserve further expanded the swap amounts in mid-October 2008 by removing the caps on its swap facilities with the four major central banks (the European Central Bank, the Bank of England, the Swiss National Bank, and the Bank of Japan). The amounts made available under the swaps peaked at US$580 billion (over 25 percent of the Federal Reserve's total assets) in mid-December 2008.

The Federal Reserve also entered into foreign-currency liquidity swap lines in April 2009 with four major central banks, and these were renewed in November 2011 (while also adding the Bank of Canada to this list).[9] These lines, which mirrored U.S.-dollar liquidity swap lines, were designed to provide the Federal Reserve with the capacity to offer liquidity to U.S. institutions in foreign currency. While the Federal Reserve did not draw on these foreign-currency swap lines, its U.S. dollar liquidity swap facilities were heavily used. At the end of October 2013, six central banks decided to convert their existing temporary bilateral liquidity swap arrangements to standing arrangements.[10] The arrangements were to remain in place until further notice, on the grounds that the existing temporary swap arrangements helped to ease strains in financial markets and to mitigate their effects on economic conditions. The standing arrangements will continue to serve as a prudent liquidity backstop.

These swap facilities instituted since 2008 have a long history. Between the 1880s and 1920s, the Bank of England drew upon gold loans from the central banks of France and Germany to protect the gold standard in lieu of raising interest rates, which would have had a negative impact on the real economy. After World War II, the Federal Reserve negotiated a network of swap lines with eight central banks during the 1960s, aggregating to US$2 billion. These swap lines were used by the United Kingdom, Canada, and the United States. The Federal Reserve fully drew the whole US$150 million swap line with the Bundesbank in the 1960s. In 1961 the advanced economies also negotiated the General Arrangements to Borrow to enable countries to borrow larger amounts of their currencies through the IMF. This was necessitated partly by the restoration of current account convertibility and the potential need for more financing.[11] The IMF has since 2009 used the New Arrangements to Borrow and the Bilateral Borrowing Agreements to expand its resources, given

---

9. The central banks were Bank of England, European Central Bank, Bank of Japan, and Swiss National Bank.

10. The central banks were Bank of Canada, Bank of England, Bank of Japan, European Central Bank, Federal Reserve, and Swiss National Bank.

11. Eichengreen (2011, 2013b).

the large financing needs in the post-2008 crisis scenario and the inability to increase its quotas in a timely manner.

Unconventional Monetary Policy: Uncoordinated

With the constraint of the zero bound on policy interest rates, central banks of the major advanced economies have turned to unconventional monetary policies to provide more monetary accommodation through quantitative easing and large-scale asset purchase policies. These actions are aimed at depressing long-term interest rates in these economies in order to boost economic activity.

As a result, the balances of these central banks have expanded significantly. Here again the response has been uncoordinated, with the Federal Reserve taking the lead. In local currency terms, the Federal Reserve and the Bank of England almost quadrupled their balances between the end of 2007 and September 2013. The Swiss National Bank also quadrupled its balance sheet in the pursuit of its policy to peg the Swiss franc. In comparison, the balance sheets of the European Central Bank and the Bank of Japan expanded relatively moderately, by around 55 percent and 87 percent, respectively. The European Central Bank's balance sheet had by mid-2012 more than doubled over its end-of-2007 level, but since then it has been scaled back with the return of some normalcy in the financial markets. The balance sheets of these banks also recorded notable increases between 2007 and 2012 in relation to their respective GDP levels: nearly doubling for the European Central Bank (to 32 percent of GDP) and almost trebling for the Bank of England, the Federal Reserve, and the Swiss National Bank (26 percent, 18 percent, and 84 percent of their GDP, respectively; see figure 5-1). The combined balance sheets of the Federal Reserve, the European Central Bank, the Bank of England, the Bank of Japan, and the Swiss National Bank more than doubled between the end of 2007 and August 2013.

Monetary Policy in the Advanced Economies: Spillovers to the EMEs

Given the near-zero short-term interest rates and also the historically low level of long-term interest rates in the advanced economies, the sharp increase in their balance sheet sizes has encouraged an aggressive search for yield and led to large capital inflows to the EMEs. This has created macroeconomic and financial stability challenges for the EMEs. The divergent interest rate cycles

Figure 5-1. *Central Bank Assets, Four Central Banks, 2004–13*

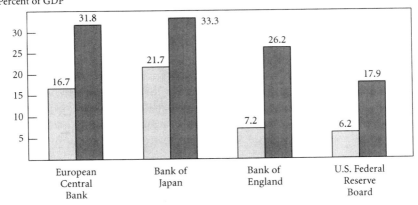

US$billions

Percent of GDP

Source: Haver Analytics.

Note: ECB = European Central Bank; BoJ = Bank of Japan; BoE = Bank of England; US Fed = U.S. Federal Reserve Board.

in the major reserve-currency advanced economies, on the one hand, and in the EMEs, on the other hand, have given a strong impetus to capital flows to the EMEs, putting appreciation pressures on the EME currencies. This led to concerns about "currency wars."

Volatile Capital Flows and Exchange Rates: Risks to Financial Stability

Capital flows have continued to exhibit their well-known volatility since the onset of the North Atlantic financial crisis, given the fluctuating risk-on and risk-off scenarios, driven by investors' perception of the macroeconomic and financial developments in the source countries rather than in the recipient countries (figure 5-2). For example, the jump in capital flows to the EMEs during 2010 was interrupted by the eurozone's sovereign debt crisis in 2011. The resumption of capital flows to the EMEs in 2012 was again interrupted in mid-2013 as investors got nervous over the Federal Reserve's plan to possibly taper its unconventional monetary policies. The monetary developments in the source countries are the primary source of the volatility in capital flows to the EMEs. This is true of not only recent decades but also historically.[12] Overall, private capital flows are volatile for all countries, advanced or emerging, and across all points of time.[13]

Such large-scale, two-way movements in capital flows create sharp adjustment costs. Large inward capital inflows during the initial phase add to nominal and real appreciation of the domestic currency and a widening of the current account deficits; large capital flows also lead to a boom in credit aggregates and asset prices and to domestic demand and output. While credit and asset price booms and stronger demand conditions might call for a monetary tightening, the appreciation of the currency helps to keep inflation low, thereby making it difficult for the central bank to make a case for monetary tightening, especially in the context of inflation-targeting frameworks. Monetary tightening is also complicated if higher domestic interest rates attract more capital flows, putting further upward pressure on the currency, which then continues to keep inflation low while pushing the current account deficit to more unsustainable levels. These challenges can be daunting for the global economy, especially if the leading reserve-currency central bank pursues a highly accommodative monetary policy on a persistent basis.

The empirical evidence indeed indicates that monetary policy in the United States has been generally accommodative since the early 2000s and not just in the postcrisis period. This then forced other central banks to pursue more-than-desired matching accommodative monetary policies of their own, resulting in low interest rates globally—the Great Deviation.[14] Deviation of the actual monetary policy from the Taylor rule has been greater in the EMEs (an average of 4 percentage points during 2003–12) than in the advanced economies (an average of 1 percentage point).[15] An assessment of the monetary

---

12. Accominotti and Eichengreen, (2013).

13. Bluedorn and others (2013).

14. Caruana (2012b); Gray (2013); Hofmann and Bogdanova (2012); Taylor (2013a).

15. BIS (2013). The Taylor rule, postulated by Taylor (1993), is a monetary policy rule that recommends an appropriate policy interest rate taking into account unemployment and inflation conditions in the economy.

Figure 5-2. *Private Capital Flows to Emerging and Developing Economies, 1980–2012*

US$billions

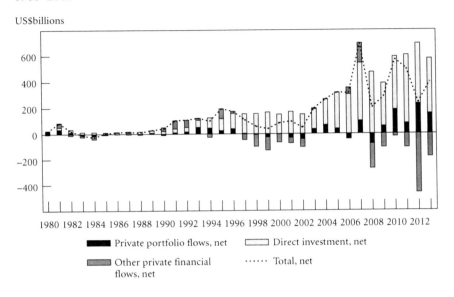

Other private financial flows, net

Private portfolio flows, net

Direct investment, net

Total, net

Percent of GDP

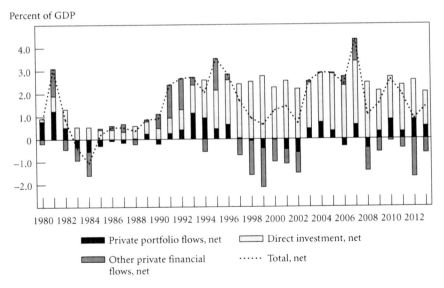

Private portfolio flows, net

Other private financial flows, net

Direct investment, net

Total, net

Source: IMF (2013c).

policy stance based on the Taylor rule is best viewed as an illustrative exercise, given that it involves assumptions about the unobservable variables (for example, equilibrium real interest rate, expected inflation and expected output) as well as unsettled debates on the universality of the policy response coefficients recommended by Taylor for inflation and output.[16] At the same time, such an assessment might underestimate the extent of the monetary accommodation at the current juncture, given the explicit objective and success of unconventional monetary policy in lowering long-term interest rates.

During the capital flows boom period, the exchange rates of high-yielding EMEs continued to exhibit appreciation, contrary to theory. But the subsequent depreciation on the back of retrenchment in capital flows tends to happen fast and in a destabilizing manner.[17] This pattern was evident during June–August 2013—the most recent episode of financial market turmoil—in several EMEs (figure 5-3). However, unlike previous such episodes of turmoil, the EMEs were able to manage the challenges relatively well, given their strong fundamentals. Nonetheless, their near-term growth prospects have suffered owing to significant volatility in financial markets.

The exchange rate movements led by unconventional monetary policy—generally appreciation in the EMEs and depreciation in the advanced economies—have contributed to some rebalancing of global imbalances, especially in the United States and China. However, no rebalancing has occurred in the large and persistent current account surpluses in Germany and Switzerland. Unconventional monetary policy, combined with relatively different growth trajectories, has generally led to lower current account surpluses (in the case of surplus EMEs) or higher deficits (in the case of deficit EMEs); this has, therefore, posed challenges to the deficit EMEs. The unconventional monetary policies of today are the modern version of the currency wars of the 1920s and the 1930s: a country puts downward pressure on its currency either directly through foreign exchange intervention or indirectly through highly accommodative monetary policies. Near-zero interest rates are a potential beggar-thy-neighbor policy.[18] Although each mature industrial country claims that it is only responding to domestic deflationary pressure and that it is not trying to devalue or conduct a beggar-thy-neighbor policy of direct devaluation, these actions could be characterized as currency warfare by stealth,

---

16. Bernanke (2010); Hofmann and Bogdanova (2012).
17. Caruana (2012a).
18. McKinnon and Liu (2013).

Figure 5-3. *Exchange Rate Movements, Four Currencies, 2000–13*

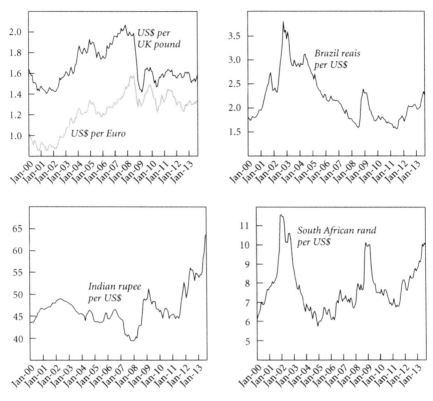

Source: Haver Analytics.

because these central banks ignore the impact of their monetary policies on the EMEs.

Overall, it is evident that fluctuations in monetary policies in the advanced economies are at the root of the volatility in capital flows to the EMEs and the concomitant boom-bust cycle in economic activity and potential financial crises. The conduct and formulation of monetary policy in the advanced economies continues to be dictated by their internal domestic macroeconomic considerations and financial conditions. Members of the Federal Open Market Committee welcomed the coordinated interest rate cut in October 2008 on the grounds that it would "yield greater economic benefits than unilateral action." If that is the case, the question that then arises is why we don't see more such coordinated actions. Similarly, it would appear that the liquidity swap facilities extended by the Federal Reserve to other central banks, mostly from the advanced economies, were motivated by the objective of minimizing the adverse impact of the U.S. dollar shortage in the global economy on the United States and other major advanced economies. It is not apparent that these were motivated by the objective of minimizing the adverse impact on the wider global economy.

Impact of Unconventional Monetary Policy on EMEs

Unconventional monetary policies have been adopted by the advanced economies to fulfil their domestic economic objectives, and these are, in theory, expected to provide a boost to their economy. Their policymakers also believe that their accommodative monetary policies provide positive spillovers to the rest of the global economy: hence these policies are claimed to be a global public good. For example, the former Federal Reserve chairman, Ben Bernanke, claims that these policies are not beggar-thy-neighbor but rather positive-sum, enrich-thy-neighbor, actions, since stronger growth in each economy confers beneficial spillovers to trading partners.[19] Similarly, the International Monetary Fund proclaims that "generally, what is good for each large, advanced economy is good for the rest of the world (and vice versa)."[20] The empirical evidence on these claims is, however, mixed.

According to the IMF, countries without unconventional monetary policies, including many EMEs, benefited from them early on.[21] Although subsequent benefits and costs, especially financial stability, are more difficult to ascertain, these policies have been beneficial, on net, both for those countries adopting the policies and on a global basis. Simulations using the Federal Reserve Board's econometric models compare the competing effects of these policies in advanced economies on the EMEs. This analysis finds that the positive spillover effects through stronger demand in advanced economies are roughly offset by the opposing negative effect through currency appreciation in the EMEs.[22]

Although unconventional monetary policies have led to buoyant financial markets, they have had limited beneficial effects on the recovery of the real economies of the advanced countries.[23] While there is a broader agreement

19. Bernanke (2013).
20. IMF (2013b, p. 28).
21. IMF (2013b).
22. Bernanke (2013).
23. Mohan (2013).

that the quantitative easing policies of 2009 had some beneficial impact on economic activity, there is skepticism about the impact of subsequent rounds of unconventional monetary policies.[24] According to Yi Wen, unconventional monetary policies cannot effectively boost domestic output and employment unless private asset purchases are highly persistent and extremely large.[25] By his estimates, the Federal Reserve's asset purchases would have to exceed 50 percent of GDP for them to have any appreciable impact on U.S. output levels. Since total asset purchases were US$3.7 trillion as of September 2013, around 22 percent of GDP, Wen's model would suggest that these policies have had no impact on U.S. output so far. John Taylor, drawing upon an IMF staff model, argues that lower interest rates in the United States, while having the expected positive impact on U.S. output, have had a negative impact on output in the Latin American and the Asian EMEs.[26] The adverse impact on the EMEs is the outcome of the exchange rate channel (negative impact) being stronger than the direct output channel (positive impact). A similar pattern of overall negative cross-border spillover was seen during the 1930s, when interest rates had approached zero and national monetary policies were viewed as beggar-thy-neighbor policies. During the 1930s, as now, the negative spillover impact from the exchange rate channel offset the direct output impact.[27]

The studies referred to above focus on the cross-border transmission of the macroeconomic impact of unconventional monetary policy through direct currency appreciation in the EMEs. In addition, the historically low interest rates in the advanced economies mean that the transmission to the EMEs also takes place through excessive foreign borrowing (whether in local currency or foreign currency), which then threatens financial stability and growth in the EMEs. This scenario played out during June–August 2013, soon after Chairman Bernanke announced the possible tapering of the Federal Reserve's unconventional monetary policy. The studies that assess the costs and benefits of this policy on the EMEs need to factor in this channel. Moreover, accommodative monetary policies in the advanced economies also boost global oil and other commodity prices, which then have an additional adverse impact on the commodity-importing EMEs. Overall, macroeconomic management in the EMEs has been rendered more complex

24. Rajan (2013).
25. Wen (2013).
26. Taylor (2013b); Carabenciov and others (2013).
27. Eichengreen (2013a).

through the effects of volatile capital flows and their consequent effects on exchange rate movements.

International Monetary Coordination: Scope and Feasibility

The conventional wisdom is that gains from international monetary policy coordination are small: a central bank's choice of a policy rule has limited impact on output and price stability in other economies.[28] Therefore, if the leading central banks were to adopt rules-based monetary policies similar to those of the 1980s and 1990s, then there may be no spillovers and hence less of a case for international coordination. However, even if the reserve-currency central banks follow rules-based policies, there may still be spillovers to the EMEs. Rules-based policies in the major advanced economies inevitably lead to changes in their monetary policies in response to domestic macroeconomic and financial shocks, which then induce spillovers to the other economies through movements in capital flows, exchange rates, commodity prices, and other asset prices. Moreover, the conventional channel stressed by Taylor focuses on only output and price stability and assumes a linear and smooth adjustment in exchange rates and other asset prices—an assumption that may not hold. Policymakers in EMEs are also concerned about the risk of over-shooting in the various asset prices on either side, which then poses additional challenges to financial stability.

Given the pace of globalization and the recurrent financial crises, it is surprising that modern international monetary theory still concludes that the gains from international coordination are negligible or may be even counterproductive. A limitation of this work is that the gains from coordination are analyzed in an isolated macroeconomic realm; in these models, by design, monetary policies do not spill over into other domains, like trade policy. Policy coordination can yield welfare gains if the international financial markets are incomplete, if the policymakers have imperfect information, and if domestic shocks are not perfectly correlated across countries.[29]

As noted earlier, accommodative monetary policy in the United States—the world's largest economy—has induced easy monetary policy globally. If instead, central banks had collectively and in coordination with each other taken an international perspective, they would all have been better off by rais-

---

28. Taylor (2013b).
29. Frieden and Broz (2013).

ing rates, thereby setting global average rates more appropriately.[30] Given the spillovers, there might be a case for the central banks in the advanced economies to internalize these spillovers in their monetary policies.

Barry Eichengreen and his colleagues propose an international monetary policy committee, composed of representatives of major central banks, that would report regularly to world leaders on the aggregate consequences of individual central bank policies.[31] The question is whether this arrangement would be effective. As the authors themselves note, central bankers might insist either that they have no control over another or that these issues are already discussed informally by the G-20, the Bank for International Settlements, and other groups. Nonetheless, these authors are hopeful that the proposed institutional arrangement could be effective and that its periodic public reports could help central bankers identify and publicly air the inconsistencies among their policies.

The efficacy of such a public reporting by a group of central banks itself is arguable.[32] If the leading central banks in the advanced economies were to recognize that there are significant spillovers of their policies, they would perhaps not pursue such policies in the first place. The case for international monetary coordination presupposes that a suitable constellation of identifiable and measurable externalities exists and that problems related to incomplete or asymmetric information across countries can be overcome.[33] The key question in this context is: Do source country central banks recognize that their interest rate policies have spillovers for the EMEs? For example, the Federal Reserve's chairman at the time, Ben Bernanke, has been skeptical of the role of interest rates in inducing capital flows to the EMEs: "It is true that interest rate differentials associated with differences in national monetary policies can promote cross-border capital flows as investors seek higher returns. But my reading of recent research makes me skeptical that these policy differences are the dominant force behind capital flows to emerging market economies; differences in growth prospects across countries and swings in investor risk sentiment seem to have played a larger role."[34]

Charlie Bean, the deputy governor of the Bank of England, while being sympathetic to the difficulties that the EMEs face in absorbing large inflows of

30. Caruana (2012a).
31. Eichengreen and others (2011).
32. Caruana (2012a).
33. IMF (2013b).
34. Bernanke (2013).

relatively short-term capital in a safe fashion, is however doubtful about the viability of the proposal to form a committee of central bankers to internalize the spillovers, as we do not "know nearly enough about the magnitude—or even the sign—of these spillovers."[35] The IMF is also agnostic on this aspect.[36] Given the sentiments on such assessments by central banks in advanced economies on the spillovers—that either there are no spillovers or that their impact is indeterminate—the proposed international monetary policy committee is unlikely to provide an effective way forward for coordination.

While a committee composed of central banks might have a limited role to play, international organizations like the BIS and the IMF have a key role to play as impartial surveyors of the global economy through enhanced surveillance and studies. The IMF's analysis can help oil the wheels of economic cooperation and coordination by illuminating potential gains from coordinated action through independent and rigorous analysis of spillovers, through candid and balanced observations, and by providing a forum devoted to exploring mutually advantageous international policy options.[37] The view that IMF surveillance is objective and candid is, however, not borne out by past experience, especially in the run-up to the North Atlantic financial crisis.[38] Neutrality and credibility of the assessor is likely to be undercut when its assessments give rise to suspicion of bias.[39] For the IMF to be an effective neutral assessor, issues related to its governance assume importance. Voting quotas of countries need to reflect their economic weights appropriately, but progress on this front has been slow and halting.

The preceding analysis focuses on the weight that the Federal Reserve puts on the outward spillovers from its monetary policy. A related issue is whether it takes into account international variables in the conduct and formulation of its monetary policy. Here, the Federal Reserve has had, since the 1970s, a policy of benign neglect of the international dimension, even as it paid significant attention to these aspects in the first two decades of its existence (the 1920s and 1930s) and the 1960s.[40] With the collapse of the Bretton Woods system in 1973, the United States was no longer required to defend the exchange rate peg or the statutory gold price, which deemphasized the need to factor in the external conditions. Thus it would appear that, even as the U.S. economy

35. Bean (2013).
36. IMF (2013b).
37. IMF (2013b); Ostry and Ghosh (2013).
38. See for example IMF (2011a).
39. Ostry and Ghosh (2013).
40. Eichengreen (2013b).

has become more integrated with the global economy, the conduct of its monetary policy is turning out to be more insular. Going forward, as the U.S. economy becomes more open and the rest of the world economy grows larger, international considerations will impinge more directly on the objectives of price and economic stability. The Federal Reserve will have to incorporate those considerations more prominently into its policy decisions.

To summarize, the EMEs and a number of observers stress the adverse spillover impacts to their economies from the monetary policies of the reserve-currency countries, and there are proposals for the reserve-currency central banks to factor such spillovers in the conduct and the formulation of their monetary policies. However, the leading reserve-currency central banks are of the view that their monetary policies do not have negative spillovers for the EMEs or are agnostic regarding such spillovers. Rather, they believe that their policies are net positive for the EMEs, although the empirical evidence for this proposition is ambiguous. Given this disconnect between the perception of the EMEs and the advanced economies on the spillovers, it is apparent that the authorities in EMEs would be better served by pursuing policies that minimize the spillovers for them, an issue that we take up in the next section.

Management of Spillovers by the EMEs

Since the conduct and formulation of monetary policy in the advanced economies continues to be dictated by their internal domestic macroeconomic considerations and financial conditions, the EMEs would be well advised to continue with their prudent approach to macroeconomic management. Given that the key channel for spillovers is through cross-border capital flows, the EMEs would benefit from the management of capital flows.

Capital Account Management

While capital flows, in theory, can add to an economy's investment and growth, the empirical evidence is typically unable to make any case for an open capital account.[41] Gains from capital flows have proved elusive in calibrated models as well as in empirical evidence.[42] Empirical studies that make a case for benefits from capital account openness often take recourse to indirect benefits, such as better financial sector development, institutions, governance, and macroeconomic stability. But this raises the issue of causality: Is it the opening

41. CGFS (2009); IMF (2012); Mohan, Patra, and Kapur (2013).
42. Rey (2013).

up of the capital account that leads to indirect benefits or is it the gradual development of domestic financial markets that allows the benefits of the subsequent opening up of the capital account to be reaped?[43] EMEs with greater restrictions on capital inflows (especially on debt liabilities) fared better during the North Atlantic financial crisis, and those with higher economy-wide capital inflow restrictions in precrisis years experienced smaller growth declines.[44]

Overall, there is strikingly little convincing documentation of a direct positive impact of financial opening on the economic welfare levels or growth rates of developing countries.[45] Available evidence is strongly in favor of a calibrated and well-sequenced approach to the opening of the capital account and its active management by authorities, along with complementary reforms in other sectors and taking into account country-specific features.[46] A new strand of the literature on the welfare theory of capital controls argues that, under certain circumstances, full capital mobility may not be desirable.[47] As a result of increased financial globalization, exchange rate flexibility no longer provides the way out of the impossible trinity or of foreign interest rate disturbances.[48]

Drawing on select country experiences, the IMF has proposed a framework for its advice on the spectrum of policy measures available to manage and liberalize inflows and to manage outflows.[49] The IMF recognizes the benefits as well as the risks associated with capital flows. It sees some role for capital controls but stresses that these should be a temporary and secondary recourse. It is interesting that the IMF suggests temporary controls and, too, as a secondary recourse, even as it recommends highly accommodative monetary policies in the advanced economies for an extended period.

It also needs to be recognized that the fast-growing EMEs have higher growth and inflation rates and, hence, higher interest rates than the advanced economies. Moreover, the demographic profile and the relatively low income levels suggest that the growth, inflation, and interest rate differentials between the EMEs and the advanced economies can be expected to persist for many years to come.[50] In the absence of any controls on debt flows, these interest rate

43. CGFS (2009).
44. Ostry and others (2010, 2011).
45. Obstfeld (2009).
46. CGFS (2009); Obstfeld (2009).
47. Korinek (2011).
48. McKinnon (2012); Rey (2013).
49. IMF (2012).
50. Mohan (2004, 2009).

differentials run the risk of the EMEs' attracting large debt flows, leading to significant real exchange rate appreciation and a boom in credit and monetary aggregates and other asset prices, which can result in a severe crisis in the future. Interest rate differentials thus reflect structural factors; of course, cyclical factors can widen or narrow the gap over the cycle, but the structural gap is likely to remain. Accordingly, capital account management measures, especially on debt flows, may have to be long lasting, at least while the growth, inflation, and interest rate differentials remain. Therefore, the notion that capital account management measures should be temporary, or a last recourse, is flawed.

Conventional wisdom seems to also suggest that capital account management measures are not effective. A number of studies that examine the efficacy of capital account management measures typically rely on the popular indexes of capital controls such as the Chinn-Ito index and the Quinn index, which suffer from serious conceptual flaws.[51] First, these indexes are often unchanged for years—in fact, for decades—for major EMEs.[52] For example, the Chinn-Ito index for India has remained unchanged since 1970, and the Quinn index has been unchanged since 1994, even as India has significantly liberalized its capital account since the early 1990s. It is evident that studies that rely on such indicators to measure the efficacy of capital controls will reach misleading conclusions. Second, these indexes are based on annual data, whereas the country authorities often fine-tune capital account measures over the course of the year, and hence the studies miss this nuanced approach. Third, some leakages in controls do not mean that they are not effective. Fourth, the costs of capital account management measures for individual corporations need to be weighed against the macroeconomic benefits for the overall economy that flow from macroeconomic and financial stability. Controls on capital inflows aimed at enhancing financial stability by preventing a buildup of currency or maturity mismatches or limiting the growth of intermediation through the domestic banking sector have a useful role.[53]

Regional Financing Arrangements

In the aftermath of the concerns emanating from the Federal Reserve's tapering its unconventional monetary policy, the EMEs had to manage the large volatility in the financial markets during June–August 2013 through the use of their foreign exchange reserves in the absence of any swap facilities from the

51. See Chinn and Ito (2008; data updated to 2009); Quinn and Toyoda (2008).
52. Mohan (2011).
53. Eichengreen and others (2011).

reserve-currency central banks. Such swap facilities, if available, would have minimized the upheavals during this period. The IMF's precautionary liquidity facilities—another short-term liquidity tool—are still viewed with caution by many EMEs on account of the stigma associated with them. Under such conditions, and in the absence of alternative policy tools, the EMEs have had to rely on their own instruments and policies to manage the turmoil. These include exchange rate flexibility, interventions in the foreign exchange market, capital account management measures, and domestic monetary and liquidity actions. Notwithstanding the large foreign exchange reserves, the exchange rates depreciated sharply and suddenly in a rather disorderly manner, although they have recovered since September 2013 from their lows. Here it is relevant to note that the IMF, based on its reserve adequacy metric, maintained that the foreign exchange reserves of the major EMEs were more than adequate, but the markets seem to have questioned this judgment.[54]

Given developments in the global financial markets since 2008, the limited resources of the IMF, the stalled progress on the IMF's voting quota and governance reforms, and the near exclusion of the EMEs from advanced economy central bank swaps, there is a growing interest among the EMEs in regional financing arrangements.[55] The Asian financial crisis of 1997–98 led to the creation of the Chiang Mai Initiative (now called the Chiang Mai Initiative Multilateralization, with a size of US$240 billion), although the fund has not been used yet. The regional financing arrangements (the European Financial Stability Facility and the European Stability Mechanism, with a combined lending capacity of EUR 700 billion) played an important role in the recent eurozone sovereign debt crises. The IMF turned out to be a small player in the financing arrangements in the region. More recently, the BRICS have proposed a currency arrangement for US$100 billion, and work is currently under way to set up this arrangement.[56] Bilateral currency swaps have also been set up or scaled up in the recent period.

Regional financing arrangements thus appear to provide an additional instrument to the EMEs to manage the volatility in international monetary conditions in the absence of any coordination by the central banks in the advanced economies. However, the efficacy of such arrangements remains to

---

54. The reserve adequacy metric was developed by the IMF to assess the foreign exchange reserves requirements of emerging market and low-income countries and the adequacy of their reserves. IMF (2011b).

55. IMF (2013a).

56. The BRICS are Brazil, Russia, India, China, and South Africa.

be tested. In many cases, these arrangements are tied to IMF arrangements above certain thresholds. Another unresolved issue is whether the bilateral or regional currency swaps that we are seeing now are an efficient or optimal alternative to multilateral systems such as the IMF.

Conclusions

The advanced economies have pursued aggressive unconventional monetary policies since 2008 to provide support to their economies. These policies have then taken interest rates, both short- and long-term, in these economies to record low levels and have encouraged large capital outflows, but with recurrent volatility, to the EMEs. The uptrend in capital flows received by the EMEs since 2008 has been interspersed with sudden retrenchments, as occurred in 2010–11 on the back of the eurozone sovereign debt crisis and in mid-2013 on the back of concerns over the Federal Reserve's tapering monetary policy stance. These sudden swings in capital flows, as in previous episodes, have complicated macroeconomic management in the EMEs. While the authorities in the advanced economies argue that unconventional monetary policies are net positive not only for them but for the EMEs as well, empirical evidence casts doubts on these claims.

Against this backdrop, this chapter looks at the feasibility for the central banks in the major advanced economies to internalize the spillovers of their policies. However, given their stance—that either there are no cross-border spillovers or, if there are spillovers, they are indeterminate or have a positive impact on EMEs—it would appear that the EMEs have to manage these spillovers on their own. The management challenges are exacerbated by the limited and discretionary liquidity swap facilities from advanced economies' central banks. Overall, judicious capital account management, exchange rate flexibility but with the capacity to intervene, supported by an appropriate level of foreign exchange reserves, prudent monetary and fiscal policies, and cautious financial market development and regulation should help the EMEs meet the challenges posed by the volatility emanating from the monetary policies of the major advanced economies.

The absence of swap facilities from the reserve-currency central banks and the sluggish pace of quota and governance reforms in the IMF are encouraging the EMEs to develop regional financing arrangements to manage volatile capital flows. But these options can reach their limitations in the presence of persistently accommodative monetary policies in the major advanced economies. So these central banks need to recognize the role of their monetary policies in inducing large fluctuations in capital flows to the EMEs and avoid excessively accommodative monetary policies.

References

Accominotti, Olivier, and Barry Eichengreen. 2013. "The Mother of All Sudden Stops: Capital Flows and Reversals in Europe, 1919–32." Working Paper 19580. Cambridge, Mass.: National Bureau of Economic Research.

Bean, Charlie. 2013. "Global Aspects of Unconventional Monetary Policies." London: Bank of England.

Bernanke, Ben. 2010. "Monetary Policy and the Housing Bubble." Washington: Board of Governors of the Federal Reserve System.

———. 2013. "Monetary Policy and the Global Economy." Washington: Board of Governors of the Federal Reserve System.

BIS (Bank for International Settlements). 2013. *Eighty-Third Annual Report.* Basel.

Bluedorn, John, Rupa Duttagupta, Jaime Guajardo, and Petia Topalova. 2013. "Capital Flows Are Fickle: Anytime, Anywhere." Working Paper WP/13/183. Washington: International Monetary Fund.

Board of Governors of the Federal Reserve System. 2008a. "Joint Statement by Central Banks." October 8. Washington.

———. 2008b. "Minutes of the Federal Open Market Committee." October 29. Washington.

Carabenciov, Ioan, Charles Freedman, Roberto Garcia-Saltos, Douglas Laxton, Ondra Kamenik, and Petar Manchev. 2013. "GPM6: The Global Projection Model with 6 Regions." Working Paper WP/13/87. Washington: International Monetary Fund.

Caruana, Jaime. 2012a. "Policymaking in an Interconnected World." Basel: Bank for International Settlements.

———. 2012b. "International Monetary Policy Interactions: Challenges and Prospects." Basel: Bank for International Settlements.

CGFS (Committee on the Global Financial System). 2009. *Capital Flows and Emerging Market Economies.* Publication 33. Basel: Bank for International Settlements.

Chinn, Menzie, and Hiro Ito. 2008. "A New Measure of Financial Openness." *Journal of Comparative Policy Analysis* 10, no. 3: 309–22.

Eichengreen, Barry. 2011. "International Policy Coordination: The Long View." Working Paper 17665. Cambridge, Mass.: National Bureau of Economic Research.

———. 2013a. "Currency War or International Policy Coordination?" *Journal of Policy Modeling* 35, no. 3: 425–33.

———. 2013b. "Does the Federal Reserve Care about the Rest of the World?" *Journal of Economic Perspectives* 27, no. 4: 87–104.

Eichengreen, Barry, and others. 2011. "Rethinking Central Banking." Report of the Committee on International Economic Policy and Reform. Brookings.

Frieden, J. A., and J. L. Broz. 2013. "The Political Economy of International Monetary Policy Coordination." In *Handbook of Safeguarding Global Financial Stabil-*

ity: Political, Social, Cultural, and Economic Theories and Models, edited by Gerard Caprio, vol. 2. Oxford: Elsevier.

G-20 leaders. 2913. "Declaration." St. Petersburg summit, September 5–6.

Gray, Colin. 2013. "Responding to a Monetary Superpower: Investigating the Behavioral Spillovers of U.S. Monetary Policy." *Atlantic Economic Journal* 41: 173–84.

Hofmann, Boris, and Bilyana Bogdanova. 2012. "Taylor Rules and Monetary Policy: A Global 'Great Deviation'?" *BIS Quarterly Review* (September): 37–49.

IMF (International Monetary Fund). 2011a. "IMF Performance in the Run-Up to the Financial and Economic Crisis." Washington: IMF Independent Evaluation Office.

———. 2011b. "Assessing Reserve Adequacy." February. Washington.

———. 2012. "The Liberalization and Management of Capital Flows: An Institutional View." November. Washington.

———. 2013a. "Stocktaking the Fund's Engagement with Regional Financing Arrangements." April. Washington.

———. 2013b. "Global Impact and Challenges of Unconventional Monetary Policies." September. Washington.

———. 2013c. "World Economic Outlook Database." October. Washington.

Korinek, A. 2011. "The New Economics of Prudential Capital Controls." *IMF Economic Review* 59, no. 3: 523–61.

McKinnon, Ronald. 2012. "Carry Trades, Interest Differentials, and International Monetary Reform." *Journal of Policy Modeling* 34, no. 4: 549–67.

McKinnon, Ronald, and Zhao Liu. 2013. "Modern Currency Wars: The United States versus Japan." Working Paper 437. Tokyo: Asian Development Bank Institute.

Mohan, Rakesh. 2004. "Challenges to Monetary Policy in a Globalizing Context." Bulletin. Mumbai: Reserve Bank of India.

———. 2009. *Monetary Policy in a Globalized Economy: A Practitioner's View.* Oxford University Press.

———. 2011. *Growth with Financial Stability: Central Banking in an Emerging Market.* Oxford University Press.

———. 2013. "Global Spillovers and Domestic Monetary Policy: An Emerging Market Perspective." Comments on Menzie Chinn, "Global Spillovers and Domestic Monetary Policy: The Impacts on Exchange Rates and Other Asset Prices." Twelfth BIS Annual Conference. Lucerne, June 21.

Mohan, Rakesh, Michael Debabrata Patra, and Muneesh Kapur. 2013. "The International Monetary System: Where Are We and Where Do We Need to Go?" Working Paper. Washington: International Monetary Fund.

Obstfeld, Maurice. 2009. "International Finance and Growth in Developing Countries: What Have We Learned?" *IMF Staff Papers* 56, no. 1: 63–111.

Ostry, J. D., and A. R. Ghosh. 2013. "Obstacles to International Policy Coordination, and How to Overcome Them?" Staff Discussion Note 13/11. Washington: International Monetary Fund.

Ostry, J. D., A. R. Ghosh, K. Habermeier, M. Chamon, M. S. Qureshi, L. Laeven, and A. Kokenyne. 2011. "Managing Capital Inflows: What Tools to Use?" Staff Discussion Note 11/06. Washington: International Monetary Fund.

Ostry, J. D., A. R. Ghosh, K. Habermeier, M. Chamon, M. S. Qureshi, and D. B. S. Reinhardt. 2010. "Capital Inflows: The Role of Controls." Staff Position Note 10/04. Washington: International Monetary Fund.

Quinn, Dennis, and A. Maria Toyoda. 2008. "Does Capital Account Liberalization Lead to Growth?" *Review of Financial Studies* 21: 1403–49.

Rajan, Raghuram. 2013. "A Step in the Dark: Unconventional Monetary Policy after the Crisis." Andrew Crockett Memorial Lecture. Basel: Bank for International Settlements.

Rey, Hélène 2013. "Dilemma not Trilemma: The Global Financial Cycle and Monetary Policy Independence." Paper prepared for the Federal Reserve Bank of Kansas City Economic Policy Symposium, Jackson Hole, Wyo.

Taylor, John. 1993. "Discretion versus Policy Rules in Practice." *Carnegie-Rochester Conference Series on Public Policy* 39: 195–214.

————. 2013a. "International Monetary Coordination and the Great Deviation." *Journal of Policy Modeling* 35: 463–72.

————. 2013b. "International Monetary Policy Coordination: Past, Present, and Future." Paper prepared for the Twelfth BIS Annual Conference. Lucerne, June 21.

Wen, Yi. 2013. "Evaluating Unconventional Monetary Policies—Why Aren't They More Effective?" Working Paper 2013-028A. Federal Reserve Bank of St. Louis.

COLIN I. BRADFORD AND WONHYUK LIM

6

Global Rebalancing and Systemic Risk Assessment: The G-20 and the International Monetary Fund

The G-20 Framework for Strong, Sustainable, and Balanced Growth was launched at the Pittsburgh G-20 summit in September 2009. "Our Framework for Strong, Sustainable, and Balanced Growth is a compact that commits us to work together to assess how our policies fit together, to evaluate whether they are collectively consistent with more sustainable and balanced growth, and to act as necessary to meet our common objectives."[1] The International Monetary Fund (IMF) was tasked with contributing the "analysis of how our respective national or regional policy frameworks fit together."[2] The focus at the time was principally on the concentration of external deficits and surpluses in the bilateral relationship between the United States and China, which was thought to manifest and contribute to global systemic imbalance.

Colin Bradford wishes to acknowledge that his work as a short-term consultant to the IMF's Independent Evaluation Office in May and June of 2013 to work on IMF roles in leading the global response to the financial crisis enabled him to read a range of publicly available IMF documents and better understand the role of the IMF in the MAP, in financial risk assessment, and in its relationship to the G-20 than would have been possible without this opportunity. The content of this paper is entirely separate from his work for the IEO. Colin Bradford would like to thank Ted Truman from PIIE for his thoughtful engagement, critical perspective, and support for this work. Ted Truman knows this terrain as well as anyone; his experience, knowledge, and good judgment are huge assets for the international community as it struggles with these issues. Wonhyuk Lim would like to thank Barry Eichengreen for his comments on global imbalances. He would also like to thank Seyeon Jang at KDI for excellent research assistance.
1. G-20 (2009), para. 15.
2. G-20 (2009), para. 5.

The G-20 leaders at Pittsburgh called upon their finance ministers and heads of central banks "to launch the new Framework by November [2009] by initiating a cooperative process of mutual assessment of our policy frameworks and the implications of those frameworks for the pattern and sustainability of global growth."[3] The Mutual Assessment Process, which would be supported by technical analysis of country medium-term trajectories submitted to the IMF by G-20 governments, is now known as the MAP. It involves peer review and policy dialogue among the G-20 countries.

Global Imbalances, Financial Crisis, and Economic Recovery

Global current account imbalances, expressed as a percent of world GDP, have narrowed considerably since 2006. According to the IMF, however, the quality of this adjustment leaves much to be desired. Most of the adjustment took place during the peak years of the global financial crisis in 2008–09, reflecting lower demand in external deficit economies. Whereas exchange rate adjustment played some role, policy adjustment contributed "disappointingly little."[4] The IMF still prescribes a broadly similar set of policies to further reduce global imbalances, compared with what it recommended initially: the two major surplus countries, China and Germany, need more consumption and investment, respectively, and the major deficit economies, including the United States, need to boost national savings through fiscal consolidation, while other deficit economies also need structural reforms to rebuild competitiveness.

Conspicuously missing from this prescription is what to do with macroeconomic financial linkages, which played a critical role in the buildup of global imbalances. Unless savings and investment perspectives on the balance of payments are complemented by financial and capital perspectives, policy prescriptions for resolving global imbalances may interfere with economic recovery and leave intact many of the factors that contributed to the global financial crisis (figure 6-1).

Before the global financial crisis, global imbalances typically referred to the persistent, large current account deficits in the United States, which were matched by persistent, large, current account surpluses in the rest of the world, especially China. Politically, the problem of global imbalances was often framed as a bilateral issue between the United States and China, focused on the nom-

---

3. G-20 (2009) para. 6.
4. IMF (2013a, p. 12).

Figure 6-1. *Global Current Account Imbalances*

Percent of world GDP

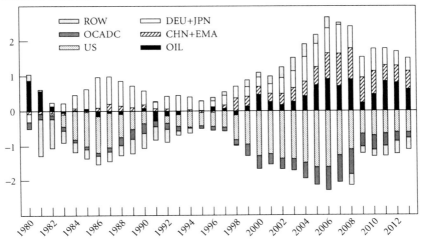

Source: International Monetary Fund, World Economic Outlook Database, October 2013.

Note: ROW = Rest of the world; OCADC (Other Current Account Deficit Countries) = Bulgaria, Croatia, Czech Republic, Estonia, Greece, Hungary, Ireland, Latvia, Lithuania, Poland, Portugal, Romania, Slovakia, Slovenia, Spain, Turkey, United Kingdom; US = United States; DEU+JPN = Germany and Japan; CHN+EMA (Emerging Market Asia) = China, Hong Kong SAR, Indonesia, Korea, Malaysia, Philippines, Singapore, Taiwan Province of China; OIL (oil exporters, 24 countries) = Algeria, Angola, Azerbaijan, Bahrain, Chad, Republic of Congo, Ecuador, Equatorial Guinea, Gabon, Iran, Kazakhstan, Kuwait, Libya, Nigeria, Oman, Qatar, Russia, Saudi Arabia, Sudan, Trinidad and Tobago, Turkmenistan, United Arab Emirates, Venezuela, Yemen.

inal exchange rate. Many economists believed at the time that the global imbalances would not be sustainable, that correction would be disruptive, and that the more the correction is delayed, the bigger the disruption would be. The dynamics leading to crisis were conceptualized as follows: The buildup of current account deficits by the United States would shake investor confidence and lead to a sudden stop of capital inflows, which in turn would precipitate a large and swift fall of the U.S. dollar and a steep rise in the U.S. interest rate and a higher risk premium. The resulting disruptions could lead to a deep recession.[5] To resolve global imbalances, it was recommended that surplus countries increase consumption and that deficit countries increase national savings, with

5. Edwards (2005).

requisite structural reforms. Policy recommendations also included exchange rate adjustment to correct "fundamental misalignment."[6]

This precrisis diagnosis of global imbalances was narrowly focused on the sustainability of the U.S. current account deficit and failed to account for the impact of financial globalization on macroeconomic and financial stability under the existing international monetary system. There are three related points. First, as international financial flows are increasingly disconnected from real transactions, the current account balance is becoming a smaller part of a country's external intertemporal budget constraint based on its net foreign assets, which is also known as net international investment position (NIIP). As a result, the current account balance is becoming an increasingly imperfect measure of external sustainability.[7] Second, the prediction of "a sudden stop" for the United States underappreciated the privileged position of the U.S. dollar as the world's leading reserve currency and safe haven currency in a time of crisis. Third, the dynamics of global imbalances are much more than a bilateral issue between the United States and China, because global imbalances are deeply influenced by country-level and regional-level policy responses to accelerating financial globalization under the existing international monetary system. Precautionary, mercantilist, and geopolitical motives also drive these policy choices.

The Current Account and International Investment Position

To have a better understanding of these points, it is useful to go back to the basics and consider a country's external intertemporal budget constraint. The key question is whether the combination of current external transactions and capital gains can prevent a country's net foreign asset position from becoming unsustainably negative.

By definition a country's current account shows flows of goods, services, primary income (such as wages and investment income from abroad) and secondary income (such as current transfers) between its residents and nonresidents.[8] By accounting identity, the current account balance should be equal to the difference between savings and investment.

Current account balance = net exports + net primary income
+ net secondary income = savings − investment.

---

6. Blustein (2012).
7. Obstfeld (2012); Serven and Nguyen (2013).
8. IMF (2009).

A country's international investment position is a statement that shows the value of the financial assets of its residents that are claims on nonresidents, or are gold bullion held as reserve assets, and the liabilities of its residents to nonresidents. Its net international investment position, or net foreign assets, is simply the difference between its residents' foreign assets and foreign liabilities. By accounting identity, a change in a country's net international investment position is equal to the sum of its current account balance and net capital gains. Incorporating exchange rate and other asset price movements, net capital gains reflect changes in the nominal market values of foreign assets and liabilities.

If for instance a country runs current account surpluses, its net international investment position will improve in the absence of capital losses. In this case, the country may accumulate foreign exchange reserves or make outward foreign investment in more risky assets with some of its surpluses. By contrast, if a country runs persistent current account deficits, its net international investment position will deteriorate in the absence of capital gains. In this case, the country must reassure foreign investors that future surpluses and capital gains should be able to make up for present deficits. If the country fails to do so, then foreign borrowing will become unsustainable, and the country will face a crisis.

Change in net international investment position
$$= \text{current account balance} + \text{net capital gains.}$$

Before the advent of financial globalization, the goods and services trade portion of the current account balance tended to account for a relatively large part of a change in a country's net international investment position, because foreign assets and liabilities disconnected from real transactions were relatively small. Now, with the increasing liberalization of international capital flows, the trade balance, or net exports, is becoming a relatively small part of the current account balance, as income from abroad takes on greater importance. Moreover, net capital gains or valuation effects are having a bigger impact on a country's net international investment position. As demonstrated by the United States since the late 1990s, even if a country runs large trade deficits (or even large current account deficits) relative to its GDP, it can maintain a decent net international investment position if net capital gains can make up for these deficits.[9] Conversely, even if a country runs small current account deficits, its

---

9. Gourinchas and Rey (2007).

NIIP may deteriorate and undermine investor confidence if it suffers significant capital losses. Indeed, the correlation coefficient between the current account balance and net international investment position, all relative to GDP, declined over the past decades—especially the correlation coefficient for high-income countries, which dropped from 0.61 in 1971–90 to 0.26 in 1991–2010.[10]

Financial globalization has made a significant impact on liquidity considerations as well. In 1953, when international financial flows were heavily restricted, the IMF advised that a country's foreign exchange reserves cover three months' current payments. With the increasing liberalization of capital flows, however, this three-month import cover became inadequate. In fact, in the 1990s the Guidotti-Greenspan rule prescribed that a country's foreign exchange reserves fully cover its short-term foreign debt. In 2004 the Bank for International Settlements went a step further and advised that some significant portion of foreign-owned stocks (say, one-third) should be covered as well.

Also, with financial globalization, a multitude of leveraged economic agents (such as nonbank financial institutions) can engage in international finance. What matters for external sustainability is the financial stability of not only the state but also systemically important leveraged economic agents in general. Looking at the national aggregates is not enough. Even if a country as a whole has a good current account balance or net international investment position, some leveraged economic agents may not have sufficient foreign assets to cover their foreign liabilities and may be faced with a liquidity or solvency crisis. If these troubled economic agents are systemically important enough, their crisis could escalate to threaten the stability of the financial system. Under financial globalization, the balance sheet mismatches—of leveraged economic agents and their exposures at risk relative to their capital buffers—provide a measure of external sustainability that cannot be captured sufficiently by the country's current account balance or net international investment position.

To sum up, this discussion of global imbalances suggests that a narrow focus on the current account, driven by the savings and investment perspective, is increasingly misguided under financial globalization. Even if the savings-investment gap is large, it can be sustained if the imbalance in the financial and capital account is equally large in the opposite direction. As long as capital flows are channeled into productive uses, for which the return on investment covers the opportunity cost of capital on a sustainable basis, a large current account deficit by itself does not lead to a crisis. A capital-poor

10. Obstfeld (2012, p. 12).

country with good growth prospects provides a prime example of a current account deficit actually being a win-win situation for borrowers and lenders alike. By contrast, even if the imbalance in the current account is not large, a sudden change in capital flows may precipitate a crisis. For example, a country even with solid growth fundamentals can get into serious trouble if it does not have enough liquidity to deal with abrupt capital outflows.

Hence an exclusive focus on achieving zero imbalances through policies that affect the savings-investment gap is misguided. Instead, policy prescriptions should also cover financial resource allocation, microeconomic and macroeconomic prudential issues, and financial safety nets to deal with capital flow reversals.

Before the advent of financial globalization, the current account balance could be employed as a measure of external sustainability, and a separate set of capital and liquidity ratios could be used to assess financial stability. With financial globalization, however, the intersection between external sustainability and financial stability has increased dramatically. As domestic and foreign financial institutions are increasingly interconnected, the question of external sustainability cannot be separated from that of financial stability, which should take into account the currency and maturity mismatches of leveraged economic agents and their exposures to risk relative to their capital buffers. It cannot be ascertained by looking at the savings-investment gap alone. In practice, this means that, in addition to the current account balance, some measures of reserve-currency liquidity (such as foreign exchange reserves relative to short-term foreign debt) and soundness of investment (such as credit growth, loan-to-deposit ratio, nonperforming loans ratio, interest coverage ratio) should be employed in assessing the external sustainability of the country as a whole and its systemically important financial institutions.[11]

Pattern of Global Imbalances

The pattern of global imbalances since the 1980s (see figure 6-1) indeed shows how financial globalization has impacted macroeconomic and financial stability under the existing international monetary system.

The United States provides the most prominent case in point. The United States does not suffer from the original sin, as it issues debt denominated in a currency under its control.[12] Because the United States can print dollars to

11. "The Capital-Freeze Index" (2013).
12. Note that the denomination nationality of the country's foreign assets and liabilities may be different for the residence nationality of the respective debtors and investors. For example,

pay off debt if necessary, a sudden stop of capital inflows would not trigger a currency crisis. Also, if the United States is concerned that the accumulation of its current account deficits would shake investor confidence and ultimately undermine the privileged position of the dollar, it has at its disposal policy tools to address the problem. Most simply, and just like any other country in the world, it could raise the interest rate, which would reduce the savings-investment gap by dampening domestic demand. However, as a superpower, the United States has other options as well. For instance, it could try to prevail on current account surplus countries to appreciate their currency or boost their economy. This would allow the United States to increase its net exports without having to raise the interest rate to dampen domestic demand across the board. In fact, the United States exercised this option in the 1980s, when its current account deficit exceeded 3 percent of GDP. Through the Plaza Accord in 1985, the United States successfully pressured Japan and Germany to revalue their currencies.

In the first half of the first decade of the 2000s, however, the United States failed on both domestic and external fronts to deal with its rising current account deficits, precariously relying on capital gains to maintain its net international investment position. In 2001, in the wake of the collapse of the information technology boom, the Federal Reserve slashed the target federal funds rate from 6.50 percent to 1.75 percent. Over the next three years, due in part to high unemployment and low inflation, the Federal Reserve made additional interest rate cuts, but the resulting interest rate of around 1 percent was well below the level consistent with the Taylor rule on ranges for interest rate adjustments. In fact, although the Federal Reserve began raising the rate in June 2004, the policy rate in real terms remained negative until late 2005. Combined with imprudent financial deregulation, the low interest rate fueled a housing market boom, where escalating asset prices helped to justify further investments. Although the return on investment appeared to cover the oppor-

---

a country like Korea would have its European assets denominated in the euro but may have to issue its foreign liabilities denominated in some reserve currency. A country that cannot issue its external debt in its own currency suffers from the "original sin" and must accumulate foreign exchange reserves to insure itself against a sudden reversal of capital flows. See Eichengreen, Hausmann, and Panizza (2003). By contrast, a country with an internationally accepted reserve currency has the fallback option of printing money to pay back its foreign liabilities in the worst-case scenario, even though its status as a reserve-currency country may be ultimately undermined if it chronically resorts to printing money and loses the confidence of investors. Under the existing international monetary system, there is a fundamental asymmetry between countries whose own currency does, and does not, serve as a reserve currency.

tunity cost of capital for some time, housing prices became unsustainably high compared with fundamentals, and borrowers' capabilities to pay back debt deteriorated over time.

On the external front, the United States did not have as much negotiating leverage over China as it had over Japan in the 1980s to craft a second Plaza Accord. The purchase of U.S. government bonds by China and other surplus countries also helped to keep long-term interest rates low, providing further support to the housing market in the United States. The year 2006 marked the peak of the U.S. current account deficit, at 6 percent of GDP. Although domestic and external adjustments had begun to be made by then, they were too late, too little.

To sum up, the popular doomsday scenario for global imbalances underappreciated the privileged international position of the U.S. dollar, on the one hand, and the risk of domestic financial resource misallocation, on the other. The U.S. current account deficits helped to trigger a financial crisis, not a currency crisis. Instead of a sudden stop of capital inflows, the United States experienced an initial appreciation of the dollar as a result of international investors' flight to safety—befitting its privileged status as the reserve currency of last resort.

As for China, it ran current account deficits nearly as often as surpluses in 1982–96, within 2 percent of GDP in most of the years. Since the Asian economic crisis of 1997, however, China has consistently run current account surpluses. Although China's initial buildup of foreign exchange reserves may be justified on the basis of precaution, other motives seem to have driven current account imbalances since 2001, when China joined the World Trade Organization. Although trade barriers fell and corporate profitability improved, China pushed ahead with a mercantilist export promotion policy, which favored firms over households and restrained domestic consumption and social welfare spending.[13] In excess of ten times short-term external debt, China's foreign exchange reserves earn low yields but provide a large pool of funds to advance its geopolitical objectives.

An argument has been made that China's financial underdevelopment might have contributed to global imbalances by being unable to provide high-quality assets for savers.[14] But this fails to account for China's small current account surpluses before 1997, when its financial markets were even more underdeveloped and the large surpluses of advanced economies, such

13. Yang (2012).
14. Caballero, Fahri, and Gourinchas (2008).

as Germany, had well-developed financial markets. Capital may flow uphill or downhill, depending on relative investment returns (proxied by the capital-output ratio, not the capital-labor ratio).[15] Relative levels of financial development, on the other hand, would tend to change too slowly to account for observed changes in global imbalances.

The buildup of global imbalances before the crisis of 2008–09 was much more than a bilateral issue between the United States and China. On the deficit side, the United States clearly dominated the scene as early as 1998. However, since the launch of the euro in 1999, the combined current account deficits of the eurozone periphery (Greece, Ireland, Portugal, Spain, and Italy) increased rapidly, from 3 percent of their combined GDP in 1999 to 8 percent in 2007. On the surplus side, although China and emerging market Asia received most of the attention in precrisis discussions on global imbalances, the current account surpluses of Germany and several Nordic countries as well as Japan and oil exporters were significant as well. In fact, the combined surpluses of Germany and other northern European economies exceeded that of China in recent years.

Driven by precautionary motives in the aftermath of the Asian economic crisis of 1997, emerging market Asia accumulated foreign exchange reserves to guard against sudden capital flow reversals. For instance, Korea began to run a current account surplus to accumulate foreign exchange reserves in the wake of the Asian economic crisis, having learned that a three-month import cover would not be enough to protect the country from sudden capital flow reversals. In fact, before the 1997 crisis, Korea consistently ran a current account deficit, except for the 1986–89 period, when Korea enjoyed the "three-low" boom driven by low oil prices, low interest rates, and a low value of the Korean won relative to the Japanese yen. Similarly, Indonesia reversed its current account position in the wake of the 1997 crisis.

Outside Asia, Argentina, Brazil, Mexico, and Russia have all improved their current account balances since the late 1990s, having gone through their own crises. In fact, foreign reserve holdings of the countries that suffered "sudden stops" in the 1990s and 2000s are, on average, twice as large as before.[16] An exception to this rule is Turkey, whose current account balance has deteriorated since 2001. Although precautionary motives seemed to play an important role in the buildup of foreign reserves in the immediate wake of crises, more recent evidence suggests that mercantilist and geopolitical motives are

15. Gros (2013).
16. Durdu, Mendoza, and Terrones (2007).

becoming more important, with foreign reserves exceeding short-term external debt by a huge margin.[17]

In the case of Germany, its current account balance swung from minus 1 percent of GDP (deficit) in 1999 to plus 7 percent (surplus) in 2007. Over the same period, Germany's international competitiveness (proxied by unit labor cost trends) improved a great deal. Had it not been for the currency union, the German mark would have appreciated to reduce its current account surplus, but the launch of the euro took away this option. Alternatively, if the corresponding capital inflows into the eurozone periphery had been invested productively on a sustainable basis, their current account deficits might not have become a problem. However, what happened instead in the eurozone periphery was a finance-driven boom and bust similar to the one in the United States. In the case of Japan, it failed to deal resolutely with deflationary pressure and zombie lending and instead opted for an odd combination of output being produced to satisfy external demand, while demand in the large domestic market stagnated.[18]

Even in the aftermath of the global financial crisis and the ensuing deleveraging shock, many of the precrisis ideas about global imbalances still had considerable influence on policymaking. Calling the eurozone crisis a "fiscal crisis" and prescribing austerity might be the most egregious example. Conveniently overlooked in this prescription is the macroeconomic-financial linkage. The eurozone periphery had benefited from lower capital costs since 1999, but massive capital inflows helped to fuel asset price escalation. When the deleveraging shock occurred, these countries had to face sharply rising interest rates and depressed growth prospects and, in some cases, had to stabilize the financial system by injecting public funds to take over nonperforming loans and recapitalize the banking sector. The combination of these factors dramatically raised the ratio of public debt to GDP, and fiscal consolidation would not solve this problem.

Fortunately, there has been important progress as well. Faced with weak economic recovery and uncertainty about fiscal policy, the Federal Reserve aggressively pushed quantitative easing. Although the Federal Reserve justified its action on the basis of its domestic mandate to promote "maximum employment, stable prices, and moderate long-term interest rates," not international bargaining, it demonstrated that the United States still has the power to create problems for others if they do not cooperate. In other words, the

17. See Aizenman and Lee (2007); Serven and Nguyen (2013).
18. Hoshi and Kashyap (2011).

United States might not have the leverage to pull off a second Plaza Accord, but it has the power to affect the global economy if others are slow to make the necessary adjustments, as was the case in 2010. If the United States can avoid a premature tapering of quantitative easing and an abrupt fiscal contraction, its recovery should gather steam as the private sector's balance sheet has improved. Faced with quantitative easing and the risk of dollar devaluation down the road, China understands that an aggressive buildup of foreign exchange reserves is unwise.

In fact China's current account surplus relative to GDP declined from the peak of 10.1 percent in 2007 to 2.3 percent in 2012. China's main concern now is minimizing the risk of financial resource misallocation by the shadow banking sector and avoiding the mistakes that the United States and Europe made before the global financial crisis. A slowdown in the rate of growth may be the price China must pay for an improvement in the quality of growth. Japan, for its part, finally began to fight deflationary pressure with an aggressive monetary and fiscal policy of its own. It remains to be seen, however, whether Japan will be as resolute in dealing with zombie lending and other structural problems. Even in the eurozone, policy discussions appear to be turning away from fiscal austerity. Due to a tepid economic recovery and the slow progress in deleveraging and restructuring, however, the eurozone faces tougher challenges than the other economies.

In sum, these patterns of global imbalances highlight the fact that the limited focus on macroeconomic imbalances without the inclusion of shifts in capital stocks and financial flows runs the risk of underestimating the actual degree of systemic risk and the fact that a wider global focus beyond the United States and China is also required.

The Analytical Focus of the Mutual Assessment Process

The 2007–08 global financial crisis was the latest in a sequence of global financial shocks from the oil crisis in the 1970s, the interest rate shock of the 1980s, and the Asia capital flows crisis in the 1990s. Each of these crises imposed huge costs on forgone economic growth, reversed progress in global poverty reduction, and created disruptions in the accumulation of global wealth, directly affecting peoples' lives everywhere. A major purpose of convening the G-20 summits at the leaders' level is to avoid another financial crisis, which would again inflict hardship on people around the world, and to achieve recovery from the current crisis. This self-imposed mandate is challenging, to say the least. Nonetheless, the core agenda for G-20 summits continues to embrace these twin objectives of recovery and crisis avoidance.

The Record

The Pittsburgh G-20 summit, on September 24–25, 2009, launched the Framework for Strong, Sustainable, and Balanced Growth. It is clear from the Pittsburgh "Leaders' Statement" that the intent was for the framework to include financial stability as a key element. The second sentence states, "We pledge to avoid destabilizing booms and busts in asset and credit prices." In the elaboration of the framework further on in the "Leaders' Statement," it says that their objectives were "to avoid both the recreation of asset bubbles and the reemergence of unsustainable global financial flows." It continues, "we will undertake macro prudential and regulatory policies to help prevent credit and asset cycles from becoming forces of destabilization" and that the mutual assessment process would "identify potential risks to financial stability."

Fast forward to 2013. The "G20 Leaders' Declaration" at the Russian G-20 summit in St. Petersburg on September 5–6, 2013, the section titled "Global Economy and G-20 Framework for Strong, Sustainable and Balanced Growth," does not emphasize the centrality of financial stability.[19] The "main challenges to the global economy" do not include global financial systemic risk or financial stability, though there is a concern for "financial market fragmentation in Europe" and "volatility of capital flows." There is no mention of financial regulatory reform under the framework at all. There is a mention of concern for financial stability in "some emerging markets" generated by "excess volatility in financial flows" and mention of the need to "ensure that policies implemented to support domestic growth also support global growth and financial stability and to manage their spillovers on other countries."

The focus on financial regulation is separate from framework except for a section titled "Towards a financial system that supports strong, sustainable and balanced economic growth." This section contains the wording, "We are fully committed to tackling systemic risk." The "G-20 Fifth Anniversary Vision Statement" does not give priority attention to financial stability, though it bows to "effective regulation," "ensuring a stable, well-functioning and transparent global financial system," and the "need to maintain the financial sector on a sound footing at the service of the real economy."[20] The "St. Petersburg Action Plan" does not integrate financial regulatory reform or

19. G-20 (2013b).
20. G-20 (2013a).

financial stability into the conceptual approach of the action plan or the framework section but only provides a list of G-20 country actions on "financial market reforms."[21]

More revealing still is the fact that the mutual assessments focus almost exclusively on real economy variables and imbalances and, apart from mentioning financial stability and financial regulatory reform, do not go into depth on them nor incorporate financial imbalances into the analysis of real economy imbalances. We base this conclusion, and the conclusion that the assessments take a largely real economy approach to spillovers and the stability of members' external sectors, on a reading of IMF staff documents.[22]

The report by the Financial Stability Board (FSB) for the St. Petersburg summit provides a comprehensive overview of the financial regulatory reform agenda.[23] It emphasizes the fact that "these reforms are an essential contribution to the G-20's primary objective of strong, sustainable and balanced growth." It concludes with a note on "a financial system that supports strong, sustainable and balanced economic growth."

When the framework was launched at the Pittsburgh 2009 summit, it was genuinely felt that the concentration of global imbalances in U.S. deficits and Chinese surpluses was potentially destabilizing, unhelpful for other countries, and a threat to global stability. At that time, the focus on "rebalancing" real economy deficits and surpluses, internal and external, was justified. One could successfully argue that these imbalances still matter, which they do. But one way to understand the origins of the framework against this background is that there was a sense of vulnerability on the part of the global economy to the continuation of these imbalances and even to their correction. The focus on global real economy imbalances was, fundamentally, a focus on systemic risk.

Those imbalances have attenuated somewhat. Now that the euro crisis has occurred and the potential for financial risk not only continues but possibly has increased with the use of unconventional monetary policies, it would seem that a framework focus on systemic risk would now have to include a focus on threats to financial stability, large and small. Recall that bank runs in Cyprus had global implications. Integrating financial risk assessment into the MAP would seem consistent with the original focus of the MAP on systemic risk.

---

21. G-20 (2013c).
22. See IMF (2010a, 2010b, 2011a, 2011b, 2011c, 2011d, 2012a, 2012b, 2012d, 2012f, 2013b, 2013c).
23. FSB (2013).

Furthermore, the framework would be the appropriate locus for focusing policymakers' attention on the explicit ways in which financial stability can contribute to growth. The traditional way of viewing financial stability and growth was to see them as trade-offs. Even today a major concern advanced by some is that financial regulation could dampen growth rather than facilitate it. But as Mike Callaghan points out, the *Global Financial Stability Report* poses a fundamental question: "whether the structural changes occurring in the financial system are not only making it safer but are doing so in a way that is promoting better economic outcomes."[24]

The October 2012 report puts it this way: "The global regulatory reform agenda aims for a safer financial system so that financial intermediation can help produce stable and sustainable economic growth."[25] In this perspective, including financial stability in the framework would highlight these linkages to growth and enhance them. Therefore, it would seem wise to consider refocusing the G-20 framework by integrating the analysis of financial imbalances with real economy policy divergences in order to better understand potential threats to the global economy, as was the original intent of the MAP, while at the same time enlarging the focus on the contributions that financial stability can make to economic growth. Financial stability could be viewed as vital to the sustainable element of the framework.

The capital account also matters. Rebalancing the real economy is the primary goal. Both integrating the analysis of capital flows through the capital account and identifying gross capital flows and their balance sheet effects would provide a window into financial sector variables that might operate independently of, but impact on, the real economy variables reflected in the current account.

Maurice Obstfeld, in an extensive and nuanced analysis, makes these points extremely clear. While not ignoring the current account, Obstfeld writes, "The same factors that dictate careful attention to global imbalances also imply that data on gross international financial flows and positions are central to any assessment of financial stability risks. The balance sheet mismatches of leveraged entities provide the most direct indicators of potential instability, much more so than global imbalances. A minimally effective financial 'architecture' would imply a higher level of global economic government than currently exists." Admitting that "the political obstacles are daunting," he still wonders

24. Callaghan (2013).
25. IMF (2012c).

"how far we can safely push globalized markets beyond the perimeter of glob-alized governance."[26]

Furthermore, such a refocus could respond to one of the most important conclusions of the IMF's Independent Evaluation Office's report on lessons learned from the current crisis, which is "to better integrate financial sector issues into macroeconomic assessments."[27] The IEO starkly concluded that the IMF, in the run-up to the crisis, "appropriately stressed the urgency of address-ing the persistent and growing current account imbalances, but it did not look at how these imbalances were linked to the systemic risks that were build-ing up in financial systems."

Three Dimensions of Systemic Risk Assessment

At this point, it is useful to clarify three different dimensions of systemic risk assessment. First, as pointed out earlier, real economy imbalances, if not addressed, can become unsustainable and generate their own global economic disruptions. Second, financial-sector analyses to assess domestic and global sources of systemic financial risk, in the aftermath of the financial crisis of 2007–08, are the new imperative for managing the global economy. And third, financial regulatory reform—to provide new institutional capacity, new sources of data, and new policy instruments (such as macroeconomic pru-dential policies) for exercising oversight, supervision, and regulation of finan-cial markets and institutions—is a cutting edge for institutional innovations in managing the global economy.

The G-20 MAP as of now is designed to only address the real economy imbalances; the IMF, with support from the FSB, has the lead in evaluating global financial risk and providing an early warning system for signaling vul-nerabilities; and the FSB has the lead in financial regulatory reform efforts by major economies.

The G-20 Working Group on the Framework for Strong, Sustainable, and Balanced Growth reports regularly to G-20 summits on global rebalancing; the IMF conveys the contents of its various assessments of financial risk to the IMF board of executive directors, the IMF board of governors of 188 IMF member countries, and the IMF ministerial-level International Monetary and Finance Committee (IMFC), which is composed of 15 G-20 members and 9 other IMF member countries; and the FSB reports regularly on progress on financial regulatory reform to the G-20 leaders' summits. This FSB report

26. Obstfeld (2012, pp. 19–20).
27. IMF/IEO (2011).

implicitly separates the regulatory reform agenda from the financial-sector analyses and macroeconomic prospects work done by the IMF.

What this means is that, even though fifteen G-20 countries are represented at the IMFC, the G-20 does not itself serve as a channel for IMF financial-sector analyses nor as a policy-level group responsible for reviewing systemic risk vulnerabilities. These analyses are done by the IMF for IMF governing bodies. Except for describing the assessment processes under way, IMF documents prepared for the G-20 do not generally analyze systemic financial risk.

With IMF work on global rebalancing and the FSB's regulatory reform reports both going to the G-20 but with the financial risk assessment work being contained largely within IMF structures and governing bodies, there is not an institutional setting for high-level policymakers to evaluate the systemic risk based on these three elements taken together. In a global economy in need of steerage, this disjointed arrangement could create voids in the perception of risk and questions about who is in charge of the global economy.

Financial Risk Assessment and the Role of the IMF

The IMF now has a complicated set of exercises and work products that address the issue of financial risk. This represents significant progress by the IMF since 2008, which is extremely important. These products and processes include the traditional bilateral article IV consultations, which are conducted with, for, and on IMF member countries. The Financial Sector Assessment Program (FSAP) is now applied to all major economies, including the United States, which before the crisis was exempt from it. There are the annual flagship publications, too. The *World Economic Outlook* focuses on the real economy, the *Global Financial Stability Report* focuses on financial aspects, and the *Fiscal Monitor* focuses on fiscal risks.

There is also the Early Warning Exercise (EWE), which attempts to assess tail risks, defined as unlikely but possible vulnerabilities that have the potential for generating systemic financial risk.[28] The EWE is based on the vulnerability assessments of advanced economies, emerging economies, and low-income countries and on spillover reports, which since 2011 have analyzed the externalities of domestic policies and their potential contagion effects of the five systemic economies (China, the eurozone, Japan, the United Kingdom, and the United States). The EWE is the most sensitive process due to the fact that it "seeks to identify the vulnerabilities and triggers that could

---

28. IMF (2009b).

precipitate systemic crises."[29] The EWE reports to the IMF board of executive directors and, twice a year confidentially to the IMFC.

In addition, since 2012 the IMF has undertaken external sector reports (ESRs), which "provide a multilateral consistent analysis of the external positions of the major economies." There is an attempt in both the spillover reports on the systemic five and the ESRs to integrate reserves, capital flows, and external balances into their analyses. But as the reports themselves make clear, these efforts are still a work in progress, and there are still limitations to the reach of the methodologies used.[30] While these two reports provide useful discussions with officials from the systemic five economies and other major economies and with the IMF executive board, it is not clear that they ever receive the scrutiny of the ministers of finance, much less heads of state or government.

A significant, if somewhat separate joint endeavor by the IMF, the FSB, and the Bank for International Settlements is the development and strengthening of macroeconomic prudential policies, which they define as a policy that uses primarily prudential tools to limit systemic or systemwide financial risk.

> The defining elements of macroprudential policy are the objective (limiting systemic or system-wide financial risk), the scope of the analysis (the financial system as a whole and its interactions with the real economy), a set of powers and instruments and their governance (prudential tools and those specifically assigned to macroprudential authorities).
>
> While a broad range of policy instruments is potentially available to address macroprudential risks, those most commonly used or proposed include: (i) Tools to address threats to financial stability arising from excessive credit expansion and asset price boom. (ii) Tools to address key amplification mechanisms of systemic risk linked to leverage (e.g., capital tools) and maturity mismatches (e.g., market and funding liquidity tools) . . . (iii) Tools to mitigate structural vulnerabilities in the system and limit systemic spillovers in times of stress.[31]

One of their conclusions is that: "monetary and fiscal policies need to continue to focus on correcting macroeconomic imbalances, with macroprudential policy focused on ensuring that systemic risk is well contained."[32]

29. IMF/FSB (2013).
30. IMF/FSB (2013, annex I).
31. IMF (2012e).
32. IMF/FSB/BIS (2011a, 2011b).

Hence, macroeconomic prudential policy formation and strengthening is a vital element in the assessment of financial risk and its mitigation.

Against this background and the analytical points discussed earlier, questions arise whether or not the "governance system" for analyzing, evaluating, and acting on potential systemic risk is not indeed hampered by too many products, processes, and focal points rather than too few, as before 2008. It is not clear that there is an IMF document, known to the outside world at least, that pulls together the different threats to the global economy, real and financial, and that incorporates the three key elements, macroeconomic risk assessment with financial risk assessment and an understanding of the adequacy of the policy tools (resources, regulatory reforms and institutions, including microeconomic and macroeconomic prudential policies). In this regard, the recommendations of the IEO flowing from its evaluation of IMF surveillance from 2004 to 2007 may still apply.[33] Its final recommendation was to

> deliver a clear, consistent message to the membership on the global outlook and risks [by ensuring] that the assessment of the global economy is consistent and comprehensive, taking a stance on a central scenario with clear specifications of risks and vulnerabilities around this scenario. . . . One way to do this is by better integrating the analysis and assessments of the WEO and the GFSR. Alternatively, the IMF could issue a self-standing global surveillance report—a short, candidly written document on the macroeconomic outlook, risks to global financial stability, and potential spillovers. On issues of systemic importance, the Fund should be ready to err more often in the direction of emphasizing risks and vulnerabilities.

Policy and Institutional Innovations for the 2014 G-20 Summit

This review leads to four recommendations for policy and institutional innovations for consideration and discussion in the run-up to the 2014 Brisbane G-20 summit. These are, first, to make financial stability essential to the sustainability dimension of the G-20 Framework for Strong, Sustainable, and Balanced Growth. Second, to more fully integrate the real economy macroeconomic outlook and the financial sector analyses of the IMF to assess systemic risk. Third, to urge the IMFC to take a proactive role in crisis avoidance by increasing the intensity of its vigilance in reviewing the results of the Early

---

33. IMF/IEO (2011).

Warning Exercise. Fourth, to intensify and highlight the G-20 summit review of G-20 national governments' implementation of their own regulatory reform plans and their relationship with FSB-generated norms and standards as well as the FSB's own work on global financial regulatory reforms.

First, financial stability. Isolating the focus of the MAP on global rebalancing seems to overemphasize the importance of the threat of macroeconomic imbalances to systemic risk and fails to allow insights into what may in fact be the crucial nexus between the real and financial sides of national economies and the global economy. The capital account, gross capital flows, and balance sheet effects need to be more fully integrated with the analysis of macroeconomic policies and variables, including the current account. This shift to a broader, more inclusive focus might reveal the root causes of the global imbalances that might otherwise be missed altogether with an exclusive focus on real-side variables or, for that matter, an exclusive focus on financial variables. What is needed, it seems, is a synthesis report that provides a comprehensive, integrated vision of the current vulnerabilities that could be sources of systemic risk if not seen as a whole and if not focused on by relevant policymakers. Global growth will not be sustainable if systemic risks are not identified; and systemic risks cannot be identified without a holistic approach.

Second, fuller integration. This is a daunting task, to be sure. This assertion is not so much a critical statement regarding the considerable progress that has indeed been made by the IMF in assessing financial risk since 2008 as it is an affirmation of the urgency and importance of this integration for the crisis avoidance role of the IMF and the G-20. The next-phase steps in strengthening the IMF's surveillance systems could be relatively simple ones. For example, integrate the *World Economic Outlook* and the *Global Financial Stability Report*; integrate the work in the external sector and spillover reports; create a pithy summary profile of systemic risk, a synthesis report that draws on all of these analyses, providing a comprehensive overview rather than a series of segmented reports that fragment the vision rather than pull it together.

There is a triennial surveillance review process that creates a comprehensive overview of the legal framework for the IMF's surveillance. The latest one was in October 2011. It led to an IMF executive board decision on bilateral and multilateral surveillance on July 18, 2012. There is no doubt but what the IMF and its members are trying to connect the dots and provide an integrated assessment of systemic risk. It is propitious that the next triennial surveillance review is scheduled for 2014, which would enable Australia to utilize its G-20 leadership to push for actions and reforms that could strengthen systemic risk assessments and also contribute to the leadership role of the G-20 in the global economy.

Third, crisis avoidance. There is some evidence that the IMFC has not come to grips with the EWE process, nor has it fully taken charge of it. This could be a wrong conclusion from outside the process. But if not, then either the IMFC should improve its vigilance at the 2014 IMFC meetings, or the G-20 should decide in Brisbane to include systemic risk in its agenda, which thus far it has not, and to take responsibility for protecting the public interest in global financial stability. This is a primordial public responsibility. To have the international institutional system, especially the IMF, generating analytical bases for assessing systemic risk and not taking full advantage of these analyses is an abdication of responsibility and a failure of global leadership. A systemic risk alert system should consist of two elements: analysis and action. There are global governance challenges in each. It is both necessary to move to the next phase in integrating the assessment work streams within the IMF and to strengthen the institutional process for focusing policy attention on systemic risk. G-20 leaders are ultimately responsible for whether the international system is sufficiently vigilant in assessing systemic risk; it is the G-20 summits that have pushed the IMF forward in their analytical work; if this work is not used, now that it exists, to make judgment calls, then the G-20 will have in effect allowed that lapse to happen. Further actions are required to bring both the risk assessment elements and the policy-level review elements to higher levels of intensity and vigilance.

Fourth, highlight reforms. The G-20 played a key role in transforming the relatively passive Financial Stability Forum into the expanded Financial Stability Board (FSB) in 2009, providing it with resources and monitoring its progress. But the G-20 summit process has not proactively reviewed their own governments' progress in financial regulatory reform to judge the degree to which progress is sufficient to effectively avoid future global financial crises or to at least buffer, cushion, and manage the impact of financial shocks on the public. It is appropriate for the FSB to take the lead on financial regulation; the IMF is not a financial regulator, nor should it be. But the G-20 is a political body, which the IMF is not, and as such needs to take public responsibility for making sure this important work is moving forward at a pace, both nationally and globally, adequate to the potential threat.

Mike Callaghan proposes creating a new position and a new committee (a central bank governors' committee on financial regulation) to ensure a focus and a force behind financial regulatory reform. He also proposes that the 2014 spring meetings of the G-20 ministers of finance be devoted to reviewing progress on the FSB agenda.[34] These are good proposals, reflecting the same underlying concern we are noting here—that without a political body charged with public responsibility, progress will be less and responsibility could be shirked.

Conclusions: G-20 Leadership on Financial Stability for the Global Economy

The fundamental issue facing the G-20 summit leaders is not only to come up with policy changes and institutional reforms that improve the global economy but also to connect to the concerns of their people, whose livelihoods depend on the stability and growth of the global economy. The issues raised here appear to us to have political leadership content and dimension.

The global financial crisis affected the jobs, incomes, pensions, and savings of people everywhere. For not the first time, the global financial system shocked the global economy on which people depend. G-20 leaders must take public responsibility for economic outcomes that affect the public interest. Therefore, G-20 leaders need to demonstrate that they have taken actions that will protect the public interest in financial stability and promote the positive linkages of financial stability to growth.

To demonstrate leadership on the downside risks of the financial system impacting again the global economy of jobs, income, and output, G-20 leaders need to assure the public that they have put in place safeguards against systemic risk. They can demonstrate that through objective evaluations of accomplishments and weaknesses in national financial regulatory reform efforts by G-20 governments and of the global financial regulatory instruments and actions of the Financial Stability Board, verifying that safeguards have been put in place and that the process is ongoing. They can assure the public that the neglected linkages among financial forces, markets and institutions, and the global economy are now under intense and integrated scrutiny by the International Monetary Fund, if the changes recommended here are implemented. And they can assure the public that this comprehensive and continuous review of the relationship between the financial system

---

34. Callaghan (2013); Lowy Institute (2013).

and the global economy will receive policy-level review by ministers of finance and oversight and responsibility by G-20 leaders.

To demonstrate leadership on the positive contribution that financial stability can make to economic growth, G-20 leaders can decide to integrate financial stability into the G-20 Framework for Strong, Sustainable, and Balanced Growth to ensure that global economy implications of financial reforms are fully present in the single most important G-20 process that prioritizes growth. Leaders can articulate a vision of the positive synergies between financial stability and growth, with reforms favoring incentives to long-run investment in productive activities rather than short-term profits and speculation. Leaders can highlight the fact that financial stability is essential for fueling investment-led growth. Leaders can articulate a vision of financial stability that requires responsibility by both private and public sector actors.

Leaders can demonstrate to the public that they have thought through and seen past the old idea that financial stability and growth are inevitably in conflict, that financial stability comes first and growth second, to a new relationship in which financial stability creates the investment climate for more dynamic and socially beneficial growth and in which safeguards against financial shocks are in place to protect the public interest.

References

Aizenman, J., and J. Lee. 2007. "International Reserves: Precautionary vs. Mercantilist Views." *Open Economies Review* 18: 191–214.

Blustein, Paul. 2012. "A Flop and a Debacle: Inside the IMF's Global Rebalancing Acts." CIGI Papers 4. Waterloo, Ont.: Centre for International Governance Innovation.

Caballero, Ricardo J., Emmanuel Fahri, and Pierre-Olivier Gourinchas. 2008. "An Equilibrium Model of 'Global Imbalances' and Low Interest Rates." *American Economic Review* 98, no. 1: 358–93.

Callaghan, Mike. 2013. "Financial Regulation and the G20: Is There a Gap in the Governance Structure?" Paper prepared for Asia Regional THINK20 Seminar, Lowy Institute. Sydney, May 22–24.

"The Capital-Freeze Index." 2013. *The Economist,* September 9.

Durdu, C., E. Mendoza, and M. Terrones. 2007. "Precautionary Demand for Foreign Assets in Sudden Stop Economies: An Assessment of the New Mercantilism." *Journal of Development Economics* 89: 194–209.

Edwards, Sebastian. 2005. "Is the U.S. Current Account Deficit Sustainable? And If Not, How Costly Is Adjustment Likely to Be?" Working Paper 11541. Cambridge, Mass.: National Bureau of Economic Research.

Eichengreen, Barry, Ricardo Hausmann, and Ugo Panizza. 2003. "Currency Mismatches, Debt Intolerance, and Original Sin: Why They Are Not the Same and Why It Matters." Working Paper 1036. Cambridge, Mass.: National Bureau of Economic Research.

FSB (Financial Stability Board). 2013. "A Narrative Progress Report on Financial Reform: Report of the Financial Stability Board to G-20 Leaders." August 30.

G-20. 2009. "Leaders' Statement." Pittsburgh, September.

———. 2013a. "G20 Fifth Anniversary Vision Statement." St. Petersburg, September.

———. 2013b. "G20 Leaders' Declaration." St. Petersburg, September.

———. 2013c. "St. Petersburg Action Plan." St. Petersburg, September.

Gourinchas, Pierre-Olivier, and Hélène Rey. 2007. "From World Banker to World Venture Capitalist: The US External Adjustment and the Exorbitant Privilege." In *G7 Current Account Imbalances: Sustainability and Adjustment,* edited by Richard H. Clarida. University of Chicago Press.

Gros, Daniel. 2013. "Why Does Capital Flow from Poor to Rich Countries?" *VOX,* August 26.

Hoshi, Takeo, and Anil Kashyap. 2011. "Why Did Japan Stop Growing?" Tokyo: National Institute for Research Advancement.

IMF (International Monetary Fund). 2009a. *Balance of Payments and International Investment Position Manual.* 6th ed. Washington.

———. 2009b. *The IMF-FSB Early Warning Exercise: Design and Methodological Toolkit.* Washington.

———. 2010a. *G-20 Mutual Assessment Process—Alternative Policy Scenarios.* Toronto, June.

———. 2010b. *G-20 Mutual Assessment Process—IMF Staff Assessments of G-20 Policies.* Seoul, November.

———. 2011a. *G-20 Accountability Report.* Washington.

———. 2011b. *G-20 Economic Outlook: Analysis and Perspectives.* Washington.

———. 2011c. *G-20 Mutual Assessment Process: From Pittsburgh to Cannes—IMF Umbrella Report.* Washington.

———. 2011d. *Sustainability Reports.* Reports on China, France, Germany, India, Japan, United Kingdom, and the United States.

———. 2012a. *Enhanced Accountability Assessment: Annex to Umbrella Report for G-20 Mutual Assessment Process.*

———. 2012b. *Euro Area Imbalances: Annex to Umbrella Report for G-20 Mutual Assessment Process.*

———. 2012c. *Global Financial Stability Report: Restoring Confidence and Progressing on Reforms.*

———. 2012d. *Global Risk Analysis: Annex to Umbrella Report for G-20 Mutual Assessment Process.*

———. 2012e. *Key Aspects of Macroprudential Policy.*

———. 2012f. *Toward Lasting Stability and Growth, Umbrella Report for G-20 Mutual Assessment Process,* June 2012, for the Los Cabos G-20 Summit.

———. 2013a. *Global Financial Stability Report: Transition Challenges to Stability.*

———. 2013b. *Imbalances and Growth: Update of Staff Sustainability Assessments for G-20 Mutual Assessment Process.*

————. 2013c. *Pilot External Sector Report*, June 29.

IMF/FSB (International Monetary Fund/Financial Stability Board). 2013. "Early Warning Exercise Factsheet." September 30.

IMF/FSB/BIS (International Monetary Fund/Financial Stability Board/Bank for International Settlements). 2011a. *Macroprudential Policy Tools and Frameworks: Progress Report to the G-20*. October 27.

————. 2011b. *Macroprudential Policy Tools and Frameworks: Update to G-20 Finance Ministers and Central Bank Governors*. February 14.

IMF/IEO (International Monetary Fund/Independent Evaluation Office). 2011. *IMF Performance in the Run-up to the Financial and Economic Crisis: IMF Surveillance in 2004–2007*.

Lowy Institute. 2013. "G20 Playbook." Sydney, October 24.

Obstfeld, Maurice. 2012. "Does the Current Account Still Matter?" *American Economic Review: Papers & Proceedings* 102, no. 3: 1–23.

Serven, Luis, and Ha Nguyen. 2013. "Global Imbalances: Origins and Prospects." *World Bank Research Observer*, February 18.

Yang, Dennis Tao. 2012. "Aggregate Savings and External Imbalances in China." *Journal of Economic Perspectives* 26, no. 4: 125–46.

CARLOS A. VEGH AND GUILLERMO VULETIN

7

Fiscal Policy Responses during Crises in Latin America and Europe: Implications for the G-20

This chapter summarizes our research on the social implications of fiscal policy responses to crises in Latin America over the last forty years and in the eurozone during the aftermath of the global financial crisis.[1] We focus on the behavior of social indicators such as the poverty rate, income inequality, unemployment rate, and domestic conflict. We find a causal link from countercyclical (and procyclical) fiscal policy responses to better (and worse) social outcomes, both in Latin America and in the eurozone. These results call into question recent claims on expansionary fiscal austerity.

It is well established by now that developing countries typically pursue procyclical fiscal policy (that is, expansionary fiscal policy in good times and contractionary fiscal policy in bad times), which tends to amplify the underlying business cycle.[2] In particular, contractionary fiscal policy in bad times increases the severity and duration of crises.[3] Ironically, the procyclicality of fiscal policy has also become a hotly debated issue in the context of the current crisis in Europe. Influential economists such as Olivier Blanchard (the chief economist for the International Monetary Fund) argue that fiscal multipliers in the eurozone have been underestimated by the IMF and others and that the contractionary effects of fiscal austerity have been considerably higher than previously thought.[4]

1. The reader is referred to Vegh and Vuletin (2014) for a detailed analysis (www.nber.org/papers/w19828).
2. See for example Gavin and Perotti (1997); Kaminsky, Reinhart, and Vegh (2004); and Vegh and Vuletin (2012).
3. See Vegh and Vuletin (2013).
4. See Blanchard and Leigh (2013).

Lost in much of the discussion on procyclical fiscal policy is its effect on social indicators, such as unemployment, income inequality, and the poverty rate. Surely part of the reason has been the lack of readily available time-series data on social indicators to match the existing macroeconomic data on fiscal variables and GDP. More generally, the fact that much of the discussion on fiscal procyclicality focuses on either the issue of causality (that is, does GDP cause government spending, or is it the other way around?) or why countries are procyclical (that is, is it imperfections in international capital markets or domestic political economy factors?) seems to have left little scope to broaden the discussion and look at the possible interaction between fiscal procyclicality and the behavior of social indicators.

Our research is the first attempt at filling this void by looking at how fiscal procyclicality during crises may affect the behavior of social indicators. For these purposes, we focus primarily on the fiscal policy response to crises in Latin America over the last forty years.[5] In our 2013 paper we argue that the evidence shows that, on average, Latin American countries "graduated" in terms of their fiscal and monetary response to crises, in the sense that they switched from procyclical policy responses before 1998 to countercyclical policy responses after 1998.[6]

In this chapter, we complement our previous analysis by looking at the way fiscal policy responses to crises affect social indicators, such as the poverty rate, income inequality, the unemployment rate, and domestic conflict. Matching the methodology in our 2013 work, we provide an operational definition of *crisis* and apply it to our sample of eight Latin American countries.[7] By so doing, we identify thirty-four crises and characterize their average duration and intensity. Since casual analysis for countries such as Chile and others in the region suggests a policy shift around the year 2000, we choose the year 1998 (a year without any GDP crisis) to divide our sample into a "before" and "after." We show that the frequency, duration, and intensity of crises in Latin America fell in the post-1998 period.

We then show that, on average, fiscal policy responses to crises in Latin America shifted from being procyclical before 1998 to being countercyclical after 1998. In this sense, therefore, we could argue that, on average, Latin America has graduated in terms of its fiscal policy response to crises. This

5. We follow Vegh and Vuletin (2013).

6. Paradoxically, we also show that several European countries have responded with a procyclical fiscal policy to the current crisis, which in itself may be of interest in the G-20 context.

7. Our definition is based on the behavior of the GDP, so these are, strictly speaking, GDP crises. However, they typically coincide with well-known crisis episodes.

average response, however, masks a great deal of heterogeneity within our sample, with countries such as Chile and Brazil (and, to some extent, Mexico) leading the way in this graduation process and countries such as Argentina, Uruguay, and Venezuela still showing heavily procyclical policy responses. We further find that countercyclical policy responses, particularly on the fiscal side, tend to reduce the duration and intensity of crises, a finding with significant policy implications in the current global economic landscape.

We then look at the behavior of social indicators during the crises. Specifically, change in the poverty rate, the ratio of the richest 10 percent to the poorest 10 percent, the unemployment rate, and domestic conflict before and after 1998. In general we see a fairly consistent picture across countries: Brazil, Chile, and Mexico are the countries where social indicators deteriorated the least during crises in the post-1998 period and, to the extent that data are available, the countries where we see a marked improvement from the pre- to the post-1998 period and also in the recent global crisis.

We then examine the role of fiscal policy in bringing about a possible improvement in the behavior of social indicators during crises. Extending the analysis from the previous section, we in fact see an absolute improvement in select social indicators for these countries during the crises in the post-1998 period. We show that there is a statistically significant relationship between the degree of cyclicality of fiscal policy and social indicators, in that the more procyclical the fiscal policy, the worse the performance in the corresponding indicator. However, since correlations do not imply causation, we construct a measure of fiscal space (which we call a fiscal readiness index) that acts as an instrument for fiscal policy. We conclude that, indeed, a more countercyclical fiscal policy response leads to an improvement in the behavior of social indicators during crises.

We turn our attention to the current eurozone crisis to argue that countries such as Greece, Ireland, Italy, and Portugal have been pursuing procyclical (that is, contractionary) fiscal policy, as Latin American countries used to do (and still do to some extent). We provide evidence in the form of a fiscal readiness index that suggests that this procyclical fiscal policy has worsened the behavior of social indicators.

We end the chapter with some concluding remarks and policy implications.

Crises in Latin America: Definition and Basic Statistics

Our sample for Latin American countries consists of what is commonly referred to as the LAC-7 (Argentina, Brazil, Chile, Colombia, Mexico, Peru, and Venezuela) and Uruguay. The combined GDP of these eight economies accounts for almost 93 percent of the Latin American and the Caribbean region's GDP. Unfortunately—and mainly due to the need to have quarterly data for our analysis—the sample period differs across countries. For Argentina, for instance, our sample starts in the first quarter of 1970, whereas for Venezuela it starts in the first quarter of 1998. For all countries except Venezuela, however, our sample starts in 1980 or earlier, which gives us at least thirty-three years of quarterly data.

Analyzing policy responses to crises naturally requires defining a crisis. For our purposes, we define a crisis as the period beginning in the quarter in which real GDP falls below the preceding four-quarter moving average and ending in the quarter in which real GDP reaches the precrisis level. Using this definition, we identify thirty-four crises in the eight Latin American countries. The countries with the largest number of crises are Argentina and Brazil (seven crises each), and the country with the least number of crises is Colombia (two crises). Given the different sample periods (and the different duration of each individual crisis), we also examine the frequency of crises (defined as the number of quarters that a given country is in crisis over the total number of quarters in the sample period). By this metric, Argentina is the country with the highest frequency of crises (a proportion of 0.49 implying that, over the last forty-three years, it has been in one crisis or another 49 percent of the time), while Colombia is the country with the lowest frequency (a proportion of 0.13). The average duration of crises is eleven quarters for the whole sample. Uruguay exhibits the longest average duration (eighteen quarters). The average intensity of crises (measured as the fall in the level of GDP from the start of the crisis to the trough) is 8.6 percent, with Uruguay also having the largest average intensity (14.8 percent).

If we take 1998 as our before-and-after demarcation date, how have the frequency, duration, and intensity of crises changed?[8] The frequency of crises before and after 1998 for each of our eight Latin American countries is, on average, higher before than after 1998. This impression is confirmed by the fact that the average frequency proportion of crises fell from 0.42 before 1998

---

8. While admittedly arbitrary, the choice of 1998 seemed a natural one. First—and as discussed in Frankel, Vegh, and Vuletin (2013)—the late 1990s appears to have been a period where one can detect (through formal regressions using institutional quality as an explanatory variable) a marked improvement in macroeconomic policy. Within this period, 1998 seemed a natural candidate, because no crisis took place in that year, providing us with a clean break in the series. We also wanted to leave a reasonably large window (fifteen years, in this case) where one can observe the aftereffects.

to 0.29 afterward and that the frequency proportion of crises after 2008 has been 0.23. It includes Peru, where the frequency proportion of crises declined sharply, from 0.72 before 1998 to 0.10 after 1998. At the other extreme is Uruguay, where the same metric increased from 0.32 before 1998 to 0.49 after 1998. The data on the average duration of crises for our eight Latin American countries before and after 1998 show that the average duration also fell after 1998, with the overall average duration of crises before 1998 being fourteen quarters, and falling to eight quarters after 1998 (figure 7-1, panel A). Finally, the average intensity of crises for our eight Latin American countries decreased, as captured by the fact that the fall in GDP (from the start of the crisis to the trough) before 1998 was 11 percent, compared to just 7 percent after 1998 (figure 7-1, panel B).

In sum, the evidence clearly suggests that the frequency, duration, and intensity of crises in Latin America fell in the post-1998 period.

Fiscal Policy Response

We now review the response of fiscal policy to crises. Data for each of the eight countries in the sample for the average correlation during crisis periods between the cyclical component of government spending and GDP before and after 1998 show that three countries, Brazil, Chile, and Mexico, clearly switched from a procyclical fiscal policy response before 1998 to a counter-cyclical policy response after 1998 (figure 7-2, panel B). Not coincidentally, these are countries that are often hailed in the financial press for having considerably improved their macroeconomic management over the years. The other five countries show a procyclical fiscal response after 1998, with Argentina, Peru, Uruguay, and Venezuela exhibiting particularly large ones.[9]

Behavior of Social Indicators

This section looks at the behavior of social indicators during the crisis episodes defined in the previous sections. The behavior of social indicators is measured by the change in poverty rate, the change in the ratio of richest 10 percent to poorest 10 percent, the change in the unemployment rate, and the change in domestic conflict before and after 1998.

---

9. We should note that Colombia did not have GDP crises before 1998, and that we do not have data for Venezuela before 1998.

Figure 7-1. *Duration and Intensity of GDP Crises, Eight Latin American Countries, before and after 1998*

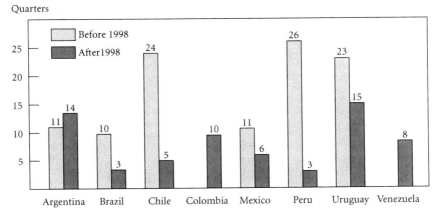

Panel A. Duration of GDP crisis (in quarters)

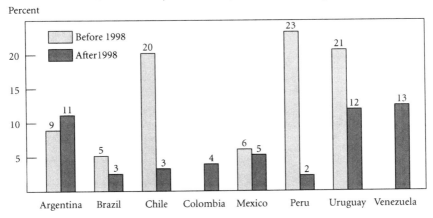

Panel B. Intensity of GDP crises(fall from start to trough)

In Brazil, Chile, and Mexico the change in the poverty rate in the post-1998 period has been in fact slightly negative, indicating a small reduction in the poverty rate during crises, in contrast to the experience of the other five Latin American countries. As we conjecture below, this could be due to counter-cyclical fiscal policies aimed at alleviating poverty in bad times. This post-1998 behavior stands in sharp contrast to the pre-1998 behavior for Brazil and Mexico (we do not have data for Chile), when increases in the poverty rate

Figure 7-2. *Changes in Unemployment Rate and Cyclicality of Fiscal Policy during GDP Crises, Eight Latin American Countries, before and after 1998*

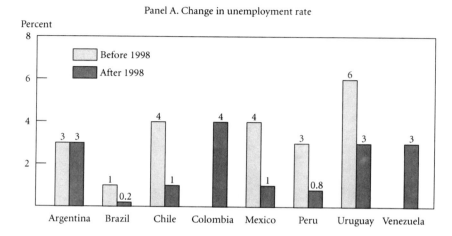

Panel A. Change in unemployment rate

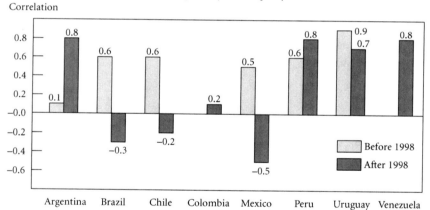

Panel B. Cyclicality of fiscal policy[a]

a. Vertical axis is the correlation between the cyclical components of government spending and GDP (during GDP crises).

were quite large. For Peru the pre- and post-1998 poverty rate is relatively low and qualitatively the same, whereas for Argentina and Venezuela the increase in the poverty rate is around 8 percent in the post-1998 period.

The change in the ratio of the richest 10 percent to the poorest 10 percent is remarkably similar. Brazil, Mexico, and Chile exhibit the smallest increases during the crises after 1998 (in fact, in Brazil and Mexico the ratio actually declined, reflecting lowering inequality during those crises), whereas the remaining five countries show consistently higher ratios, indicating worsening inequality.

In terms of changes in unemployment, the increase in the unemployment rate is significantly smaller in the post-1998 than in the pre-1998 period in Brazil, Chile, Mexico, Peru, and Uruguay (figure 7-2, panel A). In terms of magnitudes, the figures are the smallest in Brazil, Chile, and Mexico as well as Peru. The change in domestic conflict (computed relative to the historic average to control for country fixed effects) again reveals a similar pattern. After 1998 domestic conflicts declined in Brazil, Chile, and Mexico—an improving social indicator even through periods of economic crises.

In sum, we see a fairly consistent picture across countries, with Brazil, Chile, and Mexico being the set of countries where social indicators have deteriorated the least during crises in the post-1998 period and, to the extent that data are available, where we see the most marked improvement from the pre- to the post-1998 period.

The Role of Fiscal Policy

On average, our four social indicators during crises improved in the post-1998 period compared to the pre-1998 period. But we see quite a bit of variation across countries. For empirical purposes, of course, this variation is welcome because it enables us to see if we can link the nature of fiscal policy during crises to the observed changes in social indicators.

Scatter plots of the cyclicality of fiscal policy capture the correlation between the cyclical components of GDP and government spending against each of the four social indicators; we find a positive and statistically significant relationship (at least at the 10 percent level). This indicates that the more procyclical the fiscal policy, the worse the performance in the corresponding social indicator.

Correlations do not imply causation. So to argue that it is actually the change in fiscal policy that is causing the change in social indicators—and specifically that a countercyclical fiscal policy leads to an improvement in the behavior of social indicators—we replicate the methodology of our earlier work.[10] We construct a fiscal readiness index, which is basically an index of initial conditions that captures the fiscal space that countries may have before a

___

10. Vegh and Vuletin (2013).

Figure 7-3. *Duration and Intensity of Last GDP Crisis, Ten Eurozone Countries*

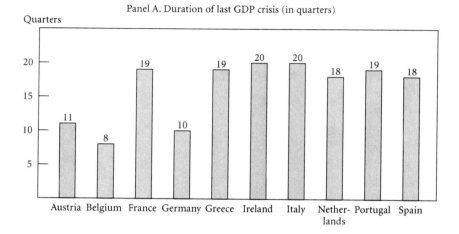

Panel A. Duration of last GDP crisis (in quarters)

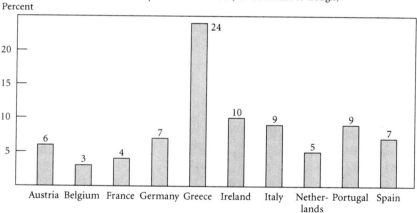

Panel B. Intensity of last GDP crisis (fall from start to trough)

crisis to pursue countercyclical fiscal policy during the crisis. This index attempts to measure the soundness of fiscal policy during the eight quarters (or two calendar years for annual indicators) preceding a crisis. The index comprises three components, each normalized between 0 and 10, such that the index ranges between 0 (lowest fiscal readiness) and 30 (highest fiscal readiness).[11] The three components are sovereign credit ratings, fiscal deficit as

11. For details on the construction of this index, see Vegh and Vuletin (2014).

percentage of GDP, and total (public plus private) external debt as a percentage of GDP.

We use the fiscal readiness index as an instrument for fiscal policy. But to do so, it needs to satisfy two conditions: first, it has to be highly correlated with the countercyclical fiscal policy response, and second, it can affect the social indicators only through its effect on the fiscal policy response. The correlation between the fiscal policy response and the fiscal readiness index is –0.50, and hence the first condition is indeed satisfied. Further, we argue that our index also satisfies the second condition because it is computed before the crisis begins and is composed of essentially backward-looking variables. Hence it cannot directly affect the change in social indicators that takes place after the crisis has begun.

The correlation between the predicted cyclicality of fiscal policy (using our instrument above) and each of the four social indicators is positive in all cases. Further, in two of the cases (poverty rate and domestic conflict), the relationship is also statistically significant at the 5 percent level. From these and other results, we conclude that our findings support the notion that the causality runs from the fiscal policy response to the behavior of social indicators.[12]

Europe: More of the Same?

We now look at the current European crisis and ask whether our main finding for Latin America—that the fiscal policy response matters for the way social indicators behave during a crisis holds for the European case (figure 7-4). Data on the duration and intensity of the current crisis for ten eurozone countries show that, as of the first quarter of 2013 (the last quarter for GDP in our sample), the crisis is ongoing for seven of the ten countries and is at least eighteen quarters old (figure 7-3).[13] The average intensity for the current eurozone crisis is 8.4 percent of GDP, which roughly coincides with the average intensity of crises in Latin America of 8.6 percent of GDP, with Greece having lost 24 percent of GDP from the start of the crisis until the trough in the first quarter of 2013; which is the last quarter in the sample.

How did fiscal policy react to the crisis? Our measure of fiscal policy cyclicality shows the correlation between the cyclical components of government spending and real GDP during crises for each of the ten countries (figure 7-4,

---

12. See Vegh and Vuletin (2014) for the data and a more detailed analysis.
13. The countries are Austria, Belgium, France, Germany, Greece, Ireland, Italy, Netherlands, Portugal, and Spain.

Figure 7-4. *Changes in Unemployment Rate and Cyclicality of Fiscal Policy during last GDP Crisis, Ten Eurozone Countries*

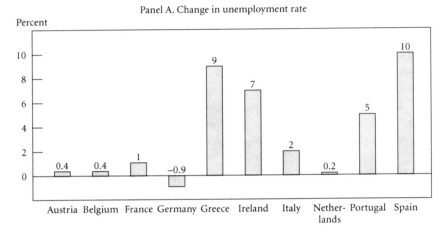

Panel A. Change in unemployment rate

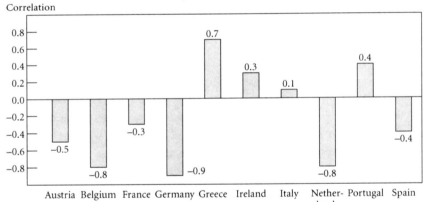

Panel B. Cyclicality of fiscal policy[a]

a. Vertical axis is the correlation between the cyclical components of government spending and GDP (during recent economic crisis).

panel B). We find that four countries—Greece, Ireland, Italy, and Portugal—have been procyclical in their fiscal policy response. In other words, they contracted fiscal spending during the crisis (as part of a "fiscal consolidation," to use today's jargon). In contrast, the other six European countries embarked on countercyclical fiscal policy, with Germany leading the way. So, as in Latin America, there is appreciable heterogeneity in the fiscal response to the crisis.

We look at social indicators for our ten eurozone countries. As expected, the biggest increases in the unemployment rate occurred in Greece, Ireland, Italy, Portugal, and Spain (figure 7-4, panel A). This is largely consistent with the observed increases in domestic conflict, with Greece and Spain truly standing out.

The question now becomes, Did procyclical fiscal policy lead to a larger deterioration in fiscal indicators during the crisis? By analyzing the relationship between the index of fiscal cyclicality and the change in unemployment and the change in domestic conflict, we find that both relationships are positive and statistically significant at, at least, the 10 percent level. In other words, these results are consistent with the idea that a procyclical fiscal response in the eurozone has led to deterioration in social indicators.

This finding, however, could reflect reverse causality. To address this issue, and as we did for Latin American countries above, we compute the fiscal readiness index for our sample of ten eurozone countries. We find a highly significant correlation between the fiscal readiness index and fiscal policy, as captured by the correlation between the cyclical component of government spending and real GDP. This is tantamount to saying that we have a valid instrument. Finally, we find a significant relation between our instrument for fiscal readiness and the duration and intensity of crises. We thus conclude that, indeed, procyclical fiscal policies in some eurozone crises contributed to making the current crisis socially costlier (both in terms of unemployment and social conflict), much as in Latin America before 1998.

Policy Conclusions and Implications for the G-20

This chapter started from the observation that the fiscal policy response to crises has dramatically shifted around the world recently. Many Latin American countries (like Chile, Brazil, and Mexico) graduated in terms of their fiscal responses to GDP crises, by switching from procyclical to countercyclical policy responses. On the other hand, many advanced economies (like Greece, Ireland, Italy, and Portugal) followed contractionary fiscal policies in the recent global financial crisis. In 2013 we presented evidence that strongly suggests that fiscal austerity policies lead to longer and deeper GDP crises, whereas fiscal stimulus policies imply shorter and shallower recessions.[14] These findings support recent evidence that fiscal multipliers are larger than

14. Vegh and Vuletin (2013).

previously thought (particularly during recessions) and do not support the so-called expansionary austerity hypothesis, put forward by many studies.[15]

Our main focus in this chapter is on the effects of fiscal policy responses to crises on social outcomes, a topic that has received little attention so far and that is of critical policy importance. If one views fiscal austerity programs as market driven, we could articulate the tension between the "need" for austerity programs and their social implications in terms of "debt versus social sustainability." We find that countercyclical fiscal policies tend to improve the undesirable effects of GDP crises on social outcomes such as poverty, income inequality, unemployment, and domestic conflict. On the other hand, austerity packages tend to worsen all of these social indicators. This evidence further supports the desirability of pursuing expansionary fiscal policies in times of distress, which may mean postponing for some time needed structural fiscal adjustment, rather than embarking on fiscal austerity in the middle of a GDP crisis.

Moreover, we also show that the ability of countries to react countercyclically during GDP crises crucially depends on their fiscal space. By constructing a simple fiscal readiness index, we show that countries that were able to follow sound fiscal and macroeconomic policies in the period before a crisis are, not surprisingly, those that are better prepared to actively use fiscal policies to reduce the length and intensity of a crisis as well as to diminish its social impact.

We argue that our findings should have important implications for G-20 members. In an increasingly uncertain world (due to, among other factors, the capital flows and financial markets implications of the expected Federal Reserve tapering, lower global demand and its effect on commodity prices, and for eurozone members, the inability to pursue an independent monetary policy), these findings suggest that countries should continue to build some fiscal policy space in order to respond effectively to future headwinds and slowdowns. Three key items in the fiscal agenda are, one, revisiting the efficiency of

---

15. Our finding that countercyclical fiscal policy has helped in reducing the duration and intensity of GDP crises is, of course, related to the issue of the size of the fiscal multipliers; see, for instance, Auerbach and Gorodnichenko (2011) and the references therein. In fact, Auerbach and Gorodnichenko argue that multipliers are larger in bad times than in good times. Riera-Crichton, Vegh, and Vuletin (2013) further suggest that it may matter whether government spending is going up or down, and they show that, at least for OECD countries, fiscal multipliers are even bigger in bad times when government spending is actually increasing. Riera-Crichton, Vegh, and Vuletin (2012) also show that (when properly measured) tax increases associated with fiscal consolidation episodes are very contractionary.

public spending; two, increasing the scope and responsiveness of social programs aimed at reducing undesired social outcomes and social conflicts; and three, focusing on public investment as a way to increase productivity in a world where favorable external conditions may come to an end. Indeed, Ethan Ilzetzki, Enrique Mendoza, and Carlos Vegh show that, while fiscal multipliers associated with government consumption are virtually zero in developing countries, increases in public investment are quite expansionary.[16] The public investment multiplier is 0.6 on impact (that is, one dollar of investment increases output by sixty cents) and about 1.5 after two years. These results support the priority on investment in infrastructure as a high-yield strategy for stimulating private sector growth and achieving sustainable development as a regional and G-20 issue for 2014. (See also chapter 13, this volume.)

In eurozone countries, our findings also point to the importance of further developing a fiscal union that would allow countries to share risk on the fiscal front. In the same way that over the last decade we have seen marked improvements on the monetary side, with many emerging markets building large chests of foreign reserves aimed at dealing with sudden stops or pressures on the domestic currency, these should be times during which fiscal authorities develop new strategies to increase their fiscal readiness.

References

Auerbach, Alan, and Yuriy Gorodnichenko. 2011. "Fiscal Multipliers in Recession and Expansion." NBER Working Paper 17447. Cambridge, Mass.: National Bureau of Economic Research.

Blanchard, Olivier, and Daniel Leigh. 2013. "Growth Forecast Errors and Fiscal Multipliers." IMF Working Paper WP/13/1. Washington: International Monetary Fund.

Frankel, Jeffrey, Carlos Vegh, and Guillermo Vuletin. 2013. "On Graduation from Fiscal Procyclicality." *Journal of Development Economics* 100 (January): 32–47.

Gavin, Michael, and Roberto Perotti. 1997. "Fiscal Policy in Latin America." *NBER Macroeconomics Annual* 12: 11–61.

Ilzetzki, Ethan, Enrique Mendoza, and Carlos Vegh. 2013. "How Big (Small?) Are Fiscal Multipliers?" *Journal of Monetary Economics* 60 (March): 239–54.

Kaminsky, Graciela, Carmen M. Reinhart, and Carlos Vegh. 2004. "When It Rains, It Pours: Procyclical Capital Flows and Macroeconomic Policies." *NBER Macroeconomics Annual,* pp. 11–82.

Riera-Crichton, Daniel, Carlos Vegh, and Guillermo Vuletin. 2012. "Tax Multipliers: Pitfalls in Measurement and Identification." NBER Working Paper 18497. Cambridge, Mass.: National Bureau of Economic Research.

16. Ilzetzki, Mendoza, and Vegh (2013).

————. 2013. "Fiscal Multipliers in Recessions and Expansions: Does It Matter Whether Government Spending Is Increasing or Decreasing?" Unpublished manuscript. Washington: World Bank.

Vegh, Carlos, and Guillermo Vuletin. 2012. "How Is Tax Policy Conducted over the Business Cycle." NBER Working Paper 17753. Cambridge, Mass.: National Bureau of Economic Research.

————. 2013. "The Road to Redemption: Policy Response to Crises in Latin America" Paper prepared for the IMF Annual Research Conference.

————. 2014. "Social Implications of Fiscal Policy Responses during Crises." NBER Working Paper 19828. Cambridge, Mass.: National Bureau of Economic Research.

YOSHIO OKUBO

8

The G-20 and Financial Market Regulation

Financial market regulation has been the core agenda of the G-20. In the immediate wake of the global financial crisis, uncertainties were abundant and tremors from the collapse of several major financial institutions were still being tangibly felt around the world. The G-20 leaders' summit was created during these tumultuous moments. Their first meeting in November 15, 2008, was focused on the glaring inadequacy of the regulations of global financial markets exposed by the crisis. The leaders sent a clear message that their regulators would work together internationally to contain the impact of the crisis and create a better financial system. They tasked their finance ministers, central bank governors, and regulators with strengthening regulatory and supervisory standards and addressing the key issues. They have worked intensively for the past five years through the Financial Stability Board (FSB) in cooperation with international financial institutions and other international bodies so that financial crises can be avoided in the future.

The inadequacy of the regulatory system for the global financial market was symbolized by the failure of Lehman Brothers, one of the largest investment banks; by the threat of collapse of other large financial institutions; and by the infusion of large amounts of public funds into large financial institutions by national governments to preserve the stability of the financial system.

The views expressed in this chapter are the author's own and should not be interpreted as views of any organization or group with which author is affiliated. The author is grateful to Colin Bradford, Kemal Derviş, and Homi Kharas of the Brookings Institution and H. K. Holdaway of the Australian Treasury for their helpful comments on an early version of this chapter.

It became evident that the national and international regulatory systems lacked an effective mechanism to alert regulators and supervisors to the risks building up in the financial system. The regulators were also found to have only limited workable tools to deal with failures of large and complex financial institutions. To contain the impact of the crisis and keep the financial system functioning, they had to rely on ad hoc measures, only made available by emergency legislation, and on large-scale backstopping by governments. The economic and social cost of such inadequacy has proved in subsequent years to be enormous in terms of government debt obligations or in the form of prolonged stagnation of economies. Along with the latter come persistently high unemployment, particularly of the young, and a loss of confidence in the future. The adverse impact is still plaguing many economies five years after the crisis.

The creation of the G-20 at that juncture was not merely a timely response to the crisis but also the beginning of a full-scale international attempt to create a robust global regulatory system over the long run. In the past, when an economy seemed to be doing well, it would have been difficult for policymakers to address the weaknesses and vulnerabilities of a national regulatory system, even if such weaknesses and vulnerabilities were partly recognized. The global nature of financial markets and financial institutions, combined with the increasing complexity of financial products, had also constrained the ability of national regulatory agencies to detect and respond to warning signals in the market and to propose regulatory reforms requiring international cooperation. The crisis and the ensuing work of the G-20 leaders of the past five years have already significantly changed the way policymakers formulate their national policies—-compelling them to consider the international implications of regulatory policies and making them accountable not only to their political leaders but also to the international regulatory community through newly created monitoring and assessment mechanisms.

Obviously, many factors other than financial regulation were also considered responsible for building the excess that led to the crisis.[1] They include

1. The leaders seem increasingly to be devoting their discussions to the global economy and to growth, employment, trade, and tax matters. Still financial market regulation is the predominant agenda item of the G-20 process; the communiqué issued by G-20 finance ministers and central bank governors in July 2013 devotes eighteen paragraphs (of thirty-eight) to financial market regulation. G-20 (2013a). This does not count the references to financial inclusion, the fight against corruption, or energy and commodity markets, which also have some relevance to financial market reform.

macroeconomic imbalances, fiscal and monetary policies, and overconfidence in the ability of markets to automatically correct excesses.[2] This overconfidence was true not only of policymakers but also of academia and the general press, which may have bred complacency, especially when markets seemed to be functioning well. While the blame tends to be directed at regulators when a crisis happens, it is also clear that reform of financial regulation alone will not bring about the stability of financial markets. Fiscal and monetary policies will play an equally important role in ensuring the stability of financial markets. The policy focus on macroeconomic prudence reflects this emerging thinking on the part of G-20 policymakers. The G-20 leaders' process on financial regulation should therefore be considered one of the several interrelated initiatives for detecting the risks that may be building up in the global financial system and for exploring the tools needed to deal with its possible instability in the future.

Over the past five years, G-20 leaders, through the FSB, agreed on a broad range of regulatory reforms that address the major fault lines that caused the crisis, and the leaders are in the process of implementing them. The reforms include, in particular, increasing the resilience of banks through the more robust capital requirements promulgated in Basel III, ending the too-big-to-fail problem by focusing on systemically important financial institutions (including through the designation of global systemically important banks and insurance companies) and subjecting them to higher loss absorbency and other requirements. Strengthened supervision of systemically important financial institutions through supervisory colleges has now become an important feature for globally active financial institutions. Reform of resolution frameworks has become an increasingly important agenda item. The work to create more transparent and robust over-the-counter derivatives markets is being undertaken. Progress is being made in addressing the issue of shadow banking, the legal entity identifier initiative, and oversight of credit rating agencies. Compensation practices have also been addressed by the FSB. Increasing attention is now being paid to more forward-looking issues, including financial regulatory factors affecting the availability of long-term investment finance, particularly in emerging markets and developing economies.

Despite these welcome developments, however, concerns have been often expressed that only modest progress has been made in the past five years in

2. For an interesting discussion and analysis of the various factors that led to the financial crisis, see Davies (2010).

creating a robust and coherent global regulatory system.[3] Some even argue that regulatory fragmentation and lack of policy coordination may be emerging.[4] On some occasions, major regulatory organizations in the United States and Europe were reported to be, if anything, less engaged in embracing coherence and harmonization, as shown in the case involving over-the-counter derivatives reform. Criticism often surfaces that the implementation of globally agreed-on standards is becoming uneven, that unilateral approaches are increasingly taken in key policy areas, that domestic bias may be emerging in supervisory practices, that extraterritorial overreach is seen in some national regulatory measures, and that protectionist tendencies may be appearing in national policies. Even within Europe, where regulatory cooperation has been advanced over many years in a drive to achieve a single market, disputes have developed, for instance, about remuneration rules, the short-selling regulation, the location of clearing houses, and taxing financial transactions. The financial press is full of news stories pointing out incoherence, complexity, and duplication in various regulatory measures, implying that divergence is arising, which may make room for more regulatory arbitrage and erode confidence in the collective approach. These concerns, real or apparent, could lead the general public to wonder if a harmonized and consistent approach to global financial market regulation is overly optimistic. These concerns may also breed cynicism about the legitimacy and relevance of the G-20 process.

It is therefore timely to review, first, the role of the G-20 in regulating globalized financial markets in a historical perspective and assessing the progress made so far; second, to identify the possible causes of the divergence and inconsistency that may emerge; and third, to suggest ways to avoid possible erosion of cohesion in the G-20 process and revitalize it going forward.

Reviewing the Role of the G-20 in International Regulatory Reform

The G-20 initiative for international regulatory reform is part of an evolutionary process, preceded by decades of efforts by international groups of supervisors and regulators in formulating the basis of international regulatory cooperation. A brief recap of the historical development of international

3. See for example Tett (2013).
4. For example, see Adams (2013).

supervisory and regulatory cooperation may highlight the potentials of the G-20 process and the challenges it faces.

Historically, supervisory cooperation was driven by the need to respond to increasing international activities of banks and to define the scope of the responsibilities of national supervisors. The establishment of the Basel Committee on Banking Supervision (BCBS) in 1974 reflects the need for supervisory cooperation in light of the growing international activities of banks due to the lifting of exchange controls and the emergence of the euro currency market.[5] It was triggered, in particular, by the failures of a German bank (Bankhaus Herstatt) and a U.S. bank (Franklin National Bank of New York) in the same year. The initial work of the BCBS was devoted, inter alia, to the division of responsibilities of home and host supervisors, as embodied in the Basel Concordat of 1975.

Subsequently, in light of the growing concern about the capital adequacy of international banks following the Latin American debt crisis in the early 1980s and about the competitive inequality arising from differences in national capital requirements, a common supervisory approach for capital adequacy requirements was pursued, driven by the desire to ensure a level playing field for internationally active banks. The first capital accord, now referred to as Basel I, was agreed on in 1988. This accord was later revised to enhance its risk sensitivity and to cover market risk and operational risk. These changes were supplemented, in the Basel II accord of 2004, by enhanced supervisory review of the internal assessment process and disclosure to strengthen market discipline.

The increasing internationalization of financial markets also led to the cooperative initiatives in securities regulation and insurance supervision. The International Organization of Securities Commissions (IOSCO) was established in 1983, and the International Association of Insurance Supervisors was established in 1994. As some of the issues were common to the BCBS and these two organizations, and as the need for coordinated supervision of financial conglomerates was heightened, the Joint Forum was established in 1996 under the aegis of the three organizations. In light of the increasing international activity in the securities and derivatives markets, the agreement within IOSCO, in 2002, on the Multilateral Memorandum of Understanding was a particularly

---

5. The BCBS was established by the central bank governors of the G-10 countries. It now reports to an oversight body, the Group of Central Bank Governors and Heads of Supervision. Its original name was Committee on Banking Regulations and Supervisory Practices. See BCBS (2013a).

important development in international regulatory cooperation, as it strengthened mutual cooperation, consultation, and exchange of information among
IOSCO members to ensure compliance with, and enforcement of, members'
securities and derivatives laws and regulations.[6] In a parallel development, the
need for high-quality and consistent accounting and auditing standards was
recognized, and in 1973 the International Accounting Standards Committee
was founded. The committee was replaced in 2001 by the International
Accounting Standards Board. Its initiatives have been aimed at an international convergence of accounting standards.

The rapid globalization of international capital markets, as well as the
European single-market plans, reinforced the drive for a global approach to
financial markets regulation. The Asian financial crisis and the collapse of a
large hedge fund in the late 1990s also accelerated the momentum for formulating and implementing supervisory and regulatory codes and standards.
In October 1998 the G-7 finance ministers and central bankers issued a communiqué calling for a new structure for enhancing cooperation among the
various national and international supervisory bodies and international financial institutions so as to promote stability in the international financial system.
The communiqué asked Hans Tietmeyer, then president of Bundesbank, to
consult the relevant international bodies on this initiative. Upon his recommendation, the Financial Stability Forum, the predecessor of the FSB, was
established by the G-7 finance ministers and central bankers in February 1999,
bringing together finance ministries and treasuries, central banks, and supervisory agencies, along with international organizations.

In the 1990s many important economies undertook the liberalization of
various restrictions and controls that had inhibited the integration of financial markets, which led to the emergence of truly global financial markets. The
launch of the G-20 process was a natural response to these developments,
based on the evolution of international cooperative initiatives. The G-20 was
initiated by G-20 finance ministers and central bank governors. Their inaugural meeting in Berlin in November 1999 reflected the growing importance
of systemically important economies and emerging market countries in the
global financial system. The group was expected to provide a new mechanism for informal dialogue in the framework of the Bretton Woods institutional system, broaden the discussions on key economic and financial policy

---

6. As of September 2013, 97 members were signatories, of 125 eligible members (www.
iosco.org).

issues among systemically significant economies, and promote cooperation to achieve stable and sustainable world economic growth.

Since their initial meetings, the G-20 finance ministers and central bank governors have focused on the development of international codes and standards in key areas—including transparency, data dissemination, and financial sector policy—and have emphasized the importance of Reports on the Observance of Standards and Codes and the Financial Sector Assessment Program, led by the IMF and the World Bank. Their focus on financial sector reform was somewhat subdued in the following years in light of the solid expansion of the world economy in the mid-2000s. But in November 2007, meeting in South Africa, they noted the "recent turbulence," recognizing that there might be important new lessons for understanding the origins of crises, the way financial shocks are transmitted, and the respective roles of regulators, rating agencies, the private sector, and the international financial community. They agreed to pursue further work to improve their understanding of these issues and their application to G-20 members in the year ahead.

A decade of work by the G-20 finance ministers and central bankers preceded the creation of the G-20 leaders' summit. Holding their tenth annual meeting in Brazil on November 8–9, 2008, amid the extremely serious financial crisis, the financial ministers and central bankers welcomed the convening of the G-20 leaders' summit in the following week (November 15), noting that a global crisis requires global solutions and a common set of principles. They pointed out that the financial crisis was largely a result of excessive risk taking and faulty risk management practices in financial markets, macroeconomic policies giving rise to domestic and external imbalances, and deficiencies in financial regulation and supervision in some advanced countries. They called for better ways to identify systemically important institutions and to ensure proper oversight of these institutions. They also said that all sectors of the financial industry, as appropriate, should be regulated or subjected to oversight. In addition, they recognized the importance of addressing the issue of procyclicality in financial market regulations and supervisory systems and agreed that financial institutions should have common accounting standards and clear internal incentives to promote stability. They added that action needed to be taken, through voluntary effort or through regulatory action, to avoid compensation schemes that reward excessive short-term returns or risk taking. All of these issues were to dominate the following G-20 leaders' discussions on financial regulation, internationally as well as domestically.

As is clear from these historical developments, the G-20 leaders' process has significantly strengthened the preexisting framework of regulatory cooperation and provided an excellent basis for regulating global financial markets in five major ways.

First, the G-20 process involves regulators and supervisors from a much broader spectrum of countries than previous groups, like the G-7 and the G-10. The involvement of systemically important and major emerging economies has enhanced the relevance and legitimacy of the agreed-on standards. It has also strengthened adherence to these standards by obtaining commitments from major jurisdictions. The most important aspect relevant to financial market regulation is the establishment of the FSB by the G-20 leaders. At their London summit in April 2009 they agreed to establish the FSB as a successor to the Financial Stability Forum and to include all G-20 countries, Financial Stability Forum members, Spain, and the European Commission.[7]

Second, by engaging the political leaders at the highest level, it strengthened the commitment of national regulators to agreed-on reform projects. The regular meetings at the highest political level have encouraged intensive communications and dialogue among regulators with different mandates and responsibilities, both internationally and domestically, utilizing their expertise in their respective areas of competence.

Third, the G-20 process, by institutionalizing peer reviews, strengthened the mechanism to monitor members' implementation of the agreed-on reform measures. Through these review processes, it was reported to the leaders, for instance, that all designated global systemically important banks were now headquartered in jurisdictions that had adopted the Basel III framework and were in the process of implementing it.[8] More important, with the G-20 leaders' endorsement, FSB member jurisdictions have committed to undergoing an assessment under the IMF-World Bank Financial Sector Assessment Program (FSAP) every five years. In addition, they have committed to submit to country peer reviews, which take place two or three years following the five-year FSAP cycle and are expected to complement those assessments.[9]

---

7. In a parallel development and with the G-20's encouragement, the key international regulatory groups, including the BCBS, IOSCO's Technical Committee, and the Committee on Payment and Settlement Systems, expanded their memberships to include systemically important economies.

8. The BCBS has put in place the Regulatory Consistency Assessment Program to monitor progress and to assess the implementation of Basel III. See also FSB (2013b), pp. 10–12.

9. See FSB (2010, 2011). Country peer reviews have been conducted and the results published for Australia, Canada, Italy, Mexico, South Africa, Spain, Switzerland, the United King-

They focus on the implementation and effectiveness of international financial standards and policies agreed on by the FSB. Furthermore, thematic peer reviews are conducted, focusing on the implementation of particular standards across the FSB membership.

Fourth, the standing nature of the G-20 process has made it possible to take up broader regulatory issues as they emerge in global financial markets. For example, in light of the scandals involving the London Interbank Offered Rate (LIBOR), the G-20 and the FSB embarked on an initiative to improve oversight and governance of widely used financial benchmarks. The FSB is now playing a major role in addressing any major regulatory issues emerging in the global financial markets, since the board has been established with a legal personality, enabling it to serve as an enduring organization, with strengthened governance, greater autonomy, and enhanced capacity to coordinate the development and implementation of financial regulatory policies. It will be in a key position to deal with issues arising from the increasingly complex and fast-moving global financial markets, driven by rapid technological change and innovation.[10]

Finally, the G-20 process has been driven and accompanied by important domestic legislative actions, particularly in large jurisdictions where sizeable and complex financial institutions are headquartered. Particularly noteworthy are the legislative actions in the United States in the form of the Dodd-Frank Act for strengthening the resolution regimes for systemically important financial institutions, contributing to the core G-20 consensus on this issue. Important legislative actions to translate the G-20 consensus into domestic regulations have been taken or are being planned in many countries, including Australia, France, Germany, Japan, Netherlands, Spain, Switzerland, and the United Kingdom.[11] The G-20 leaders clearly recognized the urgent need to create robust resolution regimes that enable authorities to resolve failing financial institutions quickly without destabilizing the financial system. While substantive challenges remain, particularly in enhancing the cross-border cooperation of crisis management and the implementation of resolution strategies, the G-20 process seems so far to have succeeded in encouraging such domestic legislative actions.

---

dom, and the United States. Thematic reviews were conducted on, among others, compensation, mortgage underwriting and origination practices, risk governance, resolution regimes, and reliance on credit rating agencies' ratings.

10. Descriptions of the progress being made are contained in Carney (2013); FSB (2013a, 2013b, 2013c).

11. See FSB (2013d, sec. 2 and app. A).

In summing up the role of the G-20 in global financial market regulation, it is important to note that the brief history of the international regulatory cooperation, culminating in the G-20 leaders' process, reveals an underlying evolution of international regulatory cooperation in three fundamental ways. First was the shift of emphasis from an even-handed supervision of financial institutions to the regulation of the market conduct of diverse market players, both regulated and unregulated. Second was the shift of focus from managing defined risks to strengthening the means to detect undefined risks in markets. And third is the shift from preventing the failures of financial institutions to managing their failures in an orderly manner. The G-20 process has embraced this underlying evolution of regulatory cooperation in an effort to stay relevant and effective, making it possible for its leaders to address inconsistencies, gaps, or duplications and to implement solutions for problems in the future global financial market.

What Drives Divergence?

While the G-20 leaders' process during the past five years has so far created a coherent approach to regulating financial markets, a number of elements still pose serious challenges over the longer term. The process of international regulatory cooperation built around the G-20 leaders seems irreversible, but progress toward a consistent global financial regulation could be hampered by many underlying factors, factors that may lead to significant fragmentation in national regulatory approaches or even to an erosion of confidence in the G-20 processes.

The most important challenge arises from the general shift from bank financing to market financing in many countries, including emerging market countries. The growth of market financing expands opportunities for firms to mobilize a large amount of funds at lower cost. The parallel development of a derivatives market may also improve their risk management capabilities. These changes also expand opportunities for investors and, together, can bring enormous benefits to economies as a whole. The diversification of financial intermediation, particularly through the development of efficient and robust capital markets, generally makes the country's financial system less vulnerable to the failure of a financial institution and more resilient in supporting innovation and growth in the economy. In addition, a jurisdiction that is actively encouraging domestic financial markets to perform a broader international intermediary role, thereby becoming an international financial center, will also expand its financial market sector, not only providing jobs but also attracting people with high skills.

But as the market becomes sophisticated, the challenge for regulators to ensure their stability, efficiency, and integrity becomes complicated. Advanced markets are broadly open to regulated and unregulated entities, domestic and foreign. The mandate of securities regulators is to protect all investors active in their own jurisdiction. But the enforcement of rules is based on domestic judiciary procedures. Of course, the nature of such market regulation does not mean that foreign players would be unfairly treated; in fact, if they were unfairly treated, the international attractiveness of the market would diminish, and its international standing would erode. Nevertheless, investors and market participants are based in a wide range of jurisdictions, where legal and regulatory philosophies may vary and their interpretations of rules may differ. The definitions or interpretations of unlawful activities may also differ, as may the manner and degree of enforcement in, for instance, insider-trading regulations and corporate disclosure requirements. In addition, just as domestic rules may not necessarily cover entities based abroad, there may be regulatory conflicts or gaps that might ultimately erode confidence in international cooperative processes.

One of the potentially most contentious aspects of financial regulation is the cross-border application of regulations, particularly those that regulate cross-border over-the-counter derivatives markets. While the collaborative efforts have produced essentially identical rules, based on shared and common objectives, the application of the rules on cross-border transactions can become complicated in practice, creating inconsistencies or uncertainties or even legal conflicts. The recent progress in over-the-counter derivatives reforms—including the agreement by the European Commission and the U.S. Commodity Futures Trading Commission—is a welcome development in this regard.[12] It was endorsed at the G-20 summit in September 2013.[13] The agreement states that jurisdictions and regulators should be able to defer to each other when it is justified by the quality of their regulatory and enforcement regimes, based on similar outcomes, in a nondiscriminatory way, paying due respect to home

12. On July 11, 2013, the European Commission and the U.S. Commodity Futures Trading Commission reached an agreement (called Path Forward) regarding their joint understandings on a package of measures for cross-border derivatives.

13. G-20 (2013b).

country regulation regimes. The G-20 regulators and the FSB are expected to report on the time line to settle remaining issues related to overlapping cross-border regulatory regimes and regulatory arbitrage.

Complicating the efforts to achieve coherent market regulation is the possibility that proper but strict rules may shift transactions from well-regulated jurisdictions to lightly regulated jurisdictions, possibly even to outside G-20 jurisdictions, draining the liquidity from their markets or making it difficult to monitor risks. The competition among markets to attract businesses may, in other words, encourage a race to the bottom, downgrading the overall quality of market regulation in the global context. Given the diversity in legal and judiciary systems among countries, a careful assessment of the implementation of agreed-on principles would be called for to ensure that international regulatory cooperation will promote the race to the top, aiming to raise the overall quality of global market regulation.

Embracing a global approach may also entail other aspects of compromising domestic regulation. The reform of over-the-counter derivatives markets, for example, will make it essential that relevant authorities have access to accurate and usable data.[14] Of course, the privacy restrictions of some countries may create barriers to reporting the information necessary for regulatory purposes. In this regard, the FSB is planning a feasibility study of how to produce and share globally aggregated trade repository data that authorities need for monitoring systemic risks. Some compromises may come easily, but others may pose serious challenges. In addition, the acceptance by the public of the primacy of financial regulation would depend on its trust and confidence in the regulators.

A related risk is the challenge of legislating internationally agreed-on principles into domestic laws and regulations. In financial market regulation, details matter, and exceptions to rules are important. It would normally take a long time to sort out these details, while resistance to reform would become strong, particularly when the cost of reform is considered to be too high. Even if it might be relatively easy to agree on the principles of market reform in the wake of crisis, it could become difficult to put these principles into practice in more normal circumstances. Turf battles among regulatory agencies may easily erupt, creating political problems that may not be readily solved. The resulting compromise could add to the complexity of regulations, blur the purposes of regulation, and breed public suspicion that the objectives of the reform have been compromised.

14. See Carney (2013, p. 4).

Another risk relates to divergence in the macroeconomic performance of countries. The prolonged recession and divergent economic performances may weaken cohesion in political leadership. The cost of dealing with the aftermath of the financial crisis differs among affected countries. In the short run, the crisis has likely enhanced disparities within the affected countries, complicating the challenges for policymakers. Criticism and resistance may emerge in some countries against collective approaches, particularly when they are seen as too complicated or too intrusive. The benefit of global approaches can be felt only in the longer term. Any reform would entail costs and affect the way the market works. In the process, the voting public or industry practitioners can become wary and may start to experience reform fatigue before any benefits are felt. Such situations may also naturally reinforce the perception that open markets and free flows of capital may benefit only a limited segment of the population, rather than the economy as a whole. Such perceptions may make protectionist and nationalistic measures popular with the voting public.

G-20 Leaders Move Forward

Solidarity among the G-20 countries is easier to manage when the leaders are facing a common global crisis. It becomes more difficult when the common threat recedes and leaders are exposed to divergent domestic political and economic situations. If significant divergence emerges in financial market regulation, financial transactions will be shifted to those jurisdictions with weaker regulation. Or they may be shifted to jurisdictions outside the G-20 markets. Such a shift may create a race to the bottom and jeopardize the longer-term stability of the global financial system. The possibility of such divergence may not be high—but also may not be remote, as discussed above, and would leave market regulation fragmented, less transparent, and undermining the purpose of reform.

What kind of leadership is needed to continue and even accelerate progress in regulating the global financial market? There are three basic areas in which the G-20 leaders can minimize the danger of fragmentation in global financial regulation; focusing on fundamentals, clarity of purpose, and the rule of law.

Focus on Fundamentals

The first priority for the G-20 leaders is to focus on the fundamental function of financial markets, namely, allocation of scarce capital for growth and innovation. Leaders should look at the issues from a higher standpoint and ask themselves how well financial markets are functioning to serve this purpose and at what cost, as argued by Benjamin Friedman.[15] A significant percentage of GDP is allocated to investment through financial markets. The performance of financial markets should therefore be judged against the success of investment in promoting growth and innovation, in encouraging well-informed risk taking, and in discouraging reckless leveraging. The G-20 leaders' role is not to micromanage specific regulatory initiatives but to ask regulators, the financial industry, and various stakeholders how they can best contribute to the better performance of the real economy.

The greatest advantage of market financing supplementing bank financing in the global market is the ability of markets to generate information. High-quality market information helps investors appreciate risks and determines the allocation of scarce capital for the real economy. For a financial market to function well and generate information in a timely manner, it needs confidence, liquidity, and efficiency. Confidence, in turn, requires transparency, fairness, and integrity. This means that the quality of regulation can therefore be judged by the availability of timely and appropriate information on market development. After all, identifying vulnerabilities in the global financial system is not a technical exercise but a high-level policy judgment, based on timely and reliable information. If G-20 leaders identify an area in which the practice is opaque and information is lacking, it will be worthwhile for them to review the regulatory system and make such changes that would allow the market to generate high-quality information.

Clarity of Purpose

Financial market regulation has become too complex. For instance, Basel III documents are voluminous, as are other documents published by international bodies. Domestic laws and regulations, such as the Dodd-Frank act, are also voluminous and complex. To the extent that they reflect the need for clarity in details, this tendency is not necessarily unwelcome. The complexities may also reflect the need for making rules less ambiguous in interpretation and the need for balancing risk sensitivity, simplicity, and comparability.[16] But the danger is that such complexity will defy the comprehension of ordinary investors, other stakeholders, and the general public, whom the financial industry and regulators are supposed to serve. Defining the purpose of regulations is essential to gaining public support of the reforms that, even though

15. Friedman (2010).
16. See BCBS (2013b).

they may seem burdensome for some stakeholders in the short term, are beneficial for the broad public in the long run. Ultimately, it is the responsibility of political leaders to communicate the purpose of regulatory reforms clearly and effectively.

To avoid major failures, catastrophes, and panics, it may also be more important to focus on what we do not know than on what we already know, as pointed out by Andrew Haldane in the now famous article, "The Dog and the Frisbee."[17] Catching a Frisbee is difficult, requiring the catcher to weigh a complex array of physical and atmospheric factors. But by keeping it simple, even a dog can catch it. A simple rule of thumb, easily mastered by ordinary human beings, can be as effective in solving a complex problem as the ability of someone with a doctorate in physics to solve an optimal control problem. The same can be said of financial regulation. Moreover, complexity breeds protectionism and opacity. Blurring the purposes of regulation may ultimately undermine confidence, a quintessential element for well-functioning financial markets.

Making rules and regulations simple, however, is more easily said than done: it requires time, energy, and judgment using high-caliber intelligence. Simpler rules would also require respecting the integrity, independence, and professional judgment of regulators. Only leaders can drive this effort on a sustained basis.

Rule of Law

As the global financial system is moving from a bank-based system to a market-based system, focus on the rule of law becomes essential. Regulating the conduct of market participants becomes as important as prudential supervision, as unregulated or lightly regulated entities play increasingly important roles in the markets. As markets become increasingly sophisticated and market practices evolve rapidly with dynamic technical changes, growing importance is attached to rules promulgated by market stakeholders, such as exchanges, clearing houses, and self-regulatory organizations. Any rules, however promulgated, will ultimately be enforced by the judiciary system of particular national jurisdictions. Fair, transparent, and efficient legal systems will thus play an essential role in supporting the functioning of these market stakeholders, whose enforcement of rules in turn relies on the effectiveness of the rule of law and the efficiency of the judiciary system.[18]

17. Haldane and Madouros (2012).
18. See Rajan and Zingales (2003), which emphasizes the importance of governments' provision of fair and robust judiciary institutions.

In addition to the quality of a judiciary system, the quality of an accounting and auditing regime is the important bedrock of a financial market, as risk taking by investors depends crucially on the quality of financial reporting. It ultimately determines the ability of capital markets to allocate scarce capital efficiently and effectively. While there may be differences in approaches and institutional arrangements in this area, the basic purposes of ensuring harmonized, high-quality standards in financial markets are broadly shared by regulators, issuers of securities, and the investing public.

An effective and transparent corporate governance regime may also be indispensable for economic growth and development. Private sector corporations play the dominant role in creating jobs and wealth through innovation. Sustained economic development beyond the middle-income trap and other stalemates will depend on how well corporate governance is managed in the economy.[19] The rules and regulations on market conduct should also include those preventing market manipulation, insider trading, money laundering, illicit selling, and fraud. While uniform approaches are difficult in these areas due to differences in legal traditions, social values, or practices, many cooperative initiatives to set minimum standards have been advanced in these areas, which should strengthen the foundation of market institutions.

It would of course be unrealistic to contemplate that the global financial market will eventually be regulated by a converged single set of rules and regulations. Even in the European Union, where movement of capital is essentially liberalized, where various institutions are in place to achieve the benefits of a single market, and where social and cultural values are commonly shared within the region, market regulations are still in the long process of convergence and essentially performed by national regulatory agencies based on national judiciary systems.

In a way, however, regulators in a jurisdiction with a high-quality and efficient judiciary system can possibly perform the function of global regulators, as transactions will essentially move to such a jurisdiction if cross-border transactions are uninhibited. To take an example from the United States, where company laws are legislated by the states, more than 50 percent of publicly traded companies and 63 percent of Fortune 500 companies are incorporated in the state of Delaware, because of its business-friendly corporate law

---

19. In this regard, the World Bank Group's "Doing Business" reports have played a prominent role in promoting legal and institutional reforms, particularly in developing countries, by evaluating legal and regulatory regimes of member countries and ranking them to highlight areas that need reform.

and the resulting existence of experts, practitioners, cases, and experiences.[20] Similarly, the use of jurisdiction agreements and the choice of court agreements for cross-border contracts in various markets may also reflect the relative competitiveness of judiciary systems. What G-20 leaders can do is to encourage healthy and transparent competition of the judiciary systems, balancing the need of the markets and their participants with national goals of economic and social development.

Conclusions

The Australian G-20 summit presents an enormous opportunity to strengthen the foundation for global financial market regulation, based on the achievement made during the past five years. The remarkable progress, particularly through the work of the FSB and other international organizations, would not have been possible without sustained G-20 leadership throughout these years. G-20 leaders will likely review the progress and pledge to continuously monitor the implementation of agreed-on principles and rules in financial regulation. They will also likely agree to take up any longer-term issues that have been identified so that the global financial system will foster the growth and development of the world economy.

At the same time, the challenges that G-20 leaders will face in the future will probably become increasingly difficult, not only because the common threat of global financial crisis recedes and the economic and political situations become divergent but also because today's financial markets are increasingly globalized while regulations remain essentially national. Reflecting the deepening of cooperative efforts, the focus of international regulatory cooperation is being broadened from prudential regulations of targeted financial institutions to market conduct regulations involving a much broader array of market players. The regulatory focus is also gradually shifting from managing defined risks to detecting undefined risks to the financial system, increasingly incorporating macroeconomic prudential approaches. Greater attention is also being paid to the resolution regimes of large and complex financial institutions. These aspects are much more closely linked to domestic legal regimes and to social values embracing the fairness, integrity, and transparency of financial markets. While the role of financial markets in allocating scare capital is widely recognized, the

---

20. See the website of the state of Delaware: corp.delaware.gov. In this regard, it is interesting to note that bankruptcy in the United States is governed by federal laws (art. 1, sec. 8, clause 4 of the U.S. Constitution).

attitudes of the voting public and the media toward financial markets may differ across countries and within jurisdictions; minor differences of opinion may easily be magnified in the media and in domestic political debates. The task of upholding coherence and solidarity for attaining better global regulation will therefore become proportionately more challenging.

The quality of financial regulations affects the long-term potentials of any economy by determining the quality of investment. Financial regulations matter not just for political leaders, bankers, financiers, regulators, and experts but also for the public at large. The investing public—including a broad array of citizens, pensions and institutional investors, and corporate and nonprofit organizations—is affected by the way international rule making is carried forward and the internationally agreed-on rules are translated into domestic rules and regulations. In order for the overall effects to be positive and supported by the public, the G-20 leaders will need to focus on the fundamental role of financial markets, clarify purposes of regulations through effective communications, and aim for transparent and effective rule of law, as discussed above.

Markets are becoming much more integrated today than most of us believed even in the wake of the global financial crisis. The need for cohesion in regulating global financial markets is probably greater now than five years ago. Going forward, G-20 leaders will need a renewed sense of mission, aiming for the higher goal of strengthening the fundamental role of financial markets in fostering innovation and growth.

References

Adams, Timothy D. 2013. "Letter to Chairman, International Monetary and Financial Committee and Chairman, Development Committee" (//iif.com/emp/article+1208.php). April 16.

BCBS (Basel Committee on Banking Supervision). 2013a. "A Brief History of the Basel Committee." July.

———. 2013b. "The Regulatory Framework: Balancing Risk Sensitivity, Simplicity, and Comparability." Discussion paper. July.

Carney, Mark. 2013. "Progress of Financial Reforms." Letter to G-20 leaders. September 5.

Davies, Howard. 2010. The Financial Crisis—Who Is to Blame? Cambridge: Polity Press.

Friedman, Benjamin M. 2010. "Is the Financial System Serving Us Well?" Daedalus 139, no. 4.

FSB (Financial Stability Board). 2010. "Framework for Strengthening Adherence to International Standards." Basel. January.

————. 2011. "Handbook for FSB Peer Reviews." Basel. December.

————. 2013a. "A Narrative Progress Report on Financial Reforms: Report of the Financial Stability Board to G20 Leaders." Basel. September.

————. 2013b. "Overview of Progress in the Implementation of the G20 Recommendations for Strengthening Financial Stability: Report of the Financial Stability Board to G20 Leaders." Basel. September.

————. 2013c. "Progress in Implementing the G20 Recommendations on Financial Regulatory Reform: Status Report by the FSB Secretariat." Basel. September.

————. 2013d. "Thematic Review on Resolution Regimes: Peer Review Report." Basel. April.

G-20. 2013a. "Communiqué." Meeting of finance ministers and central bank governors. Moscow. July.

————. 2013b. "Leaders' Declaration." St. Petersburg. September.

Haldane, Andrew G., and Vasileios Madouros. 2012. "The Dog and the Frisbee." Speech. Federal Reserve Bank of Kansas City symposium. Jackson Hole, Wyo. August 31.

Rajan, Raghuram G., and Luigi Zingales. 2003. *Saving Capitalism from the Capitalist*. New York: Crown Business.

Schiller, Robert J. 2012. *Finance and the Good Society.* Princeton University Press.

Tett, Gillian. 2013. "Insane Financial System Lives on Post-Lehman." *Financial Times*, September 13.

HOMI KHARAS

9

The G-20 and Sustainable Development

The publication "St. Petersburg Development Outlook" is the G-20's most recent assertion that the group can add value to nonmember countries in general and to low-income countries in particular.[1] It emphasizes the role of the G-20 on measures to promote growth and resilience and adds to the framework of strong, sustainable, and balanced growth by calling for economic growth to be "inclusive and resilient" as well.

This broader framework for growth helps the G-20 to link development and growth more tightly in a way that is critical to meet the group's self-stated objectives of "ending poverty and boosting shared prosperity." But at the same time, a broader framework can generate a problem of agenda creep. Indeed, an expansive agenda has bedeviled the G-20's approach to development since its inception. Agenda creep follows from the fact that the G-20 tries to address issues that matter to all 195 countries in the world. It is difficult to craft a focused and actionable agenda that is relevant in so many different circumstances. The problem is made even harder by the fact that the G-20 should add value to existing multilateral processes, such as the Millennium Development Goals (MDGs), the World Bank/IMF Development Committee, the Global Partnership for Effective Development Cooperation, and the governing boards of the more than 200 multilateral development organizations that are currently active.

The difficulty in generating a focused and actionable development agenda raises a fundamental question: Should a dialogue forum like the G-20, that

---

1. G-20 Development Working Group (2013b).

does not include a single low-income country in its membership, even try to take on broad development issues at all? Here, the G-20 is clear. Because the actions of its members have such an important impact on the global economy, affecting everyone, it is their responsibility to consider nonmembers' interests.

The G-20 has its origins as a discussion forum for finance ministers and central bank governors to address the Asian financial crises of the 1990s. Resolving these crises, and halting their spillover to the rest of the global economy, was the first task of the group. The purpose was to create a space for informal dialogue between advanced countries and systemically important emerging economies—those of sufficient size, openness, and interconnectedness to affect the global economy. The focus on ending poverty and boosting shared prosperity and reaching out to listen to and address the concerns of low-income countries came later. This chapter focuses on how to relate these two agendas in a more compelling way.

Given that the development agenda was never as focused as, say, the agenda for global financial stability, it is not surprising that it has left many critics unimpressed with its impact. An accountability report was produced for the St. Petersburg summit, assessing progress against sixty-seven specific actions contained in the multiyear action plan agreed to in Seoul in 2010 and in ensuing meetings.[2] Only one action is deemed to have stalled, and eight others are off track. All the others have been completed or are well under way. For most international agreements, such performance would be considered a resounding success. Yet critics call the G-20 development agenda "invertebrate, flabby, and toothless" and "lacking a coherent narrative and disconnected from the central concerns of leaders and finance ministers."[3] Many concur that "the Development Working Group almost immediately started to fall short of its potential."[4] Anecdotal evidence confirms the discontent—the seniority of civil servants attending Development Working Group meetings seems to be on the decline. And there has been little serious discussion of development at the leaders' level since 2010; first the eurozone crisis, and then Syria, shortchanged development's place in the agenda in 2011, 2012, and 2013.

The Australian chairmanship of the G-20 in 2014 offers an opportunity to reframe the development agenda into one that has the real economy at its heart and that focuses on the macroeconomic and structural policies that will create the desired real outcomes. Australia has clearly identified its own self-interest as

2. G-20 Development Working Group (2013a).
3. Davies (2013).
4. Brodie (2013).

being linked with development success in Asia.[5] It has a strong focus on efficient economic growth and on the power of well-regulated markets to drive prosperity for all. Like emerging economies, Australia is not part of the G-8 and hence has an interest in ensuring that the G-20 remains the preeminent forum for global economic cooperation. Australia has good relationships and shared interests with many countries, developed and developing—Indonesia, the United States and Europe, Pacific and East Asian countries, and important agricultural producers like Brazil and Argentina.

This chapter argues that, under the Australian chair, the G-20 needs to differentiate the development agenda between issues that leaders can and should discuss and those that can best be tackled by technocrats, in the context of the Development Working Group. It recommends that the leaders' track take charge of a new development narrative—one that emphasizes the need for sustainable development in every country in the world. This would shift the development narrative from something that is done "by" rich and systemically important countries "for" less advanced and smaller countries, to a narrative that emphasizes the universal nature of sustainable development for all countries, including advanced economies. This would be a significant departure from the focus of the Millennium Development Goals, which in the end largely addressed outcomes in developing countries and a few policy actions by developed countries.

The sustainable development narrative focuses on each country putting its own house in order, thereby creating the global conditions for successful development everywhere. Its focus would also be on global collective action. Development would be characterized as a process of sustainable growth, linking economic, financial, social, and environmental issues. It would be achieved by domestic actions to support sustainable growth as well as by collective action to improve the global economic, social, and environmental context within which development occurs. It would be implemented by national and multilateral actions.

A key feature distinguishing sustainable development from traditional development is that sustainable development is a universal agenda, not limited to developing countries. This concept of universality fits with the G-20's approach to deliver positive outcomes for all countries. It is a concept that enjoys wide support. Already, a High-Level Panel advising the United Nations' secretary general has recommended that the post-2015 development agenda

---

5. Australian government (2012).

be universal, applicable to, and relevant for all countries. A new agreement on sustainable post-2015 development goals is likely to call for a transition to a new era, requiring profound economic transformations and a new global partnership.[6] These two themes should be the heart of the leaders' summit discussions. If this were to happen, development would be automatically mainstreamed into broader discussions of sustainable growth.

Separately, the Development Working Group needs to continue to narrow its agenda and build on its track record of success in focused, technical areas. Clear advances have been made in food security, infrastructure finance, and financial inclusion. Initiatives to support domestic resource mobilization, partly through tax policies aimed at tackling base erosion and profit shifting, also appear promising. These agenda items mesh with finance minister concerns, helping to reinforce the notion that sustainable development and strong, sustained, and balanced growth can and should be integrated into the activities of the G-20.

A Brief History of Development in the G-20

Development concerns have always been central to the G-20.[7] The first meetings of finance ministers focused on crisis prevention and resolution, globalization, and combating the financing of terrorism, all themes for which the participation of emerging and developing countries was central.[8] When the global financial crisis hit in 2008, and the G-20 was transformed into a leaders' summit, one concern was to ensure adequate liquidity so that recession would not spread to emerging economies that were, at the time, generating two-thirds of global growth.

By the time of the London summit in 2009, there was a further risk that a contraction in bank lending in general and cross-border lending in particular would freeze trade credits. So multilateral agencies were encouraged to develop a range of new credit lines, and the G-20 agreed to support additional concessional finance to low-income countries through the sale of IMF gold stocks as well as a large replenishment of IMF resources to help all other countries weather the storm. In Pittsburgh, G-20 leaders addressed the triple crises of diminishing access to (and higher prices of) food, fuel, and finance, each of which threatened the stability of a range of developing countries. Taken

6. UN General Assembly (2013).
7. This section draws on G-20 Foundation (2014).
8. Kharas and Lombardi (2012).

together, they threatened to reverse gains in poverty reduction in the poorest countries. Based on the agreements in Pittsburgh, a Global Agriculture and Food Security Program was established, administered by the World Bank.

By the Toronto summit, the immediate fears of a twenty-first-century Great Depression had receded, and it became apparent that countries had emerged from the crisis with very different structural and macroeconomic positions. There was a need for greater flexibility in country response to replace the collective programs of fiscal and monetary stimulus that had been instituted at London. At the same time, it was clear that financing mechanisms to mitigate the impact of the crisis on low-income countries had been particularly inadequate. Not only were low-income countries subject to the worst effects of the flight to safety that ensued after the crisis, but their dependence on official development assistance put them at risk, given the budgetary pressures on many donors and their aid cutbacks.

The Toronto G-20 summit was also unique in taking place immediately after the G-8 meeting, also hosted by Canada. At the G-8, Prime Minister Harper received support for a new initiative on maternal mortality, one of the Millennium Development Goals that was falling off track. The juxtaposition of these two meetings served to highlight the fact that global responsibility for development remained a gray area, with significant aspects of the development agenda remaining within the purview of the G-8 in the areas of security, aid, and meeting the MDGs.[9]

More focus on development, therefore, became central to the G-20's effort to assert itself as the preeminent forum for international economic cooperation. If the G-20 ceded development to the G-8, it would sharply circumscribe its legitimacy to be the main forum for dialogue on global economic issues. Against this backdrop, the Toronto G-20 meeting agreed to establish the Development Working Group to provide a focused action agenda for leaders to discuss at the next summit.

At Seoul, leaders agreed on a Seoul Development Consensus and a multi-year action plan, along with a set of principles to guide the G-20's development initiatives. Although sensible, the principles have not been strictly applied in

9. This overlap persists today and continues to cause confusion. For example, the G-8 originally agreed to create the Global Agriculture and Food Security Program at L'Aquila and has since formed the New Alliance for Food Security and Nutrition, while the G-20 picked up on actual implementation of the GAFSP. More recently, the 2013 G-8 meeting announced commitments to crack down on tax avoidance, followed by a G-20 endorsement of an ambitious and comprehensive plan. The G-20 also, controversially, moved to include a foreign ministers' track for the Los Cabos meeting.

practice. For example, principle one—to focus on economic growth—did not stop the G-20 from endorsing actions to promote nationally determined social protection floors (including for low-income countries) at its Los Cabos meeting. Principle six—to have an outcome orientation that looks for activities with "tangible outcomes with significant impact" has not led to more infrastructure but rather to a study of the constraints to infrastructure investment in the developing world (an input).

In Cannes and Los Cabos the agenda turned to specific sectors: initiatives in infrastructure, food security, and green growth have been launched. But by the time of the St. Petersburg summit, the development agenda was widely seen as unwieldy, lacking focus, and devoid of major accomplishments or ideas worthy of leaders' attention. At that summit, the first accountability report for development was discussed, and recommendations were made and accepted to narrow the focus of the agenda.

Part of the dissatisfaction with implementation of the development agenda is that the G-20 has not been strategic in how it uses its main instruments for action. Table 9-1 summarizes the main development activities undertaken by the G-20 since the inception of the summit meetings. It shows that the G-20 has used three main modalities to engage in development activities. It has encouraged change and reform in multilateral institutions, especially at the beginning of the crisis. It has also engaged in collective action among G-20 members to spearhead initiatives that are implemented through new multilateral platforms, like the Agricultural Market Information System, the Tropical Agriculture Platform, and the Africa50 Fund (see below). Last, it has encouraged individual members of the G-20 to make commitments and share their experiences to change norms and expectations and to generate positive spillovers to nonmembers—unilateral measures with win-win consequences, like demonstrating the positive economic and environmental returns to green growth.

The G-20 track record on multilateral reform is mixed. While the provision of larger resources to the IMF in London is widely hailed as one of the greatest achievements of the G-20 to date, the reform of multilateral institutions' governance has been slow. IMF voice and quota reform, changes in World Bank shareholdings and board representation, greater coordination and rationalization of the activities of multilateral organizations, and a more strategic approach to the replenishment of multilateral funds have not progressed rapidly. The G-20 has not tried to push for major increases in aid or to expand the capital of multilateral development banks to meet the enormous needs for infrastructure financing and other development investments.

Table 9-1. *G-20 Development Actions and Agreements, Eight Summits, 2008–13*

G-20 summit	Notable development action or agreement	Modality of engagement
Washington, 2008	—Including emerging economies in global discussions	—Individual member country dialogue and commitments
	—Helping emerging and developing countries access finance through new facilities and greater resources for IFIs	—Multilateral institution reform
London, 2009	—Supporting new trade credit facilities in IFIs —Using IMF gold sales for additional concessional finance —Increasing total resources available to IMF	—Multilateral institution reform
Pittsburgh, 2009	—Allowing the poor more access to food, fuel, and finance; clamping down on illicit outflows —Maintaining trade openness	—Collective action
Toronto, 2010	—Completing reforms of IFIs —Establishing the Development Working Group	—Multilateral reform —Collective action
Seoul, 2010	—Agreeing on Seoul Development Consensus and Multi-Year Action Plan	—Collective action
Cannes, 2011	—Enhancing food security (AMIS, RRF) —High-Level Panel on Infrastructure Recommendations	—Collective action
Los Cabos, 2012	—Supporting multilateralism —Supporting infrastructure investments —Supporting green growth	—Multilateral reform —Collective action —Individual member country commitments
St. Petersburg, 2013	—Agreeing to focus the Development Working Group agenda on fewer items (St. Petersburg Development Outcome and Accountability reports) —Endorsing post-2015 High-Level Panel Report	—Collective action

Source: Author.

The G-20 has in fact been very cautious not to step into areas where multilateral institutions have their own governance processes. Similarly, they have shied away from trying to negotiate breakthroughs in stalled global negotiations on trade or climate change. Indeed, President Lula is said to have wanted to bring trade negotiations to the table at the first G-20 summit, in Washington, but was rebuffed by President Bush, who argued that the G-20 was not a forum for negotiations but for dialogue.

Where the G-20 has been somewhat more successful is in spurring collective action among its members. Selected new multilateral platforms, common approaches to problems, and norms of behavior (such as the promise to have a standstill on trade protectionism) have all proven their value. But the magnitude and impact of most of these actions, in development-specific areas, has been small.

The third modality, use of individual country commitments to new forms of sustainable development, has been the least well used. The G-20 monitors the impact of structural reform commitments on growth, budget, and current account balances of its own members, but it does not systematically monitor the spillover effects of structural reforms onto other countries, nor has it brought the voice of nonmember countries into spillover discussions in a central way. To take just one example, questions about the impact of implementation of Basel III regulations on long-term finance for development have not been broadly discussed with developing countries.

What is noteworthy about table 9-1 is that many of the most important issues for development actually occurred outside the Development Working Group stream, reinforcing the idea that development should be mainstreamed into all G-20 activities. In this way, the G-20 should discuss how national policies, alongside collective action and multilateral activities, can provide a global economic context that is conducive to rapid and sustained growth, with channels for trade, investments, and knowledge that are accessible to all countries.[10]

These issues are currently handled by the G-20 through the implementation of the framework for strong, sustainable, and balanced growth and through the fiscal, monetary, and structural policies that support it. But while it is obvious that the actions of G-20 countries have substantial spillovers onto developing countries, these are not systematically monitored. Currency wars, quantitative easing, tapering, coordinated fiscal adjustments, trade restriction standstills,

10. Winters and others (2010).

and the array of issues that need to be tackled to promote global financial stability have still not received sufficient articulation as critical initiatives that
affect sustainability in all countries. The impact on individual countries is not
yet sufficiently considered in developing global norms and standards and
informing individual country actions. Although there has been an unprecedented outreach to low-income countries, starting with the Seoul summit, to
ensure that their concerns were properly addressed, these countries still do not
have a significant voice in the core discussions of the G-20.

As a matter of practice, the reform commitments made by G-20 members
are still assessed in terms of the implications for their own countries. For
example, the IMF's background documentation on global growth provides
detailed information on individual G-20 member country growth prospects,
within the overall envelope of global growth forecasts, but does not comment
on any non-G-20 country or country groups in terms of specific risks or
issues they may be facing.

Similarly, the OECD and the World Bank provide background documentation on assessing the G-20's commitments to structural reform, but they do this
without any commentary on the impact of these commitments on other countries—the spillovers.[11] G-20 member countries' structural reforms are assessed
against growth, within-country income distribution, the environment, the
budget, and the current account balance.[12] They are not assessed against the
contribution to global rebalancing, trade creation and diversion, stability in
international financial flows, volatility of global economic conditions, or the
transfer and dissemination of knowledge, science, and technology to other
countries. They are not assessed in terms of their impact on the global context
in which non-G-20 countries are struggling to achieve sustainable economic
growth, financial stability, social inclusion, and environmental balance. The
global sustainability agenda cannot be achieved if the major economies continue to focus their actions only upon their own sustainability trajectory, without including their impact on the sustainability trajectory of other countries.

The Broad Scope of the G-20 Development Agenda

Part of the problem with the way the G-20 approaches development is that
the agenda is broad. A review of G-20 leaders' communiqués from each summit shows the range of development initiatives that have been discussed

11. OECD (2013b).
12. OECD (2013a).

(table 9-2).[13] On average, between nine and ten development topics are mentioned in each leaders' communiqué, with the St. Petersburg communiqué having the largest number of topics, at fourteen. Sustainable development topics, such as climate change, green growth, jobs, and development of small and medium enterprises are the most frequently mentioned items by leaders. In sharp contrast to the G-8, aid and debt relief are comparatively neglected.

Despite the diffuseness of the development agenda and the difficulties in delivering concrete, high-level results that can resonate with publics, G-20 leaders have kept a strong focus on development in their communiqués. Figure 9-1 shows the percentage of paragraphs in the leaders' communiqués devoted to some specific development topic. After the initial meeting in Washington 30–40 percent of the content of the communiqué has been relevant to development-specific issues. That figure would be even higher if all topics that have an impact on developing countries, like anticorruption, global growth, and global financial stability, were included.

Why do leaders pay so much attention to development? Partly, it would seem, because this is popular with their public. A 2012 survey by the European Commission finds that 85 percent of European adults felt it was important to help people in developing countries, with more than 60 percent advocating more aid and even more supporting a "beyond aid" agenda of trade and investment.[14] Americans, too, are broadly supportive of international engagement, especially in Africa, for which 60 percent of Americans favor maintaining or increasing aid levels. However, attitudes toward aid did track households' personal circumstances: those who felt their own prospects were bleak or declining were less favorable toward global cooperation.[15] In the United Kingdom, too, there is broad support for development cooperation, and as in the United States, support is weaker in the face of domestic fiscal austerity.[16] The informed public support global campaigns to address global poverty and humanitarian crises. But informed citizens are also wary of aid resources being wasted (with citizens in developing countries like China being most forgiving on this score), so alternative mechanisms for development cooperation are preferred.[17]

13. A topic is defined as having a notable mention if it is explicitly included in the leaders' communiqué. Nondevelopment specific topics, such as anticorruption, financial stability and regulation, and global growth are excluded from the analysis even though they have a large impact on development.

14. European Commission (2012).

15. Chicago Council on Global Affairs (2012).

16. Glennie, Straw, and Wild (2012).

17. Debeljak and others (2012).

Table 9-2. *Development Topics Included in G-20 Leaders' Communiqués*

Development topic	Washington	London	Pittsburgh	Toronto	Seoul	Cannes	Los Cabos	St. Petersburg
Job creation and labor market reform	...	...	x	x	x	x	x	x
Infrastructure financing	x	...	...	...	...	x	x	x
Gender equity	...	x	...	...	...	...	x	x
Sustainable development and green growth	...	x	...	x	x	x	x	x
Food security	x	...	x	x	x	x	x	x
Climate change	x	x	x	x	x	x	x	x
Trade liberalization and antiprotectionism	x	x	x	...	x	x	...	...
Millennium Development Goals	...	...	x	x	...	...	x	x
Social protection	...	...	...	x	x	x	...	...
Financial inclusion	...	...	x	...	x	...	x	x
Transparent tax systems	...	...	...	...	x	...	...	x
Private sector and public-private partnerships	...	x	...	...	x	...	...	x
Overseas development commitments	...	x	x	...	...	x	...	...
Debt relief and management	...	x	...	...	...	...	...	x
Data and quantification	...	...	...	x	x	...	...	...
Ending fossil fuel subsidies	...	x	x	...	...	x	...	x
Role of small and medium enterprises	...	...	x	x	x	x	x	x
Narrowing development gap	...	...	x	x	x	...	...	x

Source: Author.

Figure 9-1. *Focus of G-20 Leaders' Communiqués on Development Issues, Five Summits, 2008–13*[a]

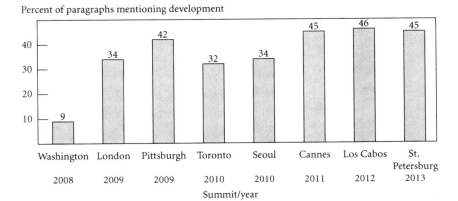

Percent of paragraphs mentioning development

Source: Author.

a. A line or subpoint in a G-20 leaders' declaration is considered to be primarily focused on development if it contains a specific action, policy, or proposal that relates to the sectoral priorities laid out in the Seoul Multi-Year Action Plan on Development (for example, food security, trade, infrastructure, green growth) or if it relates to the list of priorities stated on the official G-20 Development Working Group Information Exchange Facility (www.g20dwg.org/).

Given the high percentage of their own publics supporting development cooperation, it is appropriate for G-20 leaders to be seen as doing something for other countries, as well as their own. That is also the expectation for a self-selected steering committee for the global economy. The problem is less the relevance of the topic than the ability to generate clear deliverables. In a survey conducted by the Center for International Governance Innovation, the general view was that there have been more declaratory statements than actual achievements.[18] On average, commentators felt that there had been some regression on development. Reversing this is central to reframing the G-20 development agenda.

The Post-2015 Sustainable Development Agenda

The post-2015 sustainable development agenda is a UN-led agreement to succeed the Millennium Development Goals. It is a narrative about the real economy, coupled with a set of real economy outcomes that should be the target of

18. Carin and Lombardi (2013).

government policies—jobs, access to infrastructure, institutions, food security, water, energy, health, education, and women's rights, to mention just a few. Although the post-2015 agenda has not yet been agreed upon by member states (that is most likely to occur at the UN General Assembly meeting in September 2015), the likely contours of the future agreement are already clear. The post-2015 agenda is to be universal (relevant to and actionable by all countries), comprehensive (integrating the economic, social, and environmental aspects of development), and outcome oriented. The global agreement on this agenda provides an opportunity for the G-20 to mainstream development into the leaders' summit and to integrate sustainable development into the Mutual Assessment Process.

It can do this by embracing the goals and targets of the post-2015 sustainable development agenda as objectives to which each G-20 member should contribute and by monitoring the structural reforms required to implement such an agenda within not only each G-20 member country but also internationally. It is important that the post-2015 agenda aspires to improve the well-being of each country according to its circumstances and access to resources.

Putting One's Own House in Order: A Structural Agenda for the G-20

Perhaps most important, the post-2015 agenda reflects an effort to build a fresh narrative, where development is no longer seen as a set of activities that advanced countries undertake to support those that are less developed (most obviously the foreign aid agenda). Instead, in the fresh narrative countries recognize their spillover effects on each other and commit to both domestic reforms and international collective action to create a global context that is supportive of sustained prosperity for all.

These ideas have already been articulated in a report presented to the UN secretary general on the post-2015 agenda by a High-Level Panel of Eminent Persons from fifteen G-20 members, along with a dozen others.[19] Two of the panel cochairs are G-20 principals (President Yudhoyono of Indonesia and Prime Minister Cameron of the United Kingdom). The G-20 welcomed the contribution of the panel report at Saint Petersburg.

While the panel report is not definitive, it provides a good yardstick to judge the direction of the final agreement that is likely to emerge from the United Nations process. It sets out illustrative goals and targets. Most of these

19. United Nations (2013).

are national, implying that the level of ambition is to be set by each country individually, but taken together they are designed to create a global context in which extreme poverty can be eradicated and the building blocks for sustained prosperity can be put in place by 2030.

The panel report makes a determined effort to avoid classifying countries as developed or developing, recognizing that these lines have become blurred. Instead, it argues that no country has yet succeeded in sustainable development, defined as a development approach that could be replicated by everyone within social and planetary boundaries. It urges all countries to make progress toward sustainable development and presents goals to be achieved by 2030, with targets that countries should quantify according to their own circumstances, priorities, and resources.

One of the key messages of the High-Level Panel report is that sustainable development cannot be deconstructed into a series of individual activities but must integrate economic, social, and environmental issues into a comprehensive program. It is a systems approach to development, recognizing the connections within countries of their policies, institutions, and resources, along with the linkages among countries in providing a supportive global economic environment.

Many of the development themes of the G-20 are picked up in the panel report. There is a goal with targets on ensuring food security and good nutrition, with an emphasis not just on improving nutrition in low-income countries but also on combating the postmarket waste of food in rich countries. The panel's call for the provision of sufficient, safe, affordable, and nutritious food for everyone is also a recognition that almost all countries in the world have pockets of poverty and groups of people—especially children—where food security has not been achieved.

The panel also proposes a goal to "create jobs, sustainable livelihoods, and equitable growth," with targets regarding skills and vocational training, youth employment, financial inclusion, and access to infrastructure that repeat past and present G-20 development agenda items and that are pertinent to G-20 countries as well as to other countries.

In short, the present G-20 development agenda is a subset of the broader agenda for sustainable development that the United Nations is likely to agree on for all member states for the post-2015 agenda. This presents an opportunity for the G-20 to align its core activities with an agenda shared by the rest of the world. It makes little sense to have a Seoul development consensus or action plan that the 193 UN member states will not agree to. The G-20 should instead fully align itself with the post-2015 agenda. The St. Petersburg development outlook has already opened this door: "We recognize the need for a flexible approach that allows future G-20 presidencies to respond to new priorities and circumstances, including the post-2015 development agenda." At the Brisbane summit—which will take place after publication of the 2014 Open Working Group report on Sustainable Development Goals—leaders should throw their weight behind the completion of an agreement on the post-2015 agenda and agree to measure their own performance against the targets established by the United Nations.

Sustainability—social, economic, and environmental—is the core agenda for the G-20 and for all countries. Defining the G-20 framework for strong, sustainable, and balanced growth in this way, and orienting the G-20 Development Working Group with the core global agenda of sustainability, would align the G-20 agenda with the commitments their leaders will make on the post-2015 agenda.

Having G-20 leaders make specific commitments on structural reforms that will help move their own countries toward meeting their country-specific targets (set in the context of the post-2015 agenda) would fit well with the existing Mutual Assessment Process. It would position the G-20 member states' contribution as being supportive of a global economic context conducive to development in other countries, rather than as something that the G-20 does for other countries. And it would respect the boundaries of G-20 country interventions as being primarily focused on putting their own houses in order.

Building a New Global Partnership and a New Multilateralism

A second motivation for aligning the G-20 development agenda with the post-2015 agenda is that the G-20 will then be able to help build the new global partnership that is needed. Even at Los Cabos there was an agreement among leaders that multilateralism is of great importance in the current climate and is one of the best assets to resolve the global economy's difficulties. Yet multilateralism has faltered recently in the economic sphere, notably in the failure to conclude the Doha trade talks and the United Nations Framework Convention on Climate Change.

Sustainable development offers one of the best chances for reaffirming the value of multilateralism, because it contains within its definition the idea that global norms on trade, financial stability, environment, knowledge sharing, and other public goods are needed for the prosperity of every country. It is of vital importance that the post-2015 agenda be successfully concluded, something that should not be taken for granted. An endorsement at Brisbane from the leaders of the world's most significant economies would go a long way to ensure a good conclusion to the negotiations.

To succeed, the post-2015 agenda needs to build a new global partnership. The High-Level Panel report calls for "a new spirit of solidarity, cooperation, and mutual accountability that must underpin the post-2015 agenda. A new partnership should be based on a common understanding of our shared humanity, underpinning mutual respect and mutual benefit in a shrinking world."[20]

The call for a new partnership follows from the perception that the existing global partnership may be the least successful element of the Millennium Development Goals. Goal 8—the agreement to foster a global partnership for development—is probably the goal on which the least progress has been made. This goal targets trade and finance; the special needs of the least-developed, landlocked, and small island states; debt problems, access to affordable essential drugs, and access to new technologies. In these areas, there has been some modest progress, but many gaps remain.

In addition, the international context for a global partnership has changed fundamentally since goal 8 was articulated, with far more countries benefiting from globalization while simultaneously being vulnerable to global shocks. By 2030 the essential nature of the global partnership will be less about providing resources for the special needs of various countries and more about a global governance that reflects the economic size of emerging economies and the changing responsibilities for providing global public goods (see chapter 1, this volume).

The G-20 has already taken responsibility for reviewing the available resources and governance of the multilateral organizations, including international financial institutions that are critical for development. But progress in changing the voice in these constituency/representative institutions has been slow, and significant unmet needs have emerged, such as the limited nonconcessional public financing available for infrastructure and the limited amounts of crisis-response concessional financing. The High-Level Panel report on the post-2015 agenda provides some clues as to where the focus of the new global partnership should be. It advocates action in six areas: trade, finance, aid, climate, tax evasion and illicit flows, and access to science and technology.

---

20. United Nations (2013).

There is a risk that, without strong G-20 leadership, these elements of a global partnership, along with the reform of multilateral institutions, will suffer the same fate as Millennium Development Goal 8—negotiations bogged down by the limited vision of national civil servants. Leaders need to instill the principles of a common humanity, mutual respect, and mutual benefit throughout these processes. They need to debate whether the existing global architecture is supportive of the post-2015 agenda and, if not, to initiate reforms in this architecture.

The responsibility for bolstering and using the multilateral architecture is already part of the core G-20 process. Leaders have agreed to provide additional resources to some institutions during the crisis, and they have asked multilateral agencies to work together to shape global responses. For example, twelve international organizations collaborated for the first time to produce the report "Sustainable Agricultural Productivity Growth and Bridging the Gap for Small Family Farms" for the Mexican chairmanship. But whenever leaders have tackled a global issue, such as food insecurity or inadequate access to infrastructure, they have found significant gaps in the multilateral system. These gaps must be addressed more systematically and forcefully.

Raising the Profile, Focusing the Agenda

The G-20's development agenda has wrestled with two problems: how to raise the profile of development interventions so as to make them a priority for leaders' discussion, and how to narrow the agenda so actionable items can be pursued. The alignment with the post-2015 agenda promises to help on both scores.

By linking to the post-2015 process, the G-20 could ensure that their development agenda reinforces other leaders' processes, thereby guaranteeing that development will receive proper attention and not be treated as an add-on to the leaders' agenda. Leaders will necessarily participate in the post-2015 agenda in the context of the General Assembly summit planned for September 2015. The High-Level Panel report further recommends that a global forum at a high political level (code words for a leaders' summit, without committing to this) be convened periodically to review progress and the challenges ahead. In other words, the post-2015 agenda, like the Millennium Development Goals, is expected to involve leaders in a sustained way over time, so the agenda will naturally be on leaders' radar screen. Having leaders set aside time at annual G-20 meetings to review their own actions with regard to the post-2015 agenda would be a commonsense way to bring continuity to the post-2015 process and to link the G-20 agenda with other agendas to which leaders will be committed.

Specifically, the Mutual Assessment Process should be extended to include actions undertaken in support of the post-2015 goals and targets, once these have been defined and agreed upon. International agencies like the World Bank, the Organization for Economic Cooperation and Development, the International Monetary Fund, and the UN (either the Department of Economic and Social Affairs or the United Nations Development Program), which are already producing annual global monitoring reports for the Millennium Development Goals, could then be asked to review whether the G-20 countries are on track to deliver on their national targets and whether the structural reforms to which they commit are adequate to meet their own sustainable development goals and targets, contributing to global sustainability.

One advantage of aligning the G-20 development agenda with a defined list of goals and targets, such as the post-2015 agenda, is that it would limit the discretion of G-20 host countries to add issues to the summit agenda. For the most part, the post-2015 targets are expected to be clear, measurable, and focused on outcomes, making it easy to assess whether countries are on track or not and providing clarity on the objectives toward which structural actions should be oriented. In other words, the post-2015 agenda will provide a ready-made accountability framework for G-20 country performance—a way to measure these countries' contributions to global sustainability.

Of course, this does not imply that action will be needed on all targets or that the G-20 should discuss all aspects of the post-2015 agenda at each meeting. But the post-2015 agenda could provide the menu from which each G-20 host chooses issues. The short list identified at the St. Petersburg summit is a good starting point.

Building on Incremental Successes: The Development Working Group

The main criticism of the Development Working Group is that it has failed to excite the imagination of leaders or to produce a set of achievements or a compelling new narrative. In spite of that criticism, the Development Working Group has quietly made progress on several process issues that could bear fruit, over time, and has put in place new mechanisms that could improve the context for development. This is as it should be. Leaders should be encouraged to reflect on the big-picture issues, monitoring progress in the context of the post-2015 agenda. They need to provide the right environment for multilateral negotiations, allowing technocrats in the Development Working Group to work out the details.

Take for example food security. In this area, the G-20 has promoted a new multilateral mechanism, the Global Agriculture and Food Security Program, and has also endorsed many lesser items that emerged from technocratic discussions. Among these items are

—The formation of an agricultural market information system

—Agreements to exclude humanitarian food purchases by the World Food Program from export bans or taxes

—The establishment of regional food stock reserves

—The establishment of the Tropical Agriculture Platform to build capacity in agriculture in least-developed countries, most of them in the tropics

—The formation of the AgResults Initiative as a prize fund to encourage innovative solutions to global food security and nutrition

—The encouragement of meetings of agricultural chief scientists.

Other measures (such as the Rapid Response Forum) also have been adopted to reduce food price volatility and to encourage smallholder productivity. Many of the mechanisms will advance the agenda of global food security and build on the core G-20 principle of focusing on areas where collective action is needed, but they are hardly worthy of leaders' time and attention. They would not necessarily be directly focused on achieving any specific target of the post-2015 agenda, but they do constitute valuable steps toward making the global environment more supportive of country actions.

Similar examples can be found in infrastructure, where the creation of the Africa50 Fund aims to provide $100 billion in public and private finance for infrastructure for that continent. Other multilateral development banks have also prepared proposals for new infrastructure platforms that can include new instruments to mitigate the risk borne by private investors. An initiative to harmonize procurement practices in cofinanced infrastructure projects is under way. The Development Working Group has also called for additional review of the adequacy of project preparation facilities and of initiatives to unblock regional projects and other complex infrastructure projects with high levels of political risk.

As these examples indicate, the Development Working Group has enjoyed the most success when it uses a variety of modalities to advance the development agenda in small ways. First, it has intervened in areas requiring multilateral platforms or where multilateral coordination can be improved. Second, it has launched initiatives where collective action is desirable. A good example of this is in the area of base erosion and profit shifting, where new norms for tax avoidance are being developed and where the exchange of tax information is valuable. Several activities of the G-20 anticorruption action plan also fall under this heading. Third, it has focused on capacity building, innovation, and knowledge sharing, especially in low-income countries, bringing to bear the experiences of G-20 members. In most of these cases, it is not necessary to involve leaders in the discussions.

It is, however, important to work in cooperation with others, as the Development Working Group does in supporting a global context in which all countries can prosper. The G-20 already has mechanisms for discussion with business leaders, civil society, think tanks, youth, and labor—all groups with which the High-Level Panel also discussed the post-2015 agenda. The G-20 has reached out to low-income countries (especially during the Korean chairmanship), regional organizations (the African Union, the New Partnership for Africa's Development, the Association of Southeast Asian Nations), and heads of major global groupings (the Commonwealth, la Francophonie, and the Global Governance Group). These consultations are vital to making sure that different perspectives are brought into the G-20 agenda and to building confidence at the global level that the steps being taken by the G-20 are significant advances.

If the Development Working Group is differentiated from the leaders' process, it can concentrate on the technocratic improvements that are needed and continue to try to move the agenda forward one step at a time. It is time, however, to rebrand the group. The Development Working Group is not about what the G-20 should do for other countries; it is more critically about how the G-20 can ensure that international mechanisms to address global problems are functioning well. It could be renamed the Managing Globalization Working Group to indicate better what it is trying to do.

Conclusions

The G-20 has been concerned with global development as a major topic ever since the first meetings of G-20 finance ministers and central bank governors, which were held to respond to the Asian financial crisis starting in 1997. There is considerable popular support for global development cooperation in each G-20 country, so it is sensible for leaders to comment on what they are doing to support global development in their final communiqués. This has been done with regularity; there is ample space given to development issues in final communiqués. But there is less evidence of actual progress and concrete achievement. As one commentator remarks, "No field suffers more international meetings resulting in elegant platitudes and irreproachable aspirational statements. To date the G-20 efforts in development have had no impact on the ground."[21]

The challenge, then, is to produce more deliverables—and more deliverables that are worthy of leaders' attention and discussion. A surprising number of development activities have actually been delivered, largely through the workings of the G-20's Development Working Group, but many of these are process activities that have yet to have measurable impact.

The gap between what the Development Working Group does and what leaders should talk about is unlikely to be narrowed. Both streams serve a purpose, but they are different and should not be conflated. The Development Working Group correctly gets involved in pushing forward a technical agenda, while the leaders should take a broader strategic perspective.

Leaders should focus on getting multilateral organizations to work together to solve global problems. They have not been bold enough to ask whether existing organizations have the right level of resources and structures to do the job that is required. For example, a major gap has been identified in infrastructure financing, but little action has been taken as yet to ensure that multilateral development banks have the resources and ambition to address these needs. In the current context, it is important for leaders to explore where there is common ground to improve the governance of multilateral organizations to make them more effective.

Leaders should also focus on presenting a fresh narrative on development to their public. The old narrative, focused on providing more aid, is less relevant in a globalized world, where trade, investment, and knowledge drive growth and prosperity. The public policy agenda is to ensure that each country implements a structural reform agenda that will lead to sustainable development, both in their own countries and overseas. This will require a deeper understanding of how spillovers from systemically important large countries affect others, not just in the economic spheres of trade and investment but in social and environmental spheres as well.

The post-2015 agenda will consist of mutually reinforcing goals and targets. The G-20 could lead by example in terms of how to approach a complex and

---

21. Carin and Lombardi (2013).

integrated sustainable development agenda by emphasizing sustainability in the core G-20 agenda and aligning it with the post-2015 focus on sustainability. At the Brisbane summit, leaders could provide a statement of support for universal, comprehensive, and sustainable development goals, with an endorsement of their readiness to use the G-20 dialogue as a supplementary mechanism to monitor their implementation in G-20 countries.

The post-2015 agenda is one that leaders will agree to in September 2015, and as it is likely to involve a periodic review mechanism involving leaders at the United Nations, it becomes a natural framework to incorporate into the G-20 itself. A process like the Mutual Assessment Process should be set up to monitor G-20 countries' progress toward meeting the relevant goals and targets, along with a register of voluntary commitments by each G-20 member country, in much the same way as is currently done for the structural reforms that lie behind implementation of the framework for strong, sustainable, and balanced growth.

The Development Working Group, on the other hand, should focus more on identifying areas in which multilateral organizations could contribute to solving global problems. It could be renamed the Managing Globalization Working Group. This dual track would provide a focused sustainability agenda for the G-20. The leaders would focus on domestic actions to respond to the G-20's strong, sustainable, and balanced growth framework and to the post-2015 agenda, along with collective actions to implement the global partnership called for in the post-2015 agenda. The Development Working Group would focus on using multilateral institutions in a coordinated way to make technical advances in implementing core critical issues, starting with the priorities laid out in the St. Petersburg development outlook. This alignment between the core agenda of the G-20 and the post-2015 agenda—and the clearer division of labor between the leaders' summits and the working groups—would provide a more compelling and coherent vision for the future.

References

Australian government. 2012. "Australia in the Asian Century." October 28.

Brodie, Ian. 2013. "Is the G20's Development Working Group on the Right Track?" School of Public Policy, University of Calgary. September 4.

Carin, Barry, and Domenico Lombardi. 2013. "CIGI Survey: Progress of International Economic Governance." Waterloo, Ont.: Center for International Governance Innovation. September 4.

Chicago Council on Global Affairs. 2012. "Foreign Policy in the New Millennium: Results of the 2012 Chicago Council Survey of American Public Opinion and U.S. Foreign Policy." 2012 Chicago Council Survey. September.

Davies, Robin. 2013. "What Plot? Rationalizing the G20's Development Agenda." *G20 Monitor*, no. 5 (August): 6–18.

Debeljak, Klara, and others. 2012. "Building Support for International Development." *InterMedia* (February).

European Commission. 2012. "Solidarity That Spans the Globe: Europeans and Development Aid." *Special Eurobarometer* 392 (October).

G-20 Development Working Group. 2013a. "St. Petersburg Accountability Report on G20 Development Commitments." September 6.

———. 2013b. "St. Petersburg Development Outlook." September 5.

G-20 Foundation. 2014. "The G-20: Its Role and Legacy."

Glennie, Alex, Will Straw, and Leni Wild. 2012. "Understanding Public Attitudes to Aid and Development." London: Overseas Development Institute/Institute for Public Policy Research. June.

Kharas, Homi, and Domenico Lombardi. 2012. "The Group of Twenty: Origins, Prospects, and Challenges for Global Governance." Global Economy and Development. Brookings. August.

OECD (Organization for Economic Cooperation and Development). 2013a. "Economic Policy Reforms 2013: Going for Growth." Washington.

———. 2013b. "Pursuing Strong, Sustainable, and Balanced Growth: A Note on G-20 Structural Reform Commitments." Washington: OECD/ World Bank. September.

UN General Assembly. 2013. "A Life of Dignity for All." Report of the Secretary General, 68th sess. July 26.

United Nations. 2013. "A New Global Partnership: Eradicate Poverty and Transform Economies through Sustainable Development." Report of the High-Level Panel of Eminent Persons on the Post-2015 Agenda. May 30.

Winters, Alan L., and others. 2010. "Economic Growth in Low-Income Countries: How the G-20 Can Help to Raise and Sustain It." G-20 High-Level Development Conference.

PART IV

Other Issues for Reform of Global Governance

MARI PANGESTU AND DAVID NELLOR

10

A G-20 Agenda for the Global Trade Regime

Few propositions in economics are so clear: the global economy would be better off with a more open trading regime supported by an adequate regulatory framework. The payoff from such multilateral liberalization would be significant. One result would be about US$2 trillion that could be committed in the near term. Yet the international community fails to make meaningful progress toward this unambiguous payoff.[1]

The G-20 had a tremendous opportunity to move the trade agenda forward following the global financial crisis. The elevation of the G-20 to the leaders' level in 2008 strengthened the legitimacy of global economic leadership. But more than that, it placed the major emerging markets in a global leadership role. These economies are symbolic of the transformational growth and development role that international trade and investment can play. This newly energized legitimacy combined with the reform opportunity that crises can provide meant that the G-20 was the best vehicle to deliver the political commitment needed to bring about a stronger, fairer, and more open trade regime. Arguably this prime reform opportunity has passed, but nonetheless the reform window is still at least partly ajar.

The authors would like to thank Philippa Dee for comments and suggestions on a draft of this chapter.

1. The ninth World Trade Organization ministerial conference in Bali in December 2013 made modest progress on the Doha agenda. In advance of that meeting, Hufbauer and Schott (2013) proposed and costed seven measures that they believed the meeting in Bali in December 2013 could deliver, with estimated benefits of US$2 trillion.

The G-20's ambitions for international trade have, at best, been modest. It has repeatedly committed to avoiding protectionist measures and voiced support for completing the Doha round. But it has been silent on strengthening delivery of a more robust and fair global trade regime. This silence on bringing the international architecture of the global trading system up-to-date is evident in the absence of references to this topic in the G-20 communiqués. The silence is even more striking when compared to the ambitious agenda and accomplishments in other areas of the international system. Simply put, international trade has been a poor cousin of global macroeconomic and financial reform on the G-20 agenda.

Various hypotheses might be employed to explain the absence of progress on trade. Yes, all can see the benefits of a more open global trade regime. But the immediate domestic political downside of the transition costs as well as the perceived risk that others will not play by the rules appear to overwhelm the payoff. This, of course, is the prisoner's dilemma, which has proven particularly paralyzing in the case of international trade; the hurdle to jump over in order to move from the inferior independent quadrant of the payoff matrix to the superior cooperative quadrant has proven to be too high.[2] It should also be noted that in the past there has been leadership by major economies to break the dilemma of narrow reciprocal negotiating interests and to look at the collective good. This leadership has lately been absent and is complicated by the rise of emerging nations.

The task of this chapter is to ask how the G-20 might resolve the prisoner's dilemma posed by reform of the international trade regime. Framing the issue in terms of the prisoner's dilemma matrix underscores that the best approach for Australia, as the G-20 chair, is to focus on creating a framework that can generate results rather than on the results themselves. We call this framework the architecture of the international trade system. This architecture is a global public good that encompasses the principles, organizations, and processes within which trade discussions take place.

It is our view that the G-20 can provide the political will to shape a new architecture for the international trade system, taking into account the realities of the multipolar world, an evolving global trading system, and regional and other trade agreements. The G-20 is not the forum to agree on specific trade measures or to undertake trade negotiations. The G-20 could, however,

---

2. This is not intended to mean that each issue on the global trade agenda has a Pareto superior cooperative outcome. Rather, a superior outcome exists based on the package of issues.

be the forum to come up with the vision for the global trade regime that accounts for these new realities. The most important challenge is to establish an architecture that will help bring about the shared goals of the international community and define a process to deliver on the vision.

We begin the chapter by evaluating the G-20's accomplishments in trade and the changing global trade environment and by defining the challenges for the international community. Thoughts on reform of the international trade system follow. We end with a proposal on the way the G-20 and Australia, as G-20 chair, can address the challenges of the international trade system.

The G-20, International Trade, and the World Trade Organization: Lost in International Space

The G-20's postglobal financial crisis focus has been twofold. The first area of focus has been on global recovery. This involved strengthening the management of the global economy through coordinated policy action undertaken at the national level, particularly in 2008–09. Subsequently these efforts were captured in the Framework for Strong, Sustainable, and Balanced Growth and monitored through the Mutual Assessment Process (MAP). This package reflects an agreement on shared values, a commitment to undertake unilateral policy actions in a coordinated way based on these shared values, and a cross-check and monitoring mechanism that acts to ensure consistency, provide peer pressure, and boost confidence.

The second area of focus has been updating the global economic and financial architecture. The task is ensuring that this architecture reflects the new challenges facing the global economic and financial system as well as the multipolar reality of today's global economy.[3] There has been no similar progress in the trade area.

The G-20 and Trade: From Communiqués to Outcomes?

The statements by G-20 leaders give some guidance on the trade outcome that they want to see but much less on how or what the World Trade Organization (WTO) needs to look like and do.

The leaders' focus was—and still is—on the role of trade in recovery from the global financial crisis, when there were concerns about the rising protectionism,

3. In fact, the raison d'être of the elevated global role of the G-20 is that global economic developments are shaped increasingly by emerging economies rather than by just large mature economies.

as occurred in the 1930s tariff wars. The outcome was that the leaders, concerned by the collapse in international trade, took a minimalist position. They did not say they would reduce trade barriers to support stronger economic activity; rather, they chose a do-no-harm strategy of agreeing simply to avoid protectionist measures. The G-20 said in Washington in November 2008, "We will refrain from raising new barriers to investment or to trade in goods and services, imposing new export restrictions, or implementing WTO-inconsistent measures to stimulate exports."[4] This commitment was renewed and extended in subsequent meetings, most recently in St. Petersburg, where the standstill commitment was extended to 2016.[5] The WTO, with the United Nations Conference on Trade and Development (UNCTAD), and the Organization for Economic Cooperation and Development (OECD), was asked to provide six monthly reports on G-20 trade and investment measures to "monitor" the actions of G-20 members.[6] These reports were commissioned as a self-notification exercise.

Arguably the G-20 has had some success relative to the expectations of increasing trade barriers. In the context of plummeting growth and mounting unemployment, there were fears about a return to 1930s-style trade restrictions, which could have had a devastating impact on trade and growth. The rush to stimulus measures and industry interventions stoked this fear by giving rise to the possibility of new discriminatory measures that do not necessarily come under the WTO framework.[7] The worst of these fears did not eventuate. However, protection measures continue to grow despite the commitment to a standstill and to a rollback of such measures. Carla Hills reported that, following the November 2008 pledge not to raise trade and investment restrictions, "within a few weeks seventeen out of the twenty breached this solemn pledge."[8] Subsequent G-20-requested monitoring by the OECD, UNCTAD, and the WTO shows some pickup in restrictive measures, and those introduced as temporary remained permanent despite the improvement in economic conditions.[9] The percentage of G-20 imports affected by more restrictive measures was 0.4 per-

4. Communiqué of the G-20 leaders, Washington, November 1998.

5. See communiqué of the G-20 leaders, Washington, November 1998, annex 1, which summarizes the relevant text.

6. WTO/UNCTAD/OECD (2009). A summary of findings of successive reports is shown in annex 2.

7. See Tussle (2010).

8. Hills (2009).

9. In early 2009, the WTO said that it would monitor and report international trade developments. At the London Summit (2009), the G-20 asked the World Trade Organization, the

cent in March 2009, and even though there has been a slowdown in imposition of new trade restrictions, by November 2013, 1.1 percent of imports were affected by restrictive measures. Furthermore, the measures undertaken are not in the WTO purview. Reports of the Global Trade Alert show a significant number of additional protective measures.[10]

Leaders' declarations have also consistently called for completion of the Doha round of negotiations and less specifically have spoken about the role to be played by trade in terms of global growth and development.[11] These statements, however, do not signal any compelling conviction to conclude the Doha round. First, the repetitive nature of the statements in the face of no progress (at least until the ninth ministerial conference) gives the impression that they are pro forma rather than having strong political endorsement. Second, until the Los Cabos and St. Petersburg summits, the absence of any recognition of the burgeoning regional arrangements and what that might mean for the international system suggested little in the way of considered discussion on the real challenges faced by the international trading system.

The G-20 has set out a goal but not the means to get there. Its statements suggest that the WTO should be the driver of a more conducive trade environment and certainly be in the lead in preventing the erection of new trade barriers. But leaders' statements give no guidance on whether the WTO is suited to these tasks. Moreover, it has not given guidance on a process to accomplish the constructive trade regime goals that have been spelled out. The almost inevitable failure of this G-20 process on trade—already evident at least in part—risks diminishing further the credibility of the WTO.

Trade and the International System

The G-20 has not spelled out a view of what a global trade regime and an associated WTO of the twenty-first century might look like. The international economic and financial architecture envisaged by its twentieth-century founders was based on three pillars: the International Monetary Fund (IMF), the World Bank, and the WTO.[12] Against this background, the G-20 has

---

UN Conference on Trade and Development, and the Organization for Economic Cooperation and Development to issue periodic reports on trade measures.

10. See Evenett (2012, 2013).

11. See annex 1.

12. The treaty for the International Trade Organization was agreed on along with that for the International Monetary Fund and the World Bank but was never ratified by the United States and some others. The General Agreement on Tariffs and Trade preceded establishment of the World Trade Organization in 1995.

focused on only two legs of this three-legged stool. It has devoted considerable effort to reforming the Bretton Woods institutions so that they reflect global economic reality; recognizing the importance of global capital and financial flows, it established the Financial Stability Board. There has been no such G-20 interest in international trade. Thus the third leg, the WTO, remains shaky, risking the stability of the system as a whole.

The lack of visibility of the WTO in the G-20 communiqués is striking, especially in contrast to the focus on the architecture of the Bretton Woods institutions. These institutions, and especially the IMF, underwent the most dramatic changes in their history driven by the G-20. The IMF was slated to be transformed through changes in its governance that were meant to enhance its global legitimacy, boost its financial muscle through a major capital increase, and strengthen its effectiveness through new lending facilities and approaches to surveillance.[13] The World Bank and development banks more generally were recapitalized significantly.

Beyond the economic and financial architecture of the international system, the IMF and the World Bank feature prominently in the ongoing activities of the G-20. The IMF participates at a senior level in the finance process and attends the sherpa meetings.[14] It plays a pivotal role by operating, de facto, as the secretariat to the G-20 on macroeconomic issues. Beyond its preparation of the surveillance notes and spillover reports that underpin the macroeconomic discussions, it supports the MAP. The IMF and the Financial Stability Board advise on financial sector reform. Likewise, the World Bank reports on the development consequences of the Framework for Strong, Sustainable, and Balanced Growth as well as supporting the Development Working Group.

The WTO has not had the same "seat at the table." Perhaps there are institutional reasons, because trade ministers are responsible for WTO issues, so finance ministers may not have the jurisdiction to direct the WTO. But this is

13. Reforms of the IMF were unprecedented. The IMF quotas (its capital) stood at 213.7 billion special drawing rights (SDR) coming into the global financial crisis. In December 2010 a doubling of quotas was agreed upon. This took quotas to about SDR 477 billion (US$715 billion). A plan to increase these further is under way. In this process, the share—and thus the voting power—of emerging markets has been increased to reflect their growing global role. New lending facilities have been established and substantive new multilateral surveillance activities have been adopted.

14. The G-20 operates largely through two channels: a finance process led by finance ministers and central bank governors and a sherpa process involving the leaders' designated representatives. Meetings outside of these channels are largely ad hoc. Before 2008, the G-20 consisted solely of the finance process.

not a particularly compelling argument for the limited WTO involvement. The WTO was asked to monitor trade measures, and in many countries the ministerial responsibility for the World Bank does not reside with finance ministers, yet the World Bank has been a full and active participant in the G-20 finance process. The WTO has attended the G-20 sherpas' process, but these meetings have not conducted much of the core work on the international economic and financial agenda.

The World Has Changed; the International Trade System and the WTO Have Not

The lack of a WTO profile in the G-20 process could reflect the ambivalent view held by many about the WTO. Despite the recognition of the benefits of trade, the conventional wisdom is that the WTO is increasingly marginalized on key international trade issues for a variety of reasons. This perception gives rise to the view that the WTO can make only a limited contribution, beyond the threat of and use of its dispute resolution mechanisms and its ability to ensure certainty and predictability in doing trade under the existing rules. The challenges faced by the WTO reflect several threads of a changing membership as well as a mismatch between today's trade and investment environment and its modus operandi. However, despite lack of an adequate mandate and meaningful political endorsement, the WTO is nonetheless called on to address issues that touch on sensitive domestic sovereignty questions.

The Changing Global Environment and Trade Arrangements

The world has changed since the Doha negotiations were started in 2001. The spirit of the negotiations then was to redress imbalances and injustices between developed and developing nations. This is the reason for the title of the negotiation, namely, the Doha Development Agenda. However, over a decade down the road, a global economic crisis and the rise of emerging economies tell us that we live in a multipolar world. Emerging economies such as China, India, Brazil, and Russia have become the new poles of growth, contributing a greater share of trade flows. The slowdown in external demand by advanced countries post-2008 was partially offset by growth of demand in emerging economies. These shifts in economic development also affect the balance of global governance and the need to account for the role of emerging economies. In the last two decades the structure of trade has changed, with the share of South-South trade increasing from 30 percent to 50 percent of world trade. The different speeds of growth in developing countries means that, while the emerging market economies are expected to give more than less-developed nations in the trade negotiations, many parts of their countries are also still developing, so they also need differential treatment and capacity building.

Regional rather than multilateral trade discussions have become the focus of most countries. There is no doubt that the credibility of the WTO has been diminished by the lack of progress on the Doha round. The "early harvest" achieved at the ninth ministerial conference in Bali has provided some optimism for progress, but of course there is still the challenge to complete the more substantial components of the Doha Development Agenda. Some also portray regional arrangements and multilateral discussions (the Doha round) as alternatives or perhaps competitors. The WTO, while making the case for its global principles, has largely been an idle bystander watching the surge in regional arrangements. The current articles in the WTO agreements to guard "consistency" with the WTO are too general; and the Committee on Regional Trade Agreements that oversees this has only achieved better reporting requirements and greater transparency.

The new regional agreements demonstrate how much the trade agenda has left Doha behind. Regional arrangements are of course not new, but the growing prominence of major trading countries in these agreements, such as the Transatlantic Trade and Investment Partnership agreement between the European Union and the United States, is striking. These new agreements will govern significant shares of global trade.[15] The agenda of these trade discussions has changed from a focus on the level of protection. The UK Center for Economic Policy Research argues that 80 percent of the potential gains from the partnership agreement will come from reducing conflict and duplication of EU and U.S. rules on regulatory issues.[16]

Global Value Chains

International trade has been evolving. A decade or so ago an export strategy based on division of the production network between low-cost, labor-intensive activities and higher value added and human-capital-intensive parts of production was the norm. One talked about graduating up the value chain,

15. Gallagher (2013) provides data on this issue.
16. See Bollyky (2013).

or the "flying geese" pattern. Today the division of production is much more fragmented, and it is not just about production of goods. Recent work done on measuring trade in value added by the OECD and others shows clearly that the global value chain is shaping today's production location and trade flows. Trade is more in tasks along the value chain and less in final goods.

The global value chain has several policy consequences, including linkages of trade and investment, protection debates around the role of imports, and behind-the-border policy, including regulation and services that support the tradable sector.[17]

Regarding trade and investment linkages: the global value chain makes it possible for more countries and companies to engage in international trade. Small and developing countries can choose to specialize in one or more segments of the value chain. This results in increased linkages between trade and investment. For instance, countries might choose where they want to be in the value chain by targeting particular investment and ensuring the availability of key services and human resources needed by investing firms. Logistics, trade and customs processes, effective factor markets, and talent pool become critical ingredients to successful participation in value chains.

Regarding the dynamics of protection debates, small and medium-sized enterprises can specialize in any one part of the value chain and benefit from the global market for a product. Local production for exports and for the domestic market is more dependent on imports than on competing with imports, as in a conventional model of trade and protection. Assessing protection levels will depend on the cumulative impact of tariffs measured on the value added at any stage in the chain.

Regarding behind-the-border policy, the global value chain will function more efficiently under a trading system with one set of rules, standards, and market-access commitments. The natural dynamics of global value chains gravitate toward agreeing on standards, but there are public goods and development policy dimensions to accomplishing common rules and standards, in which the WTO could play a larger role.[18] The lack of decisiveness on the WTO's role in areas such as this has resulted in its being a bystander rather than a participant.

17. See OECD/WTO/UNCTAD (2013) for a discussion of global value chains and policy implications.
18. Baldwin (2012) is one of few voices on this issue. Baldwin argues for a WTO 2.0 based on the rise of supply-chain-related trade.

WTO and Emerging Issues

The WTO has been challenged on how it should manage or participate in emerging global issues. The nexus between climate change and trade, the impacts of trade policy on food security, the link between exchange-rate management and trade competitiveness, the link between investment and trade, and the lack of progress in the trade in services agenda are some of the issues that have emerged in recent years but that the system has struggled to address. The global financial crisis underlined the need for better coordination between international institutions to address issues such as availability of trade finance and currency tensions, which can affect trade flows.

The WTO has failed to articulate a vision and strategy either for a multilateral agenda or to enable it to be responsive to the changing global environment. Perhaps the WTO's structure and its secretariat are too locked into a model characterized by negotiation and dispute resolution. The current WTO model does not appear well suited to address the changing realities of the global trade and investment agenda, including the challenge of multilateral, single-undertaking, trade discussions, of the emerging value chains, and of other evolving issues in the international system.

Elements of a New Architecture

The challenge for the international community is to adopt an architecture for the international trade and investment system that helps deliver a global economy supported by free, fair, and open trade that boosts growth, drives development, and promotes sustainability. This section offers our views on some elements of this architecture.

Multiple Pathways

We see nothing inherently good or bad about trade arrangements that come about as a result of unilateral national policy action, of regional or like-trade arrangements, or of multilateral trade negotiations. Different approaches—especially multilateral and regional agreements—are often presented as alternatives or even competitors. In our view they are not alternatives. We refer elsewhere to the various pathways to the desired global or multilateral outcome.[19]

19. Pangestu (2013).

The key issue is what role various agreements play in helping to move the system toward the effective provision of the global public good of a robust and fair trade regime. Bilateral and regional agreements by WTO members need not be contradictory to a sound global system. Countries have entered into comprehensive free trade or economic partnership agreements that range from agreement on specific issues, such as trade in goods, to comprehensive agreements, which include goods and services, investment, trade facilitation, competition policy, and intellectual property rights. Some also touch on the more sensitive areas of government procurement, environment, and even labor. In other words, many if not most of these agreements are well beyond the scope of current WTO negotiations.

The challenge is to establish consistency and linkages among the different approaches, the agreements, and the multilateral system. In essence, there have to be pathways for making agreements consistent with a desired global or multilateral outcome. Some basic principles could include open architecture norms, such as open accession, transparency, and best standards and practices. This multiple pathway model also lends itself well to the trade and development principle of differentiated pathways, which are combined with capacity building to account for various levels of development while ensuring inclusiveness. This principle of aid for trade and capacity building has been a parallel process to the WTO negotiations.

Regional Agreements

In the Asian region, the ASEAN Free Trade Area started with tariff elimination for intra-ASEAN trade and evolved into the comprehensive ASEAN Economic Community by 2015. Similar ASEAN Free Trade Agreements with each of its main dialogue partners followed. These agreements started as the classic form of trade agreement designed to establish free trade on a preferential basis among the parties. They commenced with goods liberalization followed by investment and services and evolved to be more comprehensive by including new issues such as the environment. The agreements took on the character of "partnerships" by incorporating capacity building in recognition of the differing levels of development of the participating economies.

In other parts of the world, new proposals for major regional agreements have been under discussion. These include the comprehensive agreement being negotiated under the Trans-Pacific Partnership agreement in the Asia Pacific region and the EU-U.S. Transatlantic Trade and Investment Partnership agreement. One could argue that comprehensive and high-quality regional or bilateral agreements, such as an EU-U.S. agreement, could complement and act as a catalyst for completing multilateral negotiations. This was the experience with the negotiation of the North American Free Trade Agreement and the creation of the Asia Pacific Economic Cooperation (APEC), which was perceived to have helped to conclude the Uruguay round when it reached a deadlock in 1993–94. To the extent that such agreements address Doha-plus issues, they can also inform possible ways of shaping future multilateral rounds.

In 2011, when Indonesia was the chair of ASEAN, we developed a proposal that was adopted by ASEAN leaders known as the East Asia Regional Comprehensive Economic Partnership (RCEP) agreement.[20] The concept underlying this proposal reflects the "pathways approach" described above as well as the new realities of the global trade and investment environment. The RCEP was drafted with open architecture norms, such as open accession, transparency, and best standards and practices. It specifically mentions the requirement to be consistent with WTO principles. The RCEP is not a single undertaking, with a beginning and end, but rather is a framework within which the current trade agenda can be agreed on, stages of development can be recognized, and unanticipated new issues, which will inevitably arise over time, can be addressed.[21] It also provides a mechanism for consolidating the six agreements that dialogue partners already have with ASEAN, by ensuring that it uses a ratcheting-up process toward the best practices out of all the six agreements.[22] There is also the possibility for new members to accede.

Sectoral Agreements

Sectoral agreements can be part of the proposed architecture. Examples under a multilateral framework include an agreement on environmental goods and services (EGS) and the information technology agreement 2 (ITA2). Another approach that has recently resurfaced is plurilateral agreements and, more specifically, an agreement on services that falls outside of the Doha mandate.

20. At the time, one of the authors was the minister of trade of the Republic of Indonesia and introduced the proposal to ASEAN members.
21. The RCEP agreement is often presented as an alternative or even a competitor of the Trans-Pacific Partnership agreement. In fact, the two agreements are qualitatively different and need not be in conflict. The TPP agreement is a single undertaking on which complete agreement is required on a defined agenda. The RCEP agreement is an ongoing framework for discussion of a range of trade and investment issues. Issues can proceed as they are agreed on. Other economies willing to meet the specific terms can accede to the agreement.
22. Dialogue partners include China, Japan, Korea, Australia, New Zealand, and India.

The purpose is to continue the process of opening up in a step-by-step manner with a subset of members. If we take the wording of the eighth WTO ministerial conference in 2012, of importance is how these different approaches can be undertaken "while respecting the principle of transparency and inclusiveness."

The important issue is whether these agreements are applied to all WTO members on a most-favored-nation basis or whether they are applied on a preferential basis—that is, only among the parties to the agreement. This is a key point in considering their consistency with WTO rules. The few examples of sectoral agreements have been based on a subset of members, which make up a critical mass of trade in the sector and come under the first category of most-favored-nation application. The information technology agreement (ITA) and any second ITA that may be agreed on, as well as the agreement on environmental goods and services, are designed to be applied to all WTO members.[23] Initial agreements on critical mass under ITA1 and the EGS agreement came about at APEC meetings in 1996 and 2012, respectively, and were then brought to the WTO for negotiations. Both were intended to be applied on a most-favored-nation basis. After the success of the ITA1, APEC tried a similar approach, called the Early Voluntary Sectoral Liberalization, which was to use the APEC platform to get critical mass on a sectoral basis and to negotiate in the WTO. However, failure to get critical mass (and with large carve-outs and exceptions), meant that Early Voluntary Sectoral Liberalization did not succeed. It was in the end abandoned.

The ITA2 currently being discussed is also potentially a critical mass agreement that can be initially agreed upon in APEC and taken to the WTO for negotiations. These approaches are good examples of complementarity between regional and multilateral processes. There are also the proposed sectoral agreements within the nonagricultural market access WTO negotiations. In the non-most-favored-nation category are formal plurilateral agreements under the auspices of the WTO. The main example is the government procurement agreement that was approved by all members in Marrakesh. Such agreements may be negotiated outside of the WTO if they do not impinge on existing WTO rights and obligations. The Anti-Counterfeiting Trade Agreement on counterfeit trade

23. The ITA, which was agreed upon in Singapore in 1996, is a most-favored-nation agreement, with tariff eliminations applied by the parties to all WTO members. A second ITA is proposed on the same basis. An agreement to eliminate tariffs and other barriers on environmental goods and services was reached in APEC in 2012. Reductions in applied rates would hold for imports that qualified on the agreed list of such goods under the most-favored-nation agreement.

(not yet in force) is an example.[24] A plurilateral agreement on services is being negotiated by a group of countries that are interested in liberalizing further trade in services, but its application to other members, and the terms on which that may be agreed, are not yet clear. The agreement may be structured as a free trade agreement under the General Agreement on Trade in Services. These agreements are mostly open to other parties to join at a later stage, but the conditions for joining (full acceptance or on terms to be negotiated) vary case to case.

The challenge is for such plurilateral agreements to be multilateralized, with the principles of transparency and inclusiveness. How can such negotiations be open to nonmembers? And how should the process of accession be designed so as not to preclude other members from ever joining? How can less-developed members prepare to join? How does one avoid free riding, which will be the major concern of the original members? These are just some of the questions that need to be answered.

Reforming the WTO

A different WTO will almost certainly be needed. In our view, the WTO needs to participate in a world of many trade forums and play a role in promoting trade agreements (multilateral and other) that progress toward the vision of an international community. The G-20 is the premier economic forum for global coordination and cooperation. It has been about coordinating national actions in responding to crisis and undertaking reforms or sustainable growth paths around shared values and principles. In the trade area, the shared value and principle has been to keep markets open and ensure transparency. In relation to the multilateral trading system, leaders could consider adopting principles that would guide members and the WTO to ensuring that alternative pathways are consistent with an open, fair, and rules-based multilateral trading system that benefits all. They could propose reform of the WTO as an organization, just as they did with international organizations around financial and macroeconomic coordination. We make three proposals:

---

24. The government procurement agreement is applied only to the parties who negotiated the terms of the agreement. It is therefore not a most favored nation agreement. But all WTO members approved the agreement in 1994 at Marrakesh as part of the results of the Uruguay round; it thus fulfills the transparency principle. The agreement is open to other members who can join the agreement by negotiation with the parties. The Anti-Counterfeiting Trade Agreement was concluded in 2012 (outside the WTO) between more than thirty countries that deal with intellectual property rights. It will be open to third parties to join at a later stage.

—Adoption of the open-architecture principles, discussed above, would ensure that trade agreements are in line with WTO principles and are open accession. G-20 members would agree to abide by these principles in their various trade and investment discussions, whether those discussions are with G-20 members or otherwise. In view of the share of G-20 members in international trade and investment, this would go a long way toward ensuring that these principles have general application.

—A second part of the principles would be about the role of the WTO, regional trade arrangements, and their interaction. These principles would explicitly recognize the multiple-pathways approach. This could involve a formal reporting to the WTO of any non-multilateral trade and investment agreement discussions and a responsibility for the WTO to actively support regional arrangements consistent with these principles. The detail of this support needs to be developed. A minimalist approach could involve the WTO providing its technical expertise.[25]

—If the WTO is to be a center of excellence on trade issues, as we believe it should, the WTO should address twenty-first-century issues. In many cases this is an advisory role based on in-depth knowledge and in other cases could involve WTO actions. The current work of the WTO has led to discussions on a number of the issues, especially through studies and regular public forums on regional and bilateral agreements. New issues such as the global value chain, value added in trade statistics, trade and food security, and trade and environment have been addressed. These efforts need to be transformed into operational activities.

The communiqué of the G-20 St. Petersburg summit on the international trade and investment system is encouraging in relation to these proposals. The communiqué opens the door to the possibility that the G-20 will take up the topic of the international trade regime. It recognizes the growing role of regional trade agreements (paragraph 47) and that there is a need for better understanding of global value chains (paragraph 49). Nonetheless, the communiqué is disappointing. The G-20 fails to exploit its comparative advantage. It should take a strategic view and tackle the issue of how the international community can deliver the global public good of a robust and fair global trade regime.

First, the thrust of the communiqué text (paragraph 41 and following) is the repeated exhortation for progress on Doha and the commitment to avoid

---

25. The G-20 has set a precedent for principles along the lines noted here. It adopted a set of principles governing the roles and interactions of the IMF with regional financial arrangements.

raising trade barriers. The communiqué fails to recognize the need for a strategic design of institutions that could make such calls meaningful.

Second, on regional agreements, the text (paragraph 47) and its annex on regional agreements is about transparency and reporting. This is at best a welcome first step and at worst a vehicle to avoid taking on the substantive issue. Paragraph 47 recognizes the importance of regional agreements. But its action points are to encourage transparency and better understand the effects of regional agreements because this is "of interest to G-20 members." The annex encourages transparency. The communiqué takes the architecture of the international trade system as given.

Third, on global value chains the communiqué (paragraph 47) is an opening, but the focus is not constructive. The focus is on improving understanding and on reporting data on global value chains. The stated purpose of this work is to "help countries . . . to decide upon appropriate policy making options" to benefit from global value chains. Countries have their own incentives to determine how they can take advantage of opportunities to participate in global value chains. The challenge for the international community is how to develop an international system both responsive to and constructively supporting the current global trading system.

The communiqué's conclusions on international trade present the G-20 as a forum that is limited to encouraging transparency, information exchange, and best practice by individual members. Our view is that the G-20 should focus more on developing a framework of global economic governance in international trade—and the process to deliver it—just as it has done with the financial and macroeconomic coordination architecture.

An Agenda for Global Trade: A Role for Australia as G-20 Chair

Australia has been an active participant, and in fact a leader, in G-20-driven reform of the Bretton Woods institutions. In our view, Australia should see the WTO as the missing piece of the international economic and financial architecture that it has worked to strengthen through the G-20 process. This observation combined with Australia's interests in trade should help make the global trade regime a priority issue for the G-20 during Australia's tenure as chair in 2014.

Australia should develop a strategy consistent with the G-20's comparative advantage, which is that it can deliver the essential high-level political endorsement and political will to adopt a shared global vision for the international trade system. This architecture of the international trade system would comprise the principles, organizations, and processes within which trade discussions would take place.[26]

Agreement on this architecture is the key challenge. As noted at the beginning of this chapter, we are looking for a path to move from the inferior quadrant of the prisoner's dilemma matrix of international trade to the superior, cooperative quadrant. By providing an architecture, the G-20 would be providing the tools for trade ministers to use in trade and investment discussions. While many observers have made specific proposals on trade measures, there is little mileage for Australia in adopting one or the other of these as part of its G-20 agenda.[27] Such an approach almost certainly ensures that the G-20 will be bogged down in detailed trade discussions, which do not address the prisoner's dilemma. The G-20's comparative advantage, as mentioned, is its ability to provide legitimate global economic and financial leadership by defining the parameters within which decisions will be made; it is not a forum for trade negotiation.

Australia should use past G-20 communiqués to start the process of articulating a vision for the global trade system. The communiqué from the St. Petersburg summit might provide not only the mandate for Australia to take forward the issue of international trade but also a G-20 mandate to recast international trade in the manner set out in this chapter. One approach would be to appoint a working group of G-20 officials, led by a G-20 sherpa, tasked with preparing terms of reference for an Eminent Persons Group (EPG) to help define a new architecture. The composition of the working group reflects the need to move trade discussions beyond a trade negotiation to reflect the broader economic "wins" of a stronger regime.

The Brisbane leaders' communiqué would set out the goal of strengthening the global trade regime. To this end, it would appoint an EPG comprising persons highly regarded in international governance, trade, and other areas tasked to make recommendations on the global trade regime and specifically on the principles to be observed by G-20 members and the new WTO. In arriving at its recommendations, the EPG can draw on resources of the WTO, but the

26. The G-20 has demonstrated sensitivity to broader legitimacy of global economic and financial rules by ensuring that most agreements are formally passed through the governance structures of the relevant international institutions.

27. Thirlwell (2013) provides a helpful literature survey of various proposals. Gallagher (2013) suggests that the G-20 define specific areas for regional trade arrangements to negotiate, for example, agreement to eliminate certain classes of nontariff measures. Williams (2013) proposes quantitative reductions in various measures with given timetables.

EPG would be a separate peer group for G-20 leaders, from which they hear respected and independent reform advice reflecting a global perspective.

The EPG's terms of reference should be unshackled from the conventional WTO process. The group would recognize that a quite different WTO both in terms of process and organization might be needed. While the group should clearly acknowledge global political realities, its membership should not be based on national representation but on skills and experience in trade, international economics and finance, and global politics.

Conclusions

This chapter asks how the G-20 might resolve the prisoners' dilemma posed by reform of the international trade regime. The dilemma is that, although the global economy could move to the unambiguously superior cooperative outcome of a stronger, fairer, and more open global trade regime, it appears to be stuck in an inferior, uncooperative outcome. How can the G-20 move the trade regime to the superior outcome?

The global economy and trade are evolving even though the international regime is little changed. Regional rather than multilateral trade discussions have become the focus of most countries, reflecting inter alia the lack of progress on multilateral trade discussions and the fact that multilateral forums are not in line with the issues facing trade today. Global value chains have changed the nature of trade and underscore the links of merchandise trade to investment and services. Emerging global issues, such as the nexus between climate change and trade, have found the system wanting. Moreover, the increasing trade share of emerging markets has changed the profile of the WTO's membership.

The G-20 has shown little ambition to tackle international trade. Focused on global recovery, it has chosen a minimalist position of do no harm by agreeing to avoid raising trade barriers. It repeatedly voices support for concluding the Doha round and the benefits of a more global trade regime but offers no compelling plan on how this might come about.

In our view, framing the challenge for international trade in terms of the prisoner's dilemma matrix underscores that the best approach for Australia, as the G-20 chair, is to focus on how we might proceed toward establishing the "architecture" of the international trade system that will deliver the global public good of a robust and fair global trade regime. This architecture comprises the principles, organizations, and processes within which trade and investment discussions take place.

We propose that Australia recognize that this architecture, including the WTO, is the missing piece of the international economic and financial architecture that it has worked to strengthen through the G-20 process. As G-20 chair in 2014, Australia should look to deliver the essential high-level political endorsement and political will to initiate the process that will culminate in the G-20 adopting a global vision for the international trade system.

The G-20 Brisbane leaders' meeting would shift the focus of the G-20 toward the need for a robust new global trade regime and appoint an EPG tasked to propose an architecture to deliver the vision for the global trade regime. The nature of the EPG's outputs could be broad principles defining a new architecture along with a sequence of next steps. The EPG should press leaders to follow up their proposals with statements on the process going forward. This cannot be left to the WTO or trade ministers alone.

Our thinking is that the architecture should establish consistency and linkages between the different approaches and agreements and the multilateral system. In essence, there have to be pathways for making agreements consistent with a desired global or multilateral outcome. The G-20 might agree to abide by open-architecture principles, which could include open accession, transparency, and best standards and practices. A different WTO will almost certainly be needed. It needs to participate in multiple trade forums and promote trade agreements (multilateral and other) that progress toward the vision of an international community.

In sum, the proverb that it is better to provide the fishing rod than the fish applies when considering the role of the G-20 in relation to international trade. It is unlikely that the G-20 can secure a short-term payoff in terms of a trade agreement; this does not play to its comparative advantage. Rather, the G-20 needs to bring the architecture of the international trade and investment regime up-to-date so that the global economy can reap the benefits of a more open, fairer, and stronger trade regime over time. This architecture should reflect the changed global environment, recognize that there are multiple pathways to global trade goals, and establish a WTO that can support this process.

References

Baldwin, Richard. 2012. "WTO 2.0: Global Governance of Supply-Chain Trade." *Policy Insight* 64. London: Centre for Economic Policy Research.

Bollyky, Thomas. 2013. "Getting to Yes on Transatlantic Trade." *Foreign Affairs*, July 10.

Evenett, Simon, ed. 2012. "Debacle: The 11th GTA Report on Protectionism." Global Trade Alert. London: Centre for Economic Policy Research.

———. 2013. "Protectionism's Quiet Return." Global Trade Alert: Pre-G8 Summit Report. London: Centre for Economic Policy Research.

Gallagher, Peter. 2013. "Mega-Regional Trade Agreements and the Next Transition." *G-20 Monitor* 3. Sydney: Lowy Institute for International Policy.

Hills, Carla. 2009. "The World Economy after London G-20: Recovery, Trade, Finance, and Governance." Speech. Sixth Anniversary of the Hills Center for Governance, Yonsei University. Seoul, April 28.

Hufbauer, Gary, and Jeffrey Schott. 2013. "Payoff from the World Trade Agenda 2013." Report prepared for the ICC Research Foundation. Washington: Peterson Institute for International Economics.

OECD/WTO/UNCTAD (Organization for Economic Cooperation and Development/World Trade Organization/United Nations Conference on Trade and Development). 2013. "Implications of Global Value Chains for Trade, Investment, Development, and Jobs."

Pangestu, Mari. 2013. "The Multilateral Trading System and WTO: Challenges and Priorities." In *Race for the WTO Director-General Job: Seven Candidates Speak,* edited by Bernard Hoekman and Petros C. Mavroidis. London: Centre for Economic Policy Research.

Thirlwell, Mark. 2013. "International Trade: What Can the G-20 Do?" *G-20 Monitor* 3. Sydney: Lowy Institute for International Policy.

Tussle, Diana. 2010. "The G-20 and the Multilateral Trade Impasse." Policy brief. FRIDE, Club de Madrid, and Government of Korea.

Williams, Brett. 2013. "Australia Must Exhort the G-20 to Lead on Multilateral Trade Liberalization by Example Not Words." *G-20 Monitor* 3. Sydney: Lowy Institute for International Policy.

WTO/UNCTAD/OECD (World Trade Organization/United Nations Conference on Trade and Development/Organization for Economic Cooperation and Development). 2009. "Report on G-20 Trade and Investment Measures."

ROSS GARNAUT

11

The G-20 and International Cooperation on Climate Change

The climate change issue makes exceptional demands on capacity for collective action at home in each country and among states. The free rider problem of collective action is never easy to overcome. Effective collective action within or between countries invariably requires intellectual and institutional innovation and new dimensions of political leadership. The emergence of ideas, institutions, and political leadership and capacity for collective action on particular issues and at particular times can never be taken for granted.

The G-20 is ideally suited as the main forum for guiding international collective action on climate change. It contains all of the world's main emitters of greenhouse gases and all of the countries that are most important to effective global effort on climate change. It contains the countries that have been most active in leadership of both developed and developing countries in the global forum, the United Nations Framework Convention on Climate Change (UNFCCC). While the G-20 contains the most influential developed and developing countries, it can stand outside the entrenched and stereotypical divisions that have become barriers to effective action within the UNFCCC, with its huge and unwieldy membership and traditions of symbolic posturing.

The timing is ideal for making the increase in momentum in global climate change discussions a central feature of the G-20 meeting in Australia in 2014. The G-20 has a track record of leadership action on the international climate change agenda, so far with positive as well as pending outcomes. The world is working toward a critical meeting of the United Nations Framework Convention in Paris in December 2015. Articulation of a firm G-20 position in

Brisbane in 2014 would be in time to influence the Lima UNFCCC meeting in December 2014, leading into Paris in 2015.

Climate change is not a new issue for the G-20, nor is influence on formal decisions of the UNFCCC a new approach. The G-20 played an important role in establishing the objective of holding the contribution of human-induced climate change to 2 degrees Celsius at the Copenhagen meeting of the UNFCCC in 2009. The G-20 formulated a strong position on removal of fossil fuel subsidies as an important contribution to climate change mitigation. This position has assisted domestic reform in some countries and so far is honored mainly in the breach in others. Reiteration of the importance of this old position would be useful to the global mitigation effort. The G-20 meeting in Russia agreed to reduce hydrofluorocarbon (HFC) emissions, under the Montreal Protocol, as a contribution to climate change mitigation. The G-20 in Australia could agree to initiate negotiations at the next meeting of the Montreal Protocol's Conference of the Parties.

The chances of the G-20 playing an important role in accelerating momentum on international climate change action at this time are improved by shifts in domestic policy in the United States and China. Over the five-year life so far of the G-20, the governments of the world's two largest economies and emitters of greenhouse gases, the United States and China, have introduced major domestic programs to implement emissions reduction targets that embody major changes in established trajectories. These realities and developments augur well for the G-20 playing an important role in accelerating momentum on international action on climate change. The pivotal importance of the Paris meeting of the United Nations Framework Convention on Climate Change in December 2015 makes the 2014 UNFCCC meeting in Lima crucial to any prospects for the G-20 being helpful to a strong outcome.

In candor, it must be said that there are also less happy portents for success. The new Australian government is the host of the G-20 heads of government meeting in 2014, and it is feeling its way on domestic and international climate change action. It is seeking to repeal legislation on domestic carbon pricing linked to international markets that has been the instrument favored in principle (although not yet in domestic action) by the international community for the achievement of ambitious emissions reduction targets. However, none of the Abbott coalition government's political commitments explicitly block the taking of positive positions in increasing momentum toward a strong outcome at Paris along the lines suggested here.

The new government has confirmed its support for Australian participation in international cooperation on greenhouse gas abatement. It has explicitly confirmed the Australian targets formally communicated to the UNFCCC in 2010: unconditional reduction of emissions by 5 percent from 2005 levels by 2020 and a reduction to as much as 25 percent in the context of international action consistent with the 2-degrees target. A precise intermediate commitment was made: to reduce emissions by 15 percent in the context of comparable commitments by other developed countries and substantial action to reduce the trajectory of emissions from developing countries. The unconditional commitment represents a sharp break in the trajectory of Australian emissions growth, influenced as it was by the developed world's most rapid growth in population and economic activity and exceptionally rapid expansion of emissions-intensive resource export industries.

And in statements leading up to the September 2013 general election victory, the Abbott opposition repeatedly referred to using Australia's hosting of the G-20 heads of government in 2014 as a vehicle for securing international action on climate change. For example, Greg Hunt, then the opposition's spokesperson on climate change and now minister for the environment in the Abbott cabinet, told a large audience at the Australian National University:

> There are two important steps we should take at the international level. First, the all-UN negotiating approach of 180 countries locked in a convention centre with up to 40,000 observers is increasingly ineffective. Need I say more than Copenhagen. In the real world, any progress will be between the United States, China, India and the EU. We should therefore task the G-20 with a special responsibility for negotiating a four-way compact between these players. If we can do that then we have a genuine base for a future global agreement.[1]

The Economic Problem

The objective is for the world as a whole to invest in reducing greenhouse gas emissions to the point where the cost of a billion dollars of increased expenditure on mitigation equals the benefit of reduced climate change damage as a consequence of that expenditure.

---

1. Hunt (2013).

What is the right amount of global warming that we should accept, given the costs of mitigation? That question has been the subject of serious analysis by academic economists since the last decade of the twentieth century.[2] It was the focus of a report commissioned by the United Kingdom government.[3] These studies calculate the interests of the international community as a whole in climate change mitigation, but policy decisions will actually be made in sovereign nation-states. Even if it were clear that a specified degree of mitigation were in the international collective interest, that perspective would be ineffective unless individual nation-states took decisions on mitigation that added up to an effort that was consistent with attainment of the global goal.

This is part of the challenge of international collective action on climate change. Individual countries are affected differently by climate change and by policies to reduce greenhouse gas emissions. Each country's calculation of its interests in climate change mitigation is affected by its assessment of its vulnerability and of the costs of its own mitigation. For a country with resource endowments that make it naturally a large exporter or importer of emissions-intensive goods, the costs of mitigation depend a great deal on whether the international mitigation regime allows international trade in emissions entitlements. A large, diverse economy with energy resource endowments relative to endowments of labor and capital that are fairly similar to the world as a whole—which is not naturally a large importer or exporter of emissions-intensive goods—is not affected directly by the presence or absence of opportunities for international trade.

Here the interests of Australia in international trade can be contrasted with those of the United States. Australia has strong comparative advantage in production and export of emissions-intensive goods, and it would benefit greatly from international trade in emissions entitlements. The United States would tend toward self-sufficiency in an open trading system. It is greatly to Australia's advantage (and not so strongly to the advantage of the United States) that the international mitigation system allows trade in emissions entitlements.

How each country comes to assess the amount of mitigation that the world should seek depends on how any global effort comes to be allocated among countries. A single country has direct control over the extent of its own mitigation effort. It has only indirect influence over the mitigation efforts of other countries. In deciding on the extent of its own effort, a single country must form and act on expectations about the efforts of other countries.

2. Cline (1992); Nordhaus (1994, 2008).
3. Stern (2007).

So the assessment of the extent of mitigation that makes sense from the perspective of a single country is at once more complex and more directly relevant to policy decisions than assessment of what makes sense for the world as a whole. It is more complex because each country's judgment about the appropriate scale of its own contribution to a global effort must embody expectations of the mitigation efforts by others. It is more important because the sovereign state is the locus of policy decisions.

With all the complexity, the international community through the UNFCCC agreed in Copenhagen on an objective of holding the human-induced increase in temperature to 2 degrees Celsius above preindustrial levels. This carries implications—that can be precise with probability distributions around the base numbers—for the capacity of the atmosphere to absorb additional greenhouse gas emissions. The agreement on the objective is one of several achievements of international cooperation so far. Immense challenges of international cooperation remain, none less than the allocation of responsibilities for emissions reduction across the members of the global community.

A system of collective action can emerge in one of three ways, in both domestic and international spheres. A system of collective action can emerge through the exercise of power by strong interests, enforced by economic sanctions or the threat or reality of violence. A system of collective action can emerge through agreement that establishes order out of an anarchic state of nature (such an agreement can extend to sanctions against breach of contract). Or a system of collective action can emerge through shared acceptance by individual citizens or states of constraints on decisions and behavior. This last system is typically established by the gradual building of norms of behavior that advance shared interests, to which individual parties conform to achieve shared goals. These norms can emerge from discussions leading to shared recognition that certain types of behavior are conducive to the advancement of shared interests. The norms are strengthened over time by observation of the conforming behavior of others and by peer pressure against nonconforming behavior.

All three systems of collective action have been important in the development of civilized domestic relations among citizens and international relations among states. All three have been important in early attempts to find a basis for effective global climate change mitigation. In 2008 I emphasised the contract.[4] That emphasis was corrected in 2011 with a nod to the gradual

---

4. Garnaut (2008).

emergence of an international system built mainly on the third of the three sources of collective action—the shared norms.[5] Mainly but not exclusively norms are being shaped by emerging implicit agreements on what constitutes reasonable efforts by individual states and by the recognition that free riding may incur costs in relations with other states, including market access.

My 2008 review discusses at length the nature of an international mitigation regime that could avoid high risks of dangerous climate change.[6] The amount of emissions over a long period of time that is consistent with avoidance of high risks of dangerous climate change would be calculated and allocated among countries according to agreed-on principles. I note in the 2008 review that convergence over time to equal per capita entitlements was likely to be the foundation principle for an agreement on the allocation of a global emissions budget.

Within such a system of contraction and convergence of greenhouse gas emissions, per capita entitlement to emit greenhouse gases would converge linearly from 2000 levels toward the low levels required for the stabilization of climate—with reductions of around 90 percent for Australia and other developed countries. I suggested that the principle be modified, to allow some additional headroom for the developing economies that were growing most rapidly. Developing countries felt and expressed concerns that "contraction and convergence" demanded too little of high-income countries, which had utilized already the greater part of the earth's capacity safely to absorb emissions. Not only had the currently developed countries exhausted much of the world's capacity to absorb greenhouse gases, but they would be allowed exceptionally high per capita emissions entitlements for a number of years yet. In response, I endorsed a suggestion by Jagdish Bhagwati that this historical legacy could be addressed by developed countries providing financing for innovation in low-emissions processes, goods, and services.[7]

It became clear at the Copenhagen meeting of the UNFCCC in late 2009 that there would be no legally binding agreement on climate change mitigation for the foreseeable future. My 2011 review update observes that effective international action on climate change mitigation was emerging without a legally enforceable agreement.[8] Developments since May 2011 confirm these observations.

5. Garnaut (2011a).
6. See Garnaut (2008, chaps. 8, 9, 10).
7. Bhagwati (2006).
8. Garnaut (2011a, chaps. 3, 4).

The Emergence of a Global Climate Change Regime

The international community's work on international cooperation on climate change began at Rio de Janeiro, two decades ago. In 1992 there seemed to be lots of time, and the problem seemed to be overwhelmingly that of excessive emissions from the developed countries. That impression guided the meeting of the UNFCCC in 1997 and the resulting Kyoto Protocol. By then there had been considerable progress in sharing perspectives within a uniquely ambitious and successful effort in international scientific cooperation, through the Intergovernmental Panel on Climate Change. Understandings were reached on which gases would be covered by efforts to reduce emissions and on how they should be measured.

An agreement was reached that all developed countries would accept constraints on emissions and that there would be penalties for breaches of commitments. There would be opportunities to reduce the costs of mitigation through joint implementation among developed countries (where countries that were falling below their emissions reduction targets would be able to buy entitlements from countries that were reducing emissions more than was required by their targets). There would be opportunities for reducing the costs of mitigation in developed countries through the Clean Development Mechanism (CDM), which would certify carbon reduction offsets generated in developing countries for sale to developed countries. Developing countries undertook to make efforts to reduce emissions; developed countries contributed funding to these efforts and also to climate change adaptation in developing countries.

The Kyoto arrangements were damaged when the United States Congress refused to ratify the agreement to which the United States government was a party. The George W. Bush government elected in 2000 announced that it would not seek ratification for the agreement. The Australian government followed the United States' lead and continued to do so until policy was reversed in 2007. But both Australia and the United States remained parties to international discussions. Progress was made on some issues in conferences of the UNFCCC in Bali (2007), Copenhagen (2009), Cancun (2010), Durban (2011), and Doha (2012), including on the global 2-degrees objective.

These early efforts in collective action on climate change contained elements of success and failure. It is important to preserve the success (the scientific cooperation, the shared objective, the agreements on how to measure and later to account for and verify emissions, the mechanisms for international trade in entitlements and for transfers of financial resources to developing countries) while correcting the failures.

Time Has Passed and Times Have Changed: Concerted Unilateral Mitigation

We no longer have time. Emissions have grown more rapidly since the turn of the century than the most widely used scenarios developed in the 1990s suggested. This is partly because China's, the former Soviet Union's, and Eastern Europe's rapid movement from central planning toward market exchange for energy and the products of heavy industry created a false impression of the pace at which the emissions intensity of economic activity could be reduced on a continuing basis in these countries. In addition—particularly in China— early twenty-first-century economic growth was stronger and more energy intensive—and energy was more emissions intensive—than had been anticipated.[9] As a consequence, there must be an early and large reduction in global emissions trajectories if likely temperature increases are to be kept to 2 degrees.

In contrast to the late twentieth century, emissions growth in the twenty-first century was overwhelmingly concentrated in developing countries. My own calculations on business-as-usual emissions suggest that, in the absence of policy action to change established trends, developing countries would account for the whole of an immense increase in global emissions from 2005 to 2030.[10] In the absence of policy action, China would account for 41 percent of global emissions in 2030 and other developing countries 70 percent. Whatever weight was given to the requirements of historical responsibility and justice—whether historical responsibility and justice were highly influential in allocating the burden of reducing emissions across countries or of only secondary importance—effective global mitigation would require major and early reductions from business-as-usual emissions in China and other developing countries.

The international community has learned slowly and painfully that a legally binding top-down agreement on allocating responsibility for reducing emissions is not within reach in the foreseeable future. This reality came within view in Copenhagen in 2009 and crystallized in Cancun in 2010. It was not possible because the major powers, first of all the United States but also China, were willing to bind themselves domestically to strong mitigation out-

9. Garnaut and others (2009).
10. Garnaut (2011a, 2011b).

comes but were not willing to enter international agreements to the same end. Would the United States Senate be more likely now to ratify a new, binding international agreement, than it was when it refused to support the Kyoto agreement (to which the Clinton-Gore government had been a party)? It was not possible also because there were no effective sanctions against breaches of commitments—as demonstrated by Canada walking away without penalty from its Kyoto Protocol pledges.

Subsequent developments raise a question about whether a legally binding, comprehensive, top-down agreement is even desirable in these early stages. In anticipation of a legally binding agreement, governments settle into a negotiating mode and seek to minimize commitments. By contrast, when considering a domestic commitment, governments are prepared to look more openly at the boundaries of the realistic and to be more ambitious in defining mitigation targets. A different approach to setting national targets began to emerge in Copenhagen, took firm shape in Cancun, and was elaborated in subsequent UNFCCC meetings in Durban and Doha.

The new approach carries some important features over from the early international discussions. Scientific cooperation remains centrally important to the collective effort. The 2-degrees objective, mechanisms for measurement and verification of emissions, and instruments for international trade in entitlements have been developed or strengthened. Ideas about mechanisms for transferring resources for mitigation and adaptation from developed to developing countries have been given substantive shape (although still little money). It must be said that additional steps need to be taken on verification of emissions: while a case can be made for developing country mitigation targets to be expressed in different ways from developed country targets (intensity rather than absolute reductions), there is no case for differentiation in measurement and verification.

The big departure from the old regime is in the setting of country targets for constraining emissions. It has been accepted that substantial developing countries will make commitments to constrain emissions, in the form of reductions in emissions intensity or business-as-usual emissions. (Intensity targets are strongly preferred to business as usual, as they are capable of objective and unambiguous calculation.) It is accepted if only by default that these and developed country commitments to absolute reductions in emissions are voluntary and represent serious domestic undertakings but are not binding under international law. The pressures to make them ambitious come from domestic politics and review and commentary from other countries—a process that is known as pledge and review. I describe the new process as concerted unilateral mitigation.

It is a feature of the Kyoto arrangements carried over into the concerted unilateral mitigation regime that each country is free to use whatever instruments it chooses in meeting its targets. It is free to acquit its commitments through the purchase of international abatement to the extent that it chooses—or not at all. It is free to introduce carbon pricing in the form of an emissions trading system or a carbon tax—or not at all. Whether or not it places a price on carbon, it can choose to regulate emissions-intensive activities and subsidize low-emissions substitutes to the extent that it chooses.

For concerted unilateral mitigation to be effective, one major gap in the international regime needs to be filled. The regime needs some framework for guiding assessments of the level of mitigation in each country that amounts to a fair share of an international effort to achieve the agreed global effort. This would need to include guidance on adjustment of targets for 2020, setting appropriate targets for 2030, and also setting long-term targets for low levels of global emissions in 2050.

It would be useful and probably necessary for heads of governments committed to strong global mitigation outcomes to appoint an independent expert group to develop such a framework for allocating the global effort among countries. Members would be appointed for their international standing in appropriate fields and would not be representing individual countries or groups of countries. The guidance would extend to indicative allocation of emissions reduction targets across countries—in the form of parameters for Nationally Appropriate Mitigation Action for developing countries. Within the context of concerted unilateral mitigation, each country would be free to accept or reject guidance provided by such a framework. The framework would become a focus of international review of each country's effort and would evolve in response to discussion and experience.

The G-20 is well placed to establish an expert group to develop this guidance for targets. The G-20 could also play an important role in the pledge and review process, building on previous G-20 mechanisms of peer reporting through expert groups. Alternatively, it could delegate the review and its interaction with the expert groups' guidance on targets to a body established by the Major Economies Forum. The aim of the G-20's building of momentum toward international agreement on targets would be to build trust across the international community that each country's decisions were being made within a context that would lead to reasonable prospects of achieving the agreed-on international objective. The specific basis for that trust would be a strong agreement on targets arrived at during the UNFCCC meeting in Paris.

The Durban conference of the UNFCCC in late 2011 agreed to launch "a process to develop a protocol, another legal instrument or an agreed outcome with legal force" to govern the international mitigation effort after 2020. The process, legal instrument, or agreed-on outcome would be settled by 2015 and come into effect in 2020. Developed and developing countries would all accept certain obligations, although the form of those obligations could vary across countries. The Durban decision is sometimes interpreted as a commitment to seek a binding, top-down agreement, although the words allow other interpretations. While there would be advantages in an internationally binding agreement if it were possible to achieve one without weakening any ambition for mitigation, the practical barriers to a good binding agreement remain as strong as they were at Copenhagen. It is important that we do not allow the search for excellent form to distract the international community from grasping immediate prospects for excellent substance.

It is understood by economists that broadly based carbon pricing achieves more carbon emissions reduction at similar cost, or similar abatement at lower cost, than large numbers of separate regulatory and fiscal interventions. Considerable emissions reductions have been achieved in recent years in many countries through regulatory and differentiated fiscal interventions. However, the cost advantages of general carbon pricing—including opportunities for international trade in emissions entitlements—become more important as mitigation targets become more ambitious. These advantages are likely to be essential to achieving the deep reductions in emissions that will be necessary to achieve the agreed-on global objective.

The longest established and best-known schemes governing domestic (the EU scheme) and international (the CDM) trade in entitlements are currently generating uneconomically low prices in domestic and international markets. These low prices raise questions about whether carbon trading will be equal to the emissions reduction task. A tightening of emissions reduction targets is necessary to restore prices that relate appropriately to the cost and value of abatement in a world that is meeting its objectives on limiting climate change.

The CDM has emerged as the most important locus for international trade in carbon units, and for a number of years the mechanism contributed substantially to incentives for investment in emissions reduction in developing countries. As analyzed in the 2012 report of an independent review panel, the CDM is experiencing chronic oversupply of abatement units. Prices have fallen to levels that barely cover transaction costs. With recent and prospective reforms, the CDM is a legitimate offset mechanism with a potentially valuable place in a global system of climate change mitigation.[11] The review panel concluded that tightening emissions reduction targets and widening access on the demand side would be necessary to correct the chronic oversupply. I would suggest as well tightening access on the abatement supply side, with only least-developed countries having unconditional access. Other developing countries would have access if they accepted domestically binding emissions constraints and were living within those constraints without double counting of abatement for which CDM credits had been awarded.

If my suggested approach to reform of the CDM were adopted by the international community, international mechanisms would need to be developed (perhaps through the established arrangements for joint implementation) to monitor double counting of emissions.

Pledges Already Made under Concerted Unilateral Mitigation

Within the framework of concerted unilateral mitigation, all substantial economies have placed before the international community pledges that would reduce emissions below business as usual. The sum of the pledges represents a marked departure from established emissions trajectories. At the same time, they are no more than a first step toward achieving the reductions in emissions that would be necessary to reach agreed-on climate change objectives.

The U.S. pledge represents a large departure from earlier perspectives. President Bush had told a meeting of representatives of large economies in 2007 that U.S. emissions would peak in 2025. The Cancun pledge was for emissions to fall from 2005 levels by 17 percent by 2020, corresponding to a 16 percent fall from 2000.

Canada pledged to match a binding commitment by the United States, a substantial undertaking unless the Canadian government had in mind bad faith—annulling the pledge by saying that the American pledge was not binding even if it were being met.

Some of the pledges contained conditional and unconditional elements, the latter being triggered if other countries take strong action. The European Union pledged to increase its emissions reductions from 20 to 30 percent (both based on 1990) in the context of strong international action.

---

11. CDM (2012).

The Chinese target was to reduce the emissions' intensity of economic output by between 40 and 45 percent between 2005 and 2020. This represented the world's largest departure from business as usual in terms of tonnes of emissions avoided. It could have had a galvanizing effect on the Copenhagen meeting. That its importance was not noticed and brought to account was a failure of diplomacy in China and other countries.

The various pledges within the context of concerted unilateral mitigation added up to a much larger departure from business as usual than the notionally binding commitments at Kyoto. However, the pledges left global emissions on trajectories that were far too high for achievement of the 2-degrees objective in the absence of much more aggressive reductions in the near future. Of course, one cannot say now what the Cancun pledges mean for the containment of global warming, because they assert nothing about what happens after 2020 and do not allow for the possibility of more ambitious goals for the period before 2020.

Encouraging Progress on Pledges

Emissions reductions generally seem to be on paths to meet or exceed the Cancun targets. They are on track to meet or exceed the pledges even in the cases of China and the United States, the world's biggest emitters of greenhouse gases, the largest and most influential economies, and the countries whose pledges represent dramatic reductions in established trajectories. The achievement of current pledges is costing less than most analysts had expected. Early and widely based progress at surprisingly low cost establishes sound foundations for a large and early increase in national mitigation ambition.

Far from reaching a peak in emissions in 2025, as President Bush foreshadowed in 2007, it now seems that U.S. emissions reached their highest level in the year in which the president was speaking—and have been declining since then. It is not a decline in economic activity that dragged emissions down: U.S. output is substantially higher than in 2007. Private American studies, by Resources for the Future and the Natural Resources Defense Council, conclude that the United States is broadly on course to meet its emissions reduction targets.[12]

The Obama government, when it came into office in the United States in 2009, was committed to acting on climate change, including legislating an

12. NRDC (2012).

emissions trading scheme (ETS). The ETS legislation was passed by the House of Representatives but failed to gain sufficient support to defeat the filibuster in the Senate. It was clear after the 2010 congressional elections that there was no early prospect of an ETS proposal becoming law. In response, the Obama government set out to use regulatory powers to achieve its goals.

Secretary of Energy Stephen Chu advised me in early 2011 that, since the government could not achieve its mitigation objectives through the most economically efficient means (an ETS), it would seek to realize them through alternative, regulatory means. This approach was forcefully endorsed by the president in his Second Inaugural Address in January 2013 and in a major address on climate change a few months later.[13]

The far-reaching U.S. regulation to control emissions is being implemented differentially, with lower requirements for states like California that are implementing emissions trading schemes. The U.S. progress in mitigation in recent years has been assisted by low natural gas prices, resulting from the combination of an expansion of shale gas reserves through application of unconventional technologies and a restriction on exports. Low natural gas prices have accelerated the decline of coal-based power generation. This contrasts with eastern Australia, where proportionately much larger increases in natural gas reserves through application of unconventional technologies has led to large increases in natural gas prices. The difference in price behavior in Australia and the United States derives from differences in trade policies: rapid expansion of Australia's export processing capacity under free trade policies is causing prices to rise to export parity levels. (I come back to the economic and environmental implications of U.S. restrictions on natural gas exports.)

In Europe slow economic growth has subdued demand for emissions-intensive goods and services, but the extent of reduction and the low price of abatement in the emissions trading scheme suggest that emissions reductions have been achieved at lower cost than had been anticipated.[14]

In Australia, too, emissions growth has been well below anticipated levels over recent years, tending around zero, despite the continuation of robust expansion of population, output, and emissions-intensive resource production for export. In the electricity sector, stagnant or declining demand—largely a response to high electricity prices—has intersected with increased renewable energy production forced by a renewable energy target to cause faster decarbonization than suggested in the earlier official forecasts. The

13. Obama (2013a, 2013b).
14. European Environment Agency (2012).

introduction of carbon pricing from July 2012 and the use of part of the associated revenue to support renewable energy innovation will extend the reduction in emissions. Emissions from electricity generation in the first year of the emissions trading scheme were 7 percent lower than in the previous year, with slowing demand growth and the renewable energy target contributing to reductions.

China's twelfth five-year plan (2011–15) embodies far-reaching measures to constrain emissions within the intensity targets that the Chinese government has communicated to the international community. In 2011 the first year of the new plan, emissions continued to grow strongly. This was deeply discouraging for the international mitigation effort. However, policies to give effect to the new plan began to bite in 2012. Together with economically driven structural change, the new policies altered the emissions trajectory in 2012 to an extent that overperformance against the pledge seems likely. New policy decisions in 2013 have extended support for low-emissions energy.

In the electricity sector, accounting for over 44 percent of China's emissions in 2010, demand growth slowed to 5.7 percent in 2012, after electricity use increased by a factor of three over the previous decade.[15] This slowing was in response to energy efficiency and structural policies as well as to a moderate easing of output growth. Energy efficiency policies and structural change are likely to keep electricity demand growth much lower than in the first decade of the twenty-first century.

There was almost no growth in Chinese thermal power generation in 2012. Output of all low-emissions ("clean" energy, in the Xinhua terminology) sources of electricity grew rapidly: hydroelectric by 20 percent, nuclear by 17 percent, and wind by 36 percent. Solar increased much more rapidly still, from a low base. While hydroelectric power generation is affected by climatic conditions (which were unfavorable in 2011 and favorable in 2012), it will fluctuate around a rising trend. Nuclear power generation is likely to continue to rapidly increase its share of power generation; wind and solar will do so at an even more rapid rate. Wind power overtook nuclear power in 2012 as the second-largest source of low-emissions power generation.

A number of Chinese policies contribute to maintaining the momentum in electricity decarbonization, which became apparent in 2012. There is still some way to go in replacing high-emissions coal generation in small, inefficient generators with ultrasupercritical plants: the International Energy

15. IEA (2012).

Agency refers to 68 gigawatts of small (less than 100 megawatts) and 138 gigawatts of medium (100–300 megawatts) coal generating capacity remaining in 2010 slated for replacement.[16] Policy is focused on substantially increasing the natural and unconventional natural gas share of thermal power generation from the current low base.

China is investing more heavily than any other country in technological development for carbon capture and storage from fossil fuel combustion. Major investment in high-voltage, long-distance, transmission and in storage is leading to more complete utilization of intermittent renewable energy generation capacity and to expanding options for new investment in renewables. The twelfth five-year plan 2011–15 greatly increases financial commitments to energy efficiency and to innovation in low-emissions technologies, including in the electricity sector, and these were increased again when a macroeconomic stimulus package in August 2013 focused mainly on energy efficiency and low-emissions energy.

Coal combustion is the main source of Chinese emissions. Limiting coal use is a major and increasing focus of Chinese policy. Emissions from coal use for thermal energy may have reached close to a peak in 2011, after a long period of growth in double digits. This takes us way outside the conventional wisdom on development of the Chinese energy market—and from the projections on Chinese emissions in the absence of policy change.[17]

The strengthening of policies and actions to change the trajectory of China's greenhouse gas emissions extend beyond electricity to all major sectors. Industrial emissions, which are largest in steel production, are experiencing much slower growth as a result of not only a policy-enhanced slowing in the rate of growth of heavy industry but also innovation to reduce emissions intensity. The forced closure of inefficient plants (32 million tonnes of steel capacity alongside 8,000 gigawatts of coal electricity generation in 2011 alone), higher costs of electricity and other inputs, export taxes, and restriction of investment in new capacity have slowed expansion in energy-intensive and emissions-intensive activities.[18] These measures were supplemented by decisions late in 2013 to force the closure of about 60 million additional tonnes of steel-making capacity in Hebei Province (adjacent to Beijing), principally for domestic environmental reasons.

16. IEA (2012).
17. Garnaut (2008).
18. NDRC (2012).

In transport, the heavy investment over the past decade in intercity and intracity rail will ease somewhat the growth of automobile traffic. Within the automotive sector, ambitious official targets for electrification are being strongly supported by a range of policies.[19] These objectives were reinforced in December 2013 with the announcement of both large consumer subsidies for purchase of electric vehicles and large domestic producer subsidies. The rapid expansion of public transport, led by rail, automotive electrification, and the decarbonization of the electricity sector are likely to add up to unexpectedly early peaking of emissions from the transport sector.

In Japan targets for emissions reductions in Tokyo have been achieved much more rapidly than anticipated within the city's emissions trading scheme. Japan had been making good progress toward its emissions reductions targets before the nuclear disaster in Fukushima; the targets are now being reassessed. Reducing the emissions intensity of Japanese economic activity is proving to be less costly and disruptive than had been anticipated by expert observers, despite the low starting points.

The Natural Gas Transformation

The new technologies for producing gas from shale and coal seams have had their largest effects so far in Australia and the United States, but they have wider application and seem set to significantly change global energy markets for at least some time. Larger natural gas supplies have enhanced energy security as well as lowering energy costs. They have therefore contributed positively to economic development. They have also contributed modestly to short-term reductions in greenhouse gas emissions, principally by replacing coal by gas-based electricity generation in the United States.

U.S. trade restrictions have led to vastly different prices for natural gas across the world. In the absence of massive liberalization of U.S. exports and corresponding increases in U.S. domestic natural gas prices, by the time current investments in Australian export capacity are in full operation, Australian domestic gas prices are likely to be two or more times current U.S. prices. East Asian prices, embodying liquefaction and international transport costs, will be higher again.

The artificial price differentials resulting from U.S. trade restrictions have the usual effects of protection on economic welfare. U.S. gas-using industries

19. NDRC (2012).

receive massive subsidies in the form of gas prices at well below international levels, and the most gas-intensive American manufacturing industries are rapidly increasing global market share. Investment in manufacturing industries that use natural gas is moving to the United States and away from Australia and other sources of natural gas. This is good for the subsidized producers, but it lowers economic welfare in the United States as a whole and in the rest of the world. Inevitably, high protection in one country (and the effective protection to U.S. petrochemical production is very high) leads to pressures for countervailing subsidies in other countries (in this case, pressures for export restrictions in Australia).

The U.S. trade restrictions are sometimes supported on the grounds that they are accelerating reductions in greenhouse gas emissions. They are certainly having this effect in the United States. But by elevating natural gas prices in East Asia—and in Australia and other countries that are supplying gas to East Asia—they are inhibiting reductions in emissions outside the United States. It would be more environmentally, as well as economically, efficient to have global free trade in natural gas, with each country making choices about optimal paths to reducing emissions on the basis of free trade prices.

Price differentials based on trade restriction as large as those separating the United States natural gas market from international realities will come under competitive as well as political pressure. There will be leakage through Canada and perhaps Mexico, which will have opportunities to develop their own gas liquefaction and export industries based directly or indirectly on U.S. reserves. Artificially low prices will inhibit investment in natural gas production.

In the absence of explicit international agreement, the corrosion of trade restrictions will take many years and may remain incomplete. Much better environmental and economic outcomes would follow from all countries allowing free trade from an early date. East Asian prices would still be above U.S. and Australian prices but would be lower than with American restrictions on exports. The various Western Pacific suppliers of natural gas to East Asia would have broadly comparable domestic prices, a good deal lower than at present. The cost of reducing emissions would be lower for the world as a whole, and U.S. economic welfare would be higher.

It is perhaps a step too far to think that the G-20 could apply pressure on its strongest member to adopt free trade policies on natural gas, when the protection that export restriction provides for domestic users has such strong and widespread support. For some free traders, hope springs eternal.

Promoting Technological Innovation and Augmenting the Free Trade Agenda

Reducing emissions involves firms and households shifting to less emissions-intensive production processes and to consuming less emissions-intensive goods and services. For most of the period of modern economic development, combustion of fossil fuels has been the lowest-cost, large-scale, source of energy for transport, household lighting, warming and cooling, and industrial processes. There has been immense investment in research and development to reduce costs and expand supply—much of it provided or subsidized by the public sector—leading to large reductions in costs over a long period of time.

Beyond some point, the need to draw upon less accessible and lower-quality coal, oil, and gas began to raise the cost of fossil energy, and opportunities for cost reductions from technological innovation diminished. Rising costs of fossil energy from the 1970s increased incentives for research and development into lower-cost alternative sources of energy. Nuclear tended to be favored as a focus for public subsidy because an important input into military capacity was a joint product.

Industries producing and using fossil energy are old, applying mature technologies with limited capacities for lowering costs through technological breakthroughs. The youth and small production scale of the alternative forms of energy have left them with much larger opportunities for reducing the costs of production of intermediate and final products through technological innovation and also through learning by doing and scale economies.

The main forms of low-emissions energy seem likely to be unaffected by resource depletion and, therefore, are less likely to be subject to rising costs over time. The rising costs of fossil energy over time, and the falling costs of alternatives, could be expected gradually to increase the share of the alternatives in the total energy mix without any deliberate policy interventions. But it is in the nature of innovation that we do not know in advance of research, development, and large-scale deployment of new technologies how costly they will turn out to be—or the time at which major reductions in costs will be achieved.

Private firms are bound to underinvest in research, development, and commercialization of new technologies, because a high proportion of the benefits of innovation cannot be captured by the investor. In the current circumstances of climate change mitigation, where achievement of internationally agreed-on objectives requires rapid structural change, there is a strong case for a public subsidy for innovation in low-emissions technologies. The presence of innovation spillovers across international borders also establishes a case for ensuring that many countries contribute to support for innovation. It is best that research, development, and commercialization occur in countries with comparative advantage in particular aspects of the work. These are most likely to be supported in countries with a strong national interest in particular innovations.

It happens that most developed countries are in fact contributing to the research, development, and commercialization of low-emissions technologies. So are some developing countries, led by China in energy and Brazil in biological sequestration. China is making immense contributions to the commercialization of new technologies with a large public subsidy, driven by perceptions of the opportunity to capture first-mover advantages as a supplier of capital goods. Massive reductions in costs of solar, wind, and nuclear power in recent years, especially in China, have been driven more by larger-scale production than by invention of new technologies. In some developed countries, protection of established domestic firms producing capital goods for solar energy production has slowed diffusion of low-cost means of reducing emissions.

Several years ago I suggested the establishment of an international low-emissions technology commitment, wherein each country would pledge to do its fair share in the global effort to provide public resources for research, development, and commercialization of low-emissions technologies.[20] It now seems that voluntary domestic commitments would be able to manage the free rider problem. Most countries are finding their own reasons for providing fiscal support for innovation in low-emissions technologies. There is therefore only a weak case for G-20 intervention to increase investment in the commercialization of low-emissions technologies. It would, however, be productive for the G-20 to establish a process for reporting on national efforts so as to show each country that others are making substantial contributions to the generation of international spillovers from investment in innovation in low-emissions technologies. The G-20 could also usefully draw attention to the opportunities for choice of infrastructure investments—likely to be the subject of other recommendations from the 2014 summit—to reduce the costs of the commercialization of new low-emissions technologies.

The G-20 could also play an important part in expanding the understanding of the new global climate change mitigation regime built around con-

20. Garnaut (2008).

certed unilateral mitigation. It could usefully affirm its commitment to phase out subsidies for fossil fuel production and use and to the inclusion of hydrofluorocarbon gases in the Montreal Protocol. It would be useful for the G-20 to establish a process for reporting on public support for research, development, and commercialization of new low-emissions technologies, with a view to giving each member confidence that others were making reasonable contributions to activities with large international spillovers.

There is one other important role for the G-20: increasing pressure for free trade in goods and services that are important inputs into activities that reduce greenhouse emissions, including such raw materials as uranium and natural gas, as well as in biofuel alternatives to fossil fuels and capital goods for generation of renewable energy. This would fit with the G-20's established interest in securing open trade on a global basis. There have been considerable discussion and some action within the Asia Pacific Economic Cooperation, the World Trade Organization, and the Trans-Pacific Partnership of the importance of free trade in goods and services that are important to the global mitigation effort. The 2014 heads of government meeting of the G-20 could focus attention on the environmental as well as the economic advantages of establishing free trade in goods and services that are important inputs, adding momentum to discussions in other forums.

Conclusion: A Chance for Global Success

It is common for commentaries to focus on the failures of international cooperation on climate change. This chapter draws attention to some successes that could become the launching pad of a strong international effort to achieve the agreed-on objective of holding temperature increases to 2 degrees Celsius.

The chapter notes that the major economies, including China, the United States, and the European Union (despite the German response to the setback to nuclear energy at Fukushima), are making unexpectedly rapid progress toward realizing their pledges to the international community. It notes the potential importance of international trade in emissions entitlements in reducing the costs of mitigation for the world as a whole. It also notes some weak points in the current international collective effort on mitigation, including some associated with low prices for carbon units in the European Union emissions trading system and in the Clean Development Mechanism. The low prices themselves reflect the unexpectedly low cost of reducing emissions as well as the

inadequacy of current emissions reduction targets in relation to the requirements of the 2-degrees objective.

The remedy for prices that are well below the cost and value of optimal
abatement is the same as the remedy for a global mitigation effort that currently falls well short of the requirements of the 2-degrees objective: an early
tightening of targets. The recent progress toward announced targets on emissions reductions in many countries, and the revelation that costs of reducing
emissions have been unexpectedly low, together provide the foundations for
an early tightening of announced targets. An international climate change
system built around concerted unilateral mitigation provides a favorable context for a renewed international effort to achieve the agreed-on objective of the
international community.

Now is the right time for the G-20 to become the center of a strong international effort. Australia's hosting of the 2014 G-20 heads of government
meeting seems at first sight to create an obstacle to the development of the
G-20 agenda along these lines. But the climate change issue is important
enough to the economic and political life of the international community, the
prospects and costs of failure of international collective action large enough,
and the possibility of successful intervention high enough to make the increase
in momentum in global climate change negotiations an important opportunity for the Australian G-20 summit.

References

Bhagwati, Jagdish. 2006. "A Global Warming Fund Could Succeed Where Kyoto
    Failed." *Financial Times*, August 16.
CDM (Clean Development Mechanism). 2012. *Climate Change, Carbon Markets
    and the CDM: A Call to Action.* Report of the High-Level Panel on the CDM Pol-
    icy Dialogue. Bonn.
Cline, W. R. 1992. *The Economics of Global Warming.* Washington: Institute of Inter-
    national Economics.
European Environment Agency. 2012. "Greenhouse Gas Emissions, Trends, and Pro-
    jections in Europe 2012: Tracking Progress towards Kyoto and 2020 Targets."
    Report 6/2012. Copenhagen.
Garnaut, R. 2008. *Garnaut Climate Change Review.* Cambridge University Press,
    Melbourne.
————. 2011a. *The Garnaut Climate Change Review 2011: Australia in the Global
    Response to Climate Change.* Cambridge University Press, Melbourne.
————. 2011b. "Global Emissions Trends." Update Paper 3. In *Garnaut Climate
    Change Review.* Paper presented to Australian Agricultural and Resource Eco-

nomic Society Annual Conference, Melbourne (www.garnautreview.org.au/update-2011/update-papers/up3-global-emissions-trends.pdf).

Garnaut, R., F. Jotzo, S. Howes, and P. Sheehan. 2009. "The Implications of Rapid Development for Emissions and Climate Change Mitigation." In *The Economics and Policy of Climate Change,* edited by D. Helm and C. Hepburn. Oxford University Press.

Hunt, G. 2013. "The Coalition's Direct Action Plan on Environment and Climate Change: Incentives for Action." Speech to the Australian National University Crawford School of Public Policy, April 18 (www.greghunt.com.au/Media/Speeches/tabid/87/articleType/ArticleView/articleId/2520/Speech-to-the-ANU-Direct-Action-Plan-on-Environment-and-Climate-Change.aspx).

IEA (International Energy Agency). 2012. "Policy Options for Low-Carbon Power Generation in China" (www.iea.org/publications/insights/name,32266,en.html).

NDRC (National Development and Reform Commission). 2012. *China's Policies and Actions for Addressing Climate Change.* Beijing (http://qhs.ndrc.gov.cn/zcfg/W020121122588539459161.pdf).

Nordhaus, W. 1994. *Managing the Global Commons: The Economics of Climate Change.* MIT Press.

———. 2008. *A Question of Balance: Weighing the Options on Global Warming Policies.* Yale University Press.

NRDC (Natural Resources Defense Council). 2012. "Closer than You Think: Latest U.S. CO_2 Pollution Data and Forecasts Show Target within Reach." New York (www.nrdc.org/globalwarming/closer-than-you-think-ib.asp).

Obama, B. 2013a. *Inaugural Address by President Barack Obama.* United States Capitol. January 21, 2013 (www.whitehouse.gov/the-press-office/2013/01/21/inaugural-address-president-barack-obama).

———. 2013b. *Remarks by the President on Climate Change.* Georgetown University, June 25, 2013 (www.whitehouse.gov/the-press-office/2013/06/25/remarks-president-climate-change)

Stern, N. 2007. *The Economics of Climate Change.* Cambridge University Press.

HUANG YIPING

12

The Chinese Economy and the Future of the G-20

When President Bush invited leaders of some industrial and developing countries to the first G-20 summit in November 2008 in Washington, many saw it as a historic opportunity for China to play a role in international economic policymaking compatible with its economic weight. Some even perceived the G-20 summit as a turning point in the international economic order. The global financial crisis revealed that the old system, established at the end of World War II by the United States and its allies, no longer worked effectively. Major developing countries like China should naturally be a part of the shaping of the new international economic system. Such expectation grew higher in the following years, as China overtook Japan to become the world's second-largest economy and contributed regularly between one-third and one-half of global GDP growth. Some experts even proposed a G-2 mechanism for China and the United States to jointly manage international economic affairs.[1]

China has made some important contributions to the reform of the international economic system, through the G-20 and other processes. For instance, the People's Bank of China governor Zhou Xiaochuan published an article in early 2009 arguing for the case of reform of the international monetary system relying on a sovereign currency.[2] Zhou's argument triggered a series of policy discussions and led to several proposals of supranational currencies, including strengthening the special drawing rights of the International Monetary Fund (IMF). Also, collaborating with other G-20 members,

1. Bergsten and others (2008); Zoellick and Lin (2009).
2. Zhou (2009).

China was able to push for some important changes in the funding composition and governance structure of such international organizations as the IMF and the World Bank.

Overall, however, China's performance at the G-20 has not been very effective, especially compared with expectations. First of all, China is not proactive in proposing new agendas for the G-20 dialogues. Most of the time it accepts the agendas put forward by the industrial countries. Second, at times different departments of the Chinese government fail to form a uniform position on international economic policy issues. One such example is the discussion of the proposed 4 percent limit for external account imbalances at the Seoul summit; while the People's Bank of China appeared to be in favor of the idea, other departments opposed it. And finally, China does not form working alliances within the G-20, although many expect China to be a leader of the developing world. In fact, on many occasions China shares no more common interests with developing countries than with developed nations.

The underperformance of China in the G-20 process so far may be explained by its lack of experience in international policymaking. Despite the fact that for centuries, until the industrial revolution, China was the largest economy in the world, it never had to make international economic policies due to its limited interactions with other countries. And during the reform years Chinese leaders kept a low profile in international affairs, a principle set by Deng Xiaoping, in order to focus on domestic economic development. Improving growth sustainability has been a key challenge for China, which kept Chinese policymakers busy, at least during the past decade. Naturally, it will take some time for Chinese leaders to learn how to be active at international dialogue tables.

Equally important, China's interests are quite dynamic and complicated. It is impossible for China to form an alliance with a fixed group of countries. For instance, China shares more similar positions with France than with the United Kingdom on issues of an international currency regime, and it shares more common views with Japan and Germany than with India and United States on external account imbalances. Differences in political systems further complicate the roles that China may be able to play in international affairs. For instance, China is already the largest export market and a very important investment partner for most of the other Asian Pacific G-20 members, such as Australia, India, Indonesia, Japan, and Korea. Politically, however, many of these countries are close allies of the United States.

However, the bottom line is that the current system cannot continue for very long. If the Chinese economy maintains relatively rapid growth, then it will likely become a high-income country and the world's largest economy by around 2020. Keeping a low profile will no longer be a viable option for China. Likewise, it will be unlikely that the G-20 will succeed without the active and constructive participation of China. According to estimates by the Organization for Economic Cooperation and Development (OECD), by 2030 developing countries are set to account for nearly 60 percent of world GDP.[3] So the case for transforming the international economic system to reflect the conditions and demands of developing and emerging market economies should be strengthened even further. This, again, calls for China to play a more prominent role in the G-20 and other international mechanisms.

But two challenges for China are also apparent. One is to make domestic economic growth sustainable; the other is to play a more constructive role in international institution building. The Chinese economy has been growing rapidly for the past thirty-five years. But it also faces important imbalance, inequality, and inefficiency problems, which seriously dampen its growth outlook. For the past decade the government has been trying to transform the growth model without much success, although rapid economic growth continued. Therefore, China's first challenge is, in other words, to introduce new reform measures to facilitate the transition of the Chinese economy to a more sustainable growth model. The second challenge is to be an effective player in international organizations despite differences and complications.

These are the two main issues that I explore in this chapter. My findings can be summarized as follows. First, if the comprehensive reform program approved by the Third Plenum is rigorously implemented, the Chinese economy will evolve into a new growth model. This would trigger sea changes in the Chinese economy, leading to slower growth, higher inflation, accelerated industrial upgrading, and more volatile economic cycles, among others. If the process is smooth, we should see by around 2020 a market economy, a high-income country, the world's largest economy, and the most vibrant consumer market. These changes would also transform the way the Chinese economy interacts with the rest of the world.

Second, China likely will play a prominent and constructive role in shaping the G-20 and the international economic system. Both Chinese and American leaders agreed to develop a new model of great-power relations, despite economic and political differences. The purposes of such an initiative are for

3. OECD (2010).

their mutual benefit and also for the avoidance of major conflict. The Chinese government's attempts to also construct a new regime of economic opening would set new standards of globalization. This is clearly evidenced by the new Shanghai free trade zone, the China-U.S. Bilateral Investment Treaty, and many other liberalization initiatives. And China may also exert itself more creatively to facilitate more effective institution building within the G-20.

Efforts to Transform China's Remarkable but Unsustainable Growth Model

To a large extent, China's future role in international affairs, including within the G-20 process, depends critically on its ability to continue rapid economic growth. Assessment of China's economic outlook is often mixed, given its imbalance, inequality, and inefficiency problems. The government made some efforts during the past decade or so to improve its growth model, without much success. However, the reform initiatives approved by the Third Plenum of the Eighteenth Party Congress, which are sometimes summarized by the term *likonomics*, may pave the way for more sustainable growth.[4] This, at the same time, could also change the way the Chinese economy interacts with the rest of the world.

   Chinese economic experience during the reform period is sometimes described as the China puzzle, which refers to a unique phenomenon whereby growth acceleration makes optimists more upbeat but makes pessimists more depressed about the future of the Chinese economy.[5] On the one hand, China's extraordinary economic success during its reform period is sometimes described as the China miracle.[6] The reform policies transformed the country from a closed, poor agrarian society into an open, dynamic, global economic power within three decades. GDP growth averaged 10 percent and GDP per capita increased from US$220 in 1980 to US$6,000 in 2012. China is already the second-largest economy in the world and is a dominant player in global manufacturing, commodity, and sovereign bond markets.

   On the other hand, growing structural risks lead some to believe that the collapse of the Chinese economy is inevitable.[7] Even some senior leaders argue

---

4. Huang (2013).
5. Huang (2010b).
6. Lin, Cai, and Li (1995).
7. Chang (2001).

that the Chinese growth model is "uncoordinated, imbalanced, inefficient and unsustainable."[8] For instance, the investment share of GDP rose from 25 percent at the beginning of the reform period to close to 50 percent after the global financial crisis. Such a situation is unsustainable because, mathematically, this share cannot go up to 100 percent. In the meantime, export share of GDP also surged, current account surplus expanded, consumption share of GDP dropped, and income inequality worsened.

The fundamental reason behind the China puzzle is its asymmetric market liberalization approach during the reform period.[9] Free markets for products ensure that production decisions are based on demand and supply conditions in the economy and that resources are allocated efficiently. Distortions in factor markets are a way of providing incentives for economic entities and, sometimes, overcoming market failures. One good example is China's foreign direct investment policy. In the early years of economic reform, the Chinese government designed a range of preferential policies to attract such investment, including tax holidays, free use of land, subsidized credit, and cheap inputs like energy and water. Government support for foreign direct investment projects also reduced problems related to an undeveloped legal system for property rights protection. In typical economic textbooks, such policies are described as policy distortions. But they have been successful. By 2010 cumulative inflows of foreign direct investment into China reached US$1.5 trillion. But China provided such "subsidies" to not only foreign investors but also domestic investors during the past decades by broadly depressing factor costs.

Factor market distortions include the household registration system limiting labor mobility between rural and urban areas, direct controls of bank deposit and lending rates, the setting of energy prices (especially oil prices) by state agencies, and discounting the land use fee for investors. In most cases, these distortions depress input costs. However, labor is a special case, as it is unclear if labor market segmentation lowers or increases labor cost. Labor cost was low for a long time because of abundant agricultural labor or unlimited labor supply in a typical Lewis dual economy. But cheap energy, cheap capital, and cheap land were important in driving development of manufacturing activities.

Low input costs contribute to the China miracle and the China puzzle. They are subsidies to companies but taxes on households. They boost profits from production, increase returns to investment, and improve the interna-

8. Wen (2006).
9. Huang and Wang (2010).

tional competitiveness of Chinese exports. Low input costs also serve as a special mechanism to redistribute income from households to companies. Over the years, corporate profits grew much faster than household income, as household income was largely capped by a stagnant wage rate.

These high corporate profits bring structural problems. One, they lead to a continuous rise in shares of exports and investment in GDP. Two, they increase the national saving rate, as the corporate saving rate is generally higher than the household saving rate. Three, they bring on income inequality, as low-income households rely on wage income, while high-income households rely on corporate profits and investment returns. Four, they cause a decline in the consumption share of GDP, as household income grows more slowly than GDP. And, five, the unusually low costs of energy, capital, and other resources behind the high profits probably result in waste.

Realizing the risks of the growth model, Premier Wen Jiabao, shortly after taking office in early 2003, vowed to shift the focus of economic growth from quantity to quality and to rebalance external and internal sectors. Unfortunately, that effort did not pay off. In retrospect, there are probably two reasons for this outcome. One, the government has at least three macroeconomic policy objectives: supporting growth, controlling inflation, and adjusting the structure. If there is a conflict among the three, officials would be most likely to sacrifice the last one, because growth and inflation could directly affect economic and political stability and might affect senior officials' chances of promotion. And, two, the government mainly used administrative measures to adjust economic structure. Without changes in incentive structures, economic agents would unlikely change their behavior.

The Third Plenum of the Eighteenth Party Congress unveiled a comprehensive reform program, covering reform measures in sixty areas. These include the financial system, fiscal policy, state-owned enterprises, the land system, factor prices, household registration, the one-child policy, and the external economic regime. The breadth and depth of the new reform initiatives surprised most observers. The program exhibits three key features: top-level authority, full market system, and equity and justice overruling efficiency and development.

Top-level authority, symbolized by the establishment of the Central Leading Group for Comprehensively Deepening Reforms, headed by the general secretary of the party and the president of the state, represents a partial departure from the current bottom-up approach. There are two rationales behind it. One, while many of the past reforms, such as adoption of household farming, were based on grassroots experiences, the bottom-up approach is no longer practical for some of the reforms, such as capital account liberalization. Future reforms have to rely more on top-level design. And, two, top-level authority is necessary for overcoming strong resistance to reforms by vested interest groups. The new reforms need to deal with not only traditional interest groups associated with the old planning system but also the new interest groups formed during the reform period.

Perhaps the most important sentence in the entire policy document is the following: "Wherever market mechanism works in allocating resources, the government should not intervene." Economic reforms during the past thirty-five years were incomplete, due to its gradualist, dual-track approach. In a way, the reform program approved by the Third Plenum may be viewed as the last kick to complete the Chinese economy's transition to the market system. It will reduce state intervention in the corporate sector, in the financial system, and in factor markets.

Changing Interactions between the Chinese and Global Economies

Even if only a portion of the planned measures is rigorously implemented, China should be a market economy, a high-income country, and the world's largest economy by around 2020. Between now and then, lots of changes will take place, which might affect us all. The central transformation is the so-called transition of the Chinese economy from economic miracle to normal development.[10] In fact, changes to the growth model have already started to occur, moderating growth and rebalancing structure. In other words, the Chinese economy is entering into a period of normal development.[11] Unfortunately this has not been widely acknowledged.

GDP growth started to decelerate in 2011, partly due to the authorities' tightening policies. Toward the end of the first quarter in 2012, however, it became clear that growth might soon fall below 8 percent. Beginning in March of that year, the government undertook a number of steps to stabilize economic growth, including support of infrastructure projects in water, power, and transportation. Despite this policy effort, GDP growth decelerated continuously from 8.1 percent during the first quarter to 7.4 percent during the third quarter. In retrospect, two special factors probably contributed to this

10. Huang, Chang, and Yang (2013).
11. Huang and others (2013).

continuous slowdown. One, export growth fell from close to 8 percent during the first half of the year to around 2 percent during July and August. And two, the housing purchase restriction introduced in April 2011 led to a slowing of residential property investment growth to below 10 percent during the third quarter of 2012 (from above 30 percent a year earlier).

The policymakers, however, stayed relatively calm and appeared to be willing to tolerate somewhat slower growth for three reasons.[12] First, many government officials were reluctant to adopt aggressive measures supporting growth after implementation of the 4-trillion-yuan stimulus package during the global financial crisis. Many economists argued that it increased fiscal risks, created nonperforming loans, contributed to overcapacity in some infrastructure areas, and caused inflation and asset bubbles. Second, various studies estimate China's growth potential to be around 6–8 percent.[13] While there are some differences among these estimates, they agree that the days of 10 percent GDP growth are over for China. Third, economic indicators such as employment also suggested no need for aggressive policy easing, despite deceleration of GDP growth to below 8 percent. The working-age population rose by 8 million in 1998 but declined by 3.5 million in 2012.

So-called normal development, however, is more about growth slowdown. The economy also shows clear signs of rebalancing in recent years. For instance, the current account surplus narrowed from 10.8 percent of GDP in 2007 to 2.8 percent in 2011 and 2.6 percent in 2012. Mainly because of this, many Chinese economists and monetary policymakers argued that the yuan exchange rate was near equilibrium. In recent years, a two-way movement of the exchange rate and a two-directional capital flow actually started to emerge in China. Although some economists expect a rebound in China's external imbalances when the global economy recovers more dramatically, the rebalancing that took place in China's external sector during the past years was quite impressive.

Another rebalancing in recent years relates to income distribution. In mid-January 2013, the National Bureau of Statistics reported estimates of Gini coefficients for 2003–12, which show a steady deterioration of income distribution from 0.479 in 2003 to 0.491 in 2008 and steady improvement after that, to 0.474 in 2012. This, if confirmed, could mark another important turning point in China's economic development, although many Chinese economists are still skeptical about the results.

---

12. Huang (2012).
13. World Bank and Development Research Center (2012); Cai and Lu (2012); Zhuang, Vandenberg, and Huang (2012).

Finally, official data also suggest that the contribution of consumption to GDP growth increased from about 33 percent in 2007 to 52 percent in 2012. Recent research finds that the consumption share of GDP began to rise after 2008, although this is not yet fully reflected in official statistics.[14] Another study reached a similar conclusion applying a different approach.[15] The official data also confirm that the consumption share of GDP stopped declining and picked up slightly in 2011 and 2012.

The transition to normal development is primarily attributable to changes in factor markets. As was pointed out before, low production costs are primarily responsible for the unique performance of the Chinese economy during the reform period, including strong economic growth and growing structural risks.[16] For the same reason, reversal of such a cost structure should help reduce structural imbalances. One of the most important changes occurring during the past years was the so-called Lewis turning point, at which the labor market turns from surplus to shortage. This change is clearly evidenced by accelerating wage increases in recent years. According to our field surveys, the monthly wage was about 1,200 yuan in 2003 in the areas around Shanghai. It rose to nearly 4,000 yuan in 2013.

Rising wages cut into production profits, investment returns, and export competitiveness. This is why activities slowed as a result of recent wage increases. Meanwhile, rising wages reduced the external account surplus but raised the consumption share of GDP, since the growth of household income outpaced that of national income. And income distribution also improved, given that low-income households rely more on wage income, while high-income households rely more on investment returns.

Clearly, rebalancing is still at an early stage. For instance, the consumption share of GDP, at 52 percent in 2010 according to our estimates, was significantly below the 70–80 percent range in most developing and developed economies. This gap may be narrowed through continuous wage adjustment. Expected interest rate liberalization, which will likely lead at least to high deposit rates, should further facilitate rebalancing. Further changes may also be required to transform the development pattern more completely. This could involve measures to improve income equality beyond the primary round of income distribution: the development of social welfare systems such

14. Huang, Chang, and Yang (2012, 2013).
15. Li and Xu (2012).
16. Huang (2010a).

as pension, medical insurance, and education reform and the liberalization of financial and capital accounts.

The comprehensive reform package approved by the Third Plenum will push the Chinese economy into a market system. The most important reform is financial liberalization: introduction of market-based interest rates, increases in the flexibility of the exchange rate, improvement in the governance of state-owned financial institutions, and freeing cross-border capital flows. Financial reform is critical for the sustainability of Chinese growth, because finance is the engine of a modern economy. More important, distortions in the financial sector are by far the most severe policy distortions in the Chinese economy.

The transition from economic miracle to normal development will likely be accompanied by some important changes. First, GDP growth likely will moderate further, as the economy's gap with the world technological frontier narrows and the labor force declines. Second, inflation pressure should escalate, as input costs experience a steady and continuous increase. Third, income distribution may improve further, due to not only wage growth and interest rate liberalization but also more proactive government policies trying to address inequality issues. Fourth, economic structure could become more balanced, with rising consumption share offsetting declines in shares of both exports and investment in GDP. Fifth, industrial upgrading should accelerate, as rapidly growing costs change industrial competitiveness. And, finally, economic cycles could become a lot more volatile, being a natural feature of a market economy.

These changes in the Chinese economy should also affect its interaction with the rest of the world. While China's contribution to global GDP growth likely will continue to increase, external recession triggered by significant downturns of the Chinese economy could become increasingly likely. If China used to be a contributor of global disinflation, it may become a new source of inflation going forward. Rapid industrial upgrading in China may regularly force new international divisions of labor, creating new job opportunities for low-cost countries but adding new competition pressures on higher-tech countries. China may also shift from the world's largest manufacturing center and commodity importer to the most vibrant consumer market.

Toward a Global Economic Institution Builder

As the world's second-largest economy, largest manufacturing producer, and largest commodity importer, China no longer has the option of keeping a low profile. Any adjustment in the Chinese economy affects the world market significantly. It is said that whatever China buys, it becomes expensive, and whatever China sells, it becomes cheap. In the meantime, there should be a stronger incentive for China to influence international economic rules. During the past decades, China benefited immensely from the globalization process of the international economy, supported by the United States. This was a very important factor in China's extraordinary growth.

What China wants now will have important implications for the future of the international economic regime, given that it is on the way to overtaking the United States to become the world's largest economy in the coming decade. Some experts predict a possible departure from globalization should China dominate the policymaking process, given the evident massive state intervention in economic activities in China today. Others even warn of a major conflict between China and the United States.

While such concerns are reasonable, they are unlikely. The simple fact is that not only has China been a main beneficiary of globalization for the past decade, but also it has the greatest stake in free trade and investment. For this reason, former and current Chinese leaders repeatedly call for collective international efforts to build a harmonious world, what I interpret as a one-system, multi-pillar, world. China may demand far greater influence as its economic weight increases, but it has no intention of challenging the existing system, let alone a separate system. In essence, all China will demand is that the international economic system better reflect the conditions in all countries, not just the established industrial economies. In fact, with the planned comprehensive reforms, the Chinese regime should converge even more with the majority of the international community in areas such as a free market and policy transparency.

Chinese and American leaders agreed to develop a new model of great-power relations. The Chinese interpretation of that is mutual respect and mutual benefit, while the American interpretation is avoiding a major conflict between an emerging superpower and an existing superpower. True, it is very difficult to completely avoid competition and tension during such a transition. But if the two superpowers are able to work together, such as through the annual U.S.-China Strategic and Economic Dialogue, then chances are greater for the transition to be smooth, which should be good news for both parties and the rest of the world.

The comprehensive reform program approved by the Third Plenum can be viewed as China's effort to converge with the international system. This is particularly evidenced by the policy goal of finally establishing a full market economy by 2020. The so-called new opening regime contains four important policy pillars: promoting inward and outward opening of the economy, realizing free and orderly flows of production factors, deepening internal and external market integration, and pushing domestic reforms through further opening to the external world.

An important step in constructing the new regime is to quickly establish a Shanghai free trade zone. According to the plan, this free trade zone will experiment with foreign entry into finance, culture, education, health care, child care, elderly care, architecture, accounting, auditing, logistics, and e-commerce. The idea is that this free trade zone will experiment with these reforms, which will then be extended to the rest of the country.

Some analysts suggest that the Shanghai free trade zone is like the Shenzhen special economic zone, which was established in the early 1980s. I think, however, that the Shanghai free trade zone is a part of a broad liberalization, which is similar to changes brought about by the World Trade Organization (WTO) accession at the end of 2001. The Shanghai free trade zone is closely linked to the China-U.S. Bilateral Investment Treaty. In fact, the free trade zone readily accepted the two terms that China agreed to in the Bilateral Investment Treaty: preentry national treatment and a negative list. At the same time, the free trade zone is also related to the negotiations of the Regional Comprehensive Economic Partnership and, potentially, those of the Trans-Pacific Partnership.

I see two clear motivations for China to move aggressively on the new opening regime. One motivation would arise from a scenario in which the direct economic benefits of WTO accession decline over time and the economy needed new stimulus. In this sense, the main purpose of both WTO accession and the new open regime is to promote domestic reform. WTO accession focused on the liberalization of the manufacturing industry. The new opening regime focuses more on the liberalization of the service sector. Another motivation is China's desire to contribute to the making of new globalization standards. Many experts believe that, through both the Trans-Pacific Partnership and the Transatlantic Trade and Investment Partnership, the United States and other developed nations can set new standards for globalization. Unfortunately, China is not a member of the Trans-Pacific Partnership, so any liberalization that comes about through a Shanghai free trade zone or other programs will be evidence of China's determination and ability to take liberalization to a new level.

With all these strategies and initiatives, we can expect a more proactive role for China in international economic policymaking, including at the G-20.

However, in the years to come, China likely will play a role of supporting and strengthening, instead of dominating, the G-20 process. In other words, the decisionmaking process will continue to be led by the United States and other industrial nations. But the Chinese voice will become louder.

Policymakers in Beijing are actively debating China's G-20 strategy. Their conclusions are not yet clear. But here are the four key areas that observers should monitor. First, China will probably participate in international organizations and international decisionmaking on a broader scale. These could include engagement in not only the G-20 but also the BRICS and many other international and regional mechanisms.[17] And the Chinese government may offer more staff and funds to support these operations. There were also proposals for China to join the OECD and to regularize the G-4 central bank coordination mechanism. Second, China may adopt a more flexible approach in forming alliances. But this requires that China clearly identify its core interests. The leaders should avoid dividing according to politics (socialism versus capitalism), region (Asia versus others), or economic development (developing versus developed). For instance, on the issue of global imbalance, China could cooperate with Japan and Germany. On the issue of development, China could cooperate with India and South Africa. On the issue of international currency, China could cooperate with France and Brazil. And on the issue of food trade, China could cooperate with South Korea and Japan.

Third, I expect the Chinese leader to propose a new agenda for the G-20 dialogue. This may include establishing new vehicles and mechanisms for infrastructure investment, reforming the funding and governance of international organizations, addressing issues of the sustainability of sovereign debt in developed and developing countries, further opening the global trading and investment system, addressing international energy and food security, and coordinating international monetary policy.

And, fourth, China likely will work on domestic coordination on important international economic issues. This will probably take time, as it requires a lot of analyzing and deliberating. China could benefit from encouraging the formation of more think tanks, which could offer independent policy analysis and policy advice. More independent analyses could assist the government to arrive at informed policy positions.

---

17. BRICS is an association of the following emerging economies: Brazil, Russia, India, China, and South Africa.

Conclusions

With the rise of China and other developing countries and the recent global financial crisis, it is time to reform the international economic order. As the second-largest economy in the world, China should play an active role in this process. The G-20 offers a mechanism for such change. However, China's performance so far has been less than encouraging. This is partly because of lack of experience and partly because of the domestic economic challenges.

The recently concluded Third Plenum of the Eighteenth Party Congress approved a comprehensive package of reform measures. These could transform China into a market economy, a high-income country, and the largest economy in the world. They will also bring about important changes in the Chinese economy, including slower growth, higher inflation, a more balanced economic structure, accelerated industrial upgrading, and more volatile economic cycles. In the meantime, they should also alter the way the Chinese economy interacts with the rest of the world.

The Chinese government already adopted proactive strategies for further opening the economy, working harmoniously with the United States, and playing a more effective role in the G-20. The G-20 and other international institutions can help ensure that China continues on the path of reform and growth. China's active participation is also critical for the G-20 and other international institutions to evolve, to reflect the changing conditions of the world.

References

Bergsten, C. Fred, Charles Freeman, Nicholas Lardy, and Derek J. Mitchell. 2008. *China's Rise: Challenges and Opportunities*. Washington: Peterson Institute for International Economics.

Cai Fang and Lu Yang. 2013. "Population Change and Resulting Slowdown in Potential GDP Growth in China." *China and World Economy* 21, no. 2: 1–14.

Chang, Gordon G. 2001. *The Coming Collapse of China*. New York: Random House.

Huang Yiping. 2010a. "Renminbi Policy and the Global Reserve System." In *The Future Global Reserve System: An Asian Perspective*, edited by Jeffrey D. Sachs, Masahiro Kawai, Jong Wha Lee, and Wing Thye Woo. Manila: Asian Development Bank.

———. 2010b. "Dissecting the China Puzzle: Asymmetric Liberalization and Cost Distortion." *Asia Economic Policy Review* 5, no. 2: 281–95.

———. 2012. "The 'New Normal' of Chinese Growth." *East Asia Forum*, October 14.

———. 2013. "What to Expect from Likonomics." *China Daily*, July 5.

Huang Yiping, Cai Fang, Xue Peng, and Qin Gou. 2013. "The New Normal of Chinese Development." In *China: A New Model for Growth and Development*, edited by Ross Garnaut, Cai Fang, and Ligang Song. ANU E-Press.

Huang Yiping, Jian Chang, and Lingxiu Yang. 2012. "China: Beyond the Miracle—Great Wave of Consumption Upgrading." *Barclays Report* (January). Hong Kong.

———. 2013. "China: Beyond the Miracle." *Barclays Report* (March). Hong Kong.

Huang Yiping and Kunyu Tao. 2010. "Factor Market Distortion and the Current Account Surplus in China." *Asian Economic Papers* 9, no. 3: 1–36.

Huang Yiping and Xun Wang. 2010. "Effectiveness of Capital Account Controls in China" [in Chinese]. *Financial Development Review*, no. 8: 23–35.

Li, David, and Sean Xu. 2012. "The Rebalancing of the Chinese Economy." Paper prepared for the CCER-NBER conference on the Chinese economy. Peking University, June 25–26.

Lin, Justin Yifu, Cai Fang, and Li Zhou. 1995. *The China Miracle: Development Strategy and Economic Reform.* Chinese University of Hong Kong Press.

OECD (Organization for Economic Cooperation and Development). 2010. *Perspective on Global Development 2010.* Paris.

Wen Jiabao. 2006. "Government Work Report." National People's Congress, March 5.

World Bank and Development Research Center. 2012. *China: 2030.* Washington.

Zhou, Xiaochuan. 2009. "Thinking on the Reform of International Currency System." Beijing: People's Bank of China.

Zhuang, Juzhong, Paul Vandenberg, and Yiping Huang. 2012. "Growing Beyond the Low-Cost Advantage: Can the People's Republic of China Avoid the Middle-Income Trap?" Asian Development Bank and Peking University.

Zoellick, Robert B., and Justin Yifu Lin. 2009. "Recovery Rides on the 'G-2.'" *Washington Post*, March 6.

ANDREW ELEK, MAHENDRA SIREGAR, AND
MARIA MONICA WIHARDJA

13

Global Infrastructure Opportunities for the G-20 and Regional Organizations in the Asia Pacific Region

W orld leaders can use the G-20 to help all economies reach their potential for sustainable development and to deal with threats to the global economy. Unfortunately, five years after its excellent start, the forum's effectiveness is already in doubt. The G-20 agenda for cooperation has become very broad, but huge threats to the prospects for inclusive and sustainable development are not receiving adequate attention.

The G-20 needs find a way to restore the momentum of global economic growth after the damage of the 2008 global financial crisis. Until there is confidence in a robust recovery, it will be difficult to devote adequate attention to other serious systemic problems, such as global warming. The capacity to deal with complex global challenges will depend on effective leadership within the G-20. A transition in the role of Asian countries at the G-20—from cautious and sometimes defensive to visionary and exemplary—was expected to unfold slowly, possibly taking a decade or more. But the continuing threats to economic recovery, due to the self-created problems of the United States and the eurozone, have created an urgent demand for Asian leadership.

ASEAN and APEC, both of which are well-established institutions for economic cooperation, are setting some examples for wider global economic cooperation and integration. ASEAN is committed to creating an ASEAN economic community, which will soon be the most integrated group of economies other than the EU. Unlike the EU, which maintains trade barriers against the rest of the world, Southeast Asian economies are reducing obstacles to commerce with all economies as well as among themselves. That is consistent with the principle of open regionalism, pioneered successfully by

APEC. Both APEC and ASEAN are integrating their economies by means of cooperative arrangements—for example, by strengthening regional transport, communications, and institutional links. These arrangements are open clubs: any other economies can join as soon as they perceive the benefits of doing so.

The prospective gains from improving physical, institutional, and people-to-people connectivity now outweigh, massively, the potential gains from marginal liberalization of remaining traditional border barriers to trade and investment. The people who are creating and expanding international production networks are, therefore, advising governments to shift attention beyond "free trade" to focus on better connectivity and on regulatory convergence, neither of which can be achieved by trade negotiations alone.

ASEAN's integration responds to these realities and priorities. Members are cooperating to increase and improve available skills and institutional capacity, the lack of which creates barriers to deep integration. With support from multilateral development banks (MDBs), Southeast Asian governments are investing in the economic infrastructure needed to create transport, communications, and energy networks. The emerging Regional Comprehensive Economic Partnership (RCEP) is likely to broaden this effort within Asia. A determined effort, including deepening and integrating Asian financial markets, is beginning to attract more international investment in productive economic infrastructure.

Within a few years, it should be possible to mobilize resources to close a significant part of the huge infrastructure gaps in the Asia Pacific economies, which account for more than half of global GDP. That investment in infrastructure will inject a new source of sustainable effective demand into the global economy, which is currently operating well below full capacity.

Many constraints will need to be addressed to attract and accelerate investment, especially investment in infrastructure from private savings. But problems related to labor force skills, institutional and administrative capacity, and financial intermediation can all be overcome gradually. International cooperation facilitates a process of learning together to solve problems, and the most effective method to find ways past constraints is to learn from experience.

China's decision to establish the Asian Infrastructure Investment Bank provides a valuable new opportunity for governments to launch significant infrastructure initiatives, including large, strategic investments to improve transport and communications links among Asian economies. The G-20 can follow this example by coordinating an even wider multilateral effort to fix the massive financial market failure that allows huge gaps in infrastructure to coexist with a comparably massive accumulation of savings and underused global economic capacity. It will take time, but it should be possible to restore the effective demand and confidence needed for robust worldwide recovery from the global financial crisis.

The Global Infrastructure Opportunity

The quick response of G-20 leaders to the global financial crisis prevented a potentially serious global depression. In 2009, all of them agreed to avoid a retreat into systematic protectionism and to stimulate demand in their economies. However, since the immediate threat of a global depression passed, the G-20 has not been able to coordinate macroeconomic policies to deal with the imbalances that contributed to the crisis or to revive confidence in a full recovery. The G-20 did agree on its Framework for Strong, Sustainable, and Balanced Growth (FSSBG). Unfortunately, excessive concern about long-term debt led too many G-20 governments to apply their fiscal brakes just as they adopted this new framework, within which they promised each other not to do so.

Searching for Recovery

The governments of the eurozone do not have a coherent strategy for eliminating the causes of uncertainty about the future of the euro, let alone for restoring confidence about sustained growth. The United States has stumbled from one self-imposed fiscal crisis to the next. The uncertainty generated by these policy mistakes has kept global production well below capacity and, despite extremely low interest rates, the private sector is reluctant to invest. At a time of excessive ex ante savings and deficient global demand, substantial private savings are looking for better returns.[1] The savings generated by emerging economies, including China, are locked up in excessive foreign exchange reserves, which are raising the risk of significant capital losses and the opportunity cost of forgone opportunities to improve productivity.

Five years after the crisis, it is becoming unsustainable to counter the perversely contractionary fiscal policy of some G-20 members by monetary stimulus. There is a pressing need for a concerted stimulus to the global economy, and G-20 coordination would be the best way to make that happen.[2] There is vast unmet demand for productive economic infrastructure, especially in the emerging economies of Asia. OECD estimated that global infrastructure

1. Grenville (2013).
2. Drysdale and Willis (2013).

requirements over the next two decades will be around US$50 trillion.[3] The Asian Development Bank (ADB) estimates that developing Asian economies need to invest US$8 trillion from 2010 to 2020 just to keep pace with expected infrastructure needs.[4] According to the American Society of Civil Engineers, the United States should spend US$3.6 trillion by 2020 on infrastructure, with US$2.2 trillion needed simply to maintain the existing quality of infrastructure. In all cases, much of this investment is needed to rehabilitate, maintain, or to extend transport networks.[5]

The supply of savings is more than adequate to begin to meet some of the demand for infrastructure. The very low cost of investment makes this an excellent time to address a large global financial market failure by redirecting some of these savings to fund some of the vast unmet need for productive economic infrastructure, especially in the emerging economies of Asia. Doing so can create a large and potentially rapidly growing source of effective demand that does not require unsustainable borrowing.

The case for accelerating investment in economic infrastructure began to attract attention after the premature end to a coordinated effort to stimulate the global economy that weakened recovery from the global financial crisis. There is an excellent opportunity for investment in infrastructure in the United States at a time when, due to underutilization of resources, the multiplier effect of additional expenditure could be expected to be above unity and the economic returns from rehabilitating some of the nation's rapidly deteriorating economic infrastructure would exceed the very low costs of any new borrowing for that purpose.

However, the United States is allowing its infrastructure to deteriorate, partly because of ideological opposition to any additional government spending by the U.S. Congress and partly because of the fear that some of the benefits of a large stimulus by any one economy would flow to others. In welcome contrast, China has sustained its efforts to meet the need for infrastructure, helping to sustain its own and global economic activity. However, Chinese investment alone should not be expected to revive the global economy. In a highly integrated world, it would be far more efficient for economies to launch a coordinated multilateral stimulus to reboot global recovery. A coordinated initiative to deal with the shortage of economic infrastructure in most G-20 economies would avoid the risks of "Keynesianism in one economy." Such an

3. OECD (2011).
4. Bhattacharyay (2010).
5. American Society of Civil Engineers (2013).

initiative could be consistent with maintaining international economic balance and need not lead to an increase in either private or government long-term debt.

The case for a significant multilateral stimulus, led by the G-20 and designed to mobilize private sector investment in productive infrastructure, was set out by Elek and Drysdale.[6] Lin and Dömeland also accepted the widespread perception that most governments have limited room for new net borrowing and proposed a way for them to support demand and employment without adding further to debt levels in the medium term.[7] Both Lin and Dömeland and Drysdale and Willis explain that investment in potentially self-financing investment can generate a virtuous cycle of higher demand, productivity, and growth consistent with long-term deleveraging without crowding out other potential investment.[8]

Boosting investment in economic infrastructure would not only ease constraints to growth in developing economies, but would also create new demand in developed economies suffering from high unemployment and excess capacity. In a world of international production networks and low border barriers to most of the products passing along international supply chains, coordinated investment in transport and communications infrastructure is also the most efficient way to reduce the costs of international commerce among economies.[9]

Overcoming Constraints

It will not be easy to steer more savings toward meeting the huge demand for infrastructure, in Asia or elsewhere. Typically the investments needed are for public goods, which require large-scale, long-term, and illiquid investment and present challenging cost-recovery problems. To turn opportunities for macrolevel stimulus into specific project funding requires sound governance, competent project appraisals, and effective intermediation between funders and spenders.[10]

PROJECT SELECTION AND PREPARATION. The cost of transforming a wish list into a pipeline of bankable project proposals backed by professional feasibility studies amounts to a very small proportion of the total investment needed to fill infrastructure gaps. Expertise, including from the MDBs, is

6. Elek (2011); Drysdale (2011).
7. Lin and Dömeland (2012).
8. Lin and Dömeland (2012); Drysdale and Willis (2013).
9. World Economic Forum (2013).
10. Grenville (2013).

available to assess the potential economic rate of return on the necessary investments and to set out an orderly sequence for implementing them. It should be possible to persuade more governments to allocate adequate resources to project preparation.

IMPLEMENTATION RISKS. No matter how well prepared, some projects will not deliver their potential returns. Some risks (such as changes in pricing or regulations and demand shortfalls) can be built into high-quality feasibility studies, but almost all projects will come up against unexpected physical, regulatory, and administrative problems, ranging from land acquisition to corruption. And most will encounter unanticipated difficulties in operating and maintaining new assets. This is an insurance issue. Some governments have already set up ways to insure investors against problems caused by changes in or the inability to implement relevant government policies or regulations.[11] Other risks can be estimated from extensive recent experience and then pooled.

FROM ECONOMIC TO FINANCIAL RETURNS. McKinsey Global Institute and many other studies have identified many opportunities for investment in economic infrastructure with high potential economic rates of return, especially investments to rehabilitate or upgrade existing assets.[12] However, policy weaknesses in many economies may prevent the true economic rates of return from being reflected in expected financial returns. All economies have some distortions in product and factor markets. It is not easy to estimate the benefit of particular investments, especially in public goods, to particular groups. Political pressure can make it hard to recover any of the costs of investment from those who benefit and governments may not be willing to subsidize either capital or recurrent costs.

WHO WILL PAY? The majority of the estimated US$0.8 to 0.9 trillion a year that is currently invested in infrastructure by developing countries is financed from domestic government budgets. Of that investment, 20 to 30 percent is financed by the private sector and less than 10 percent from official development assistance or MDB sources.[13] A significant acceleration of investment will need a greater share of direct or indirect financing from private sources. The capacity to design public-private partnerships (PPPs) for investment in economic infrastructure is improving, drawing on international experience with many recent investments. Some governments are cre-

11. For example, the Indonesia Infrastructure Guarantee Fund (www.iigf.co.id).
12. McKinsey Global Institute (2013).
13. Grenville (2013).

ating and strengthening the institutional capacity for forming PPPs and, as part of the APEC process, working toward more consistent sets of policies for drawing in private investment in infrastructure.

The many well-established MDBs and the new Asian Infrastructure Investment Bank can make a significant contribution to lending, on a commercial basis, to economic infrastructure projects with acceptable rates of return. If the MDBs adjust their governance to reflect recent changes in the world economy, they can expect to enlarge their capacity for lending significantly. They also can do a lot more to leverage private sector investment by innovative cofinancing, pooling risks and underwriting.[14]

Whatever progress is made in terms of attracting finance from development banks or from private sources, governments will need to finance a significant share of the investment in infrastructure.[15] Public investment may be limited by the same excessive concern about budget deficits and official debt that has already weakened the prospects of recovery from the global financial crisis. Clarifying whether government borrowing is being used for consumption or for investment in projects that can be expected to generate revenue (directly or indirectly) to service new debt can help governments make sound assessments of the capacity for net public sector borrowing.[16]

INTERMEDIATION CHALLENGES. To raise the volume of investment in economic infrastructure to a level sufficient to provide a significant boost to global economic demand will require expanded and new forms of financial intermediation. Fortunately, it is neither necessary nor desirable to wait for optimal forms of financing or sweeping reforms of domestic and international financial markets before taking some initiatives for investment in some well-prepared infrastructure projects. Many governments, especially in East Asia, have large accumulated savings or the capacity to borrow to finance some infrastructure (or both). Existing and new development banks can support investment in economic infrastructure directly or help governments leverage financing from the world's huge pool of savings. In the short term, finance is not the binding constraint to beginning to fill some of the huge gaps in infrastructure.

LEARNING BY DOING. All of the constraints to accelerating investment in infrastructure are formidable, but all of them are soluble. Governments

---

14. G-20 (2011).

15. As explained in Streeter (2011), not all investments in public goods are suited to public-private partnerships; governments will need to make some contributions to any PPPs.

16. Grenville (2013).

committed to raising living standards and willing to listen to and work with the business sector can overcome them, at least for some investments, and learn from the experience gained to ease the constraints facing subsequent investments. Evidence of successful private sector investment in projects will increase the incentives for finding innovative forms of financial intermediation. Research on the nature of financial markets will help, but new modes of intermediation will not be discovered by studies alone—there is no theoretical solution for overcoming any of the many constraints to additional long-term investment. The pragmatic approach to accelerating investment is to launch economic infrastructure initiatives, then to build on the practical experience thus acquired to improve access to long-term finance for infrastructure.

Individual governments will have to implement the policy decisions and institutional upgrading needed to create an enabling and attractive environment by easing the constraints on accelerating private sector investment in infrastructure. Consulting and sharing relevant experiences and expertise in the G-20 process can help them do so and promote progressive convergence in policies, especially where they facilitate efficient investment in and operation of infrastructure to connect economies.[17] Cooperation will be essential to seize the opportunity to scale up worldwide investment in economic infrastructure. No single economy can be expected to undertake the investment in infrastructure needed to deliver a large positive shock to effective demand and to instill the confidence needed to ensure a robust recovery of the currently underperforming global economy. The G-20 has the potential to coordinate and accelerate investment in infrastructure on the required scale.

The G-20 Agenda for Financing Infrastructure

Initially, the G-20 focused on infrastructure only as it related to projects on the group's development agenda. The 2011 report by the High-Level Panel on Infrastructure made some useful recommendations for improving the investment environment and presented some innovative ideas for attracting financing, including the potentially catalytic contribution of development banks.[18] The MDBs helped the panel to draw up an action plan for investment in economic infrastructure in low-income countries, with an emphasis on connecting economies. G-20 leaders then undertook to sponsor eleven pilot

17. Drysdale and Simandjuntak (2013).
18. G-20 (2011).

investment projects in low-income countries, selected on the basis of agreed, sound criteria.

Spotting the Global Opportunity

In 2011, Indonesia suggested that the G-20's efforts to promote infrastructure should be "mainstreamed" rather than restricted to low-income countries. Issues of institutional capacity, innovative financing, and risk management need attention everywhere, especially in emerging economies, which have the widest gaps in their economic infrastructure. In 2011, Indonesia initiated a G-20 discussion of the opportunity to boost investment in economic infrastructure, explaining its potential contribution to economic recovery. It also pointed out the need for extensive policy development to attract private as well as public investment, to narrow infrastructure gaps, and to make more productive use of global savings.

Mainstreaming infrastructure investment will also strengthen the legitimacy of the G-20. The current G-20 development agenda is no more than a new, small, "foreign aid" program. Restoring the momentum of the global economy by injecting new demand will deliver far greater benefits to low-income economies than any marginal improvements in the current, mostly poorly designed suite of foreign aid activities managed by the Development Working Group. The potential benefits of that program are greatly outweighed by the cost of the policy failures of the G-20 governments, which led to the global financial crisis and the subsequent weak recovery.[19] Indonesia's recommendation to include global infrastructure in the FSSBG swiftly gained a critical mass of support, including from other Asian economies, and has become part of the G-20's core agenda.

In 2012, G-20 leaders called for work to ensure the availability of adequate funding for infrastructure. G-20 finance ministers have set up a new working group on financing for investment, which is working closely with relevant international organizations. Their research will examine infrastructure investments (successes and failures) in developing economies by the private sector, including institutional investors who have accumulated global assets of US$85 trillion. Very few of those investments have been made in infrastructure, but multilateral development banks and other financial institutions could steer a growing proportion in that direction consistent with the G-20/OECD High-Level Principles of Long-Term Investment Financing by Institutional Investors.[20]

19. Elek (2013).
20. G-20/OECD (2013).

At the 2013 G-20 summit, leaders endorsed and welcomed work by MDBs to mobilize and catalyze additional financing for infrastructure investment and called for research on ways to improve PPP arrangements.[21] As host of the G-20 process, Australia has made investment in infrastructure one of the top priorities for 2014.[22]

From Hope to Action?

Although cooperative policy development to steer more savings toward productive investment in economic infrastructure is welcome, it is not enough to bring about a measurable increase in the volume of infrastructure investment. It will never be possible to remove all constraints on all investments in all places. In reality, all infrastructure projects will come up against unexpected problems. However, a strong political commitment to a few carefully selected initiatives can overcome, at least in those cases, the constraints discussed above as well as the unexpected problems inevitably encountered during construction. Having examples of how difficulties can be resolved should then create the confidence needed to launch more initiatives to rehabilitate currently deteriorating assets and to close well-known gaps in global economic infrastructure.

The World Bank and the Asian Development Bank Institute have assessed the potential benefits of two significant projects to improve transport and communications links among Asian economies. One of them is a coordinated program to improve the efficiency of Asia Pacific ports and airports. Because Asia Pacific governments already are eager to improve their trade logistics, the investments needed to enhance the efficiency of ports and airports will eventually be made. Discussion, sharing of information and experience, and cooperation among economies interested in making improvements can result in investments that happen sooner and at less cost than investments by individual economies. International cooperation can also enhance the efficiency of investments to upgrade existing assets by encouraging the use of interoperable software for processing the movement of products.

A coordinated upgrading of ports and airports would lead to significant economic gains. In 2003 the World Bank estimated that the region would gain US$280 billion a year if the performance of all major ports in the Asia Pacific could be raised to half of the highest level of performance already achieved in the region.[23] The potential gain would be even greater if the effi-

21. Grenville (2013).
22. Australian Government (2013).
23. Wilson, Mann, and Otsuki (2003).

ciency of airports and currently minor shipping ports also could be raised to half of the efficiency of facilities using current best practices.

A second opportunity for internationally coordinated investment has been created by Myanmar's recent decision to engage with the international economy. That decision presents an opportunity to construct a set of very large transport and communications projects designed to cope with high levels of road and rail traffic and to limit operation and maintenance costs. High-quality links would dramatically reduce the costs of trade and investment among three major groups of Asian economies: those in Southeast Asia, Northeast Asia, and South Asia. The potential benefits have been set out in recent reports by the Asian Development Bank Institute and by the Center for Strategic and International Studies.[24] The scale of the initiatives should be sufficient to generate a welcome boost to effective demand in the economy during their construction phase and to contribute significantly to regional productivity when implemented. Sound policies for cost recovery and risk sharing can draw in private sector investment and encourage PPPs to finance more worthwhile investments in economic infrastructure, enhancing the confidence needed for sustained recovery from the global financial crisis.

The G-20 can support productive investments in such economic infrastructure projects without becoming an implementing agency. There is a precedent for G-20 commitment to investment in economic infrastructure. In 2011, G-20 leaders decided to support eleven pilot projects in low-income countries—most of which were designed to improve their connectivity with other economies and to help them engage in international production networks—mostly indirectly by approving support to the projects from the MDBs. Until now, the G-20 leaders have not paid adequate attention to these rather small initiatives.[25] They are somewhat more likely to take an interest in big ideas that can make a significant contribution to economic integration through investment in better connectivity.

Representatives of G-20 governments on the boards of the MDBs can steer them to take advantage of opportunities for making internationally coordinated investments, starting with professional feasibility studies and financing plans that include policies for cost recovery and sharing of political and implementation risks. Some of the construction costs can be financed by lending to the governments directly involved or to G-20 governments that can expect to obtain significant indirect benefits from improved economic infrastructure.

24. ADBI (2013); CSIS (2013).
25. Davies (2013).

The commitment of governments and policies to generating adequate cash flows should prove sufficient to mobilize private sector investment. Once financing is obtained, development banks can manage the awarding of contracts for project preparation, construction, and operation on behalf of the governments committed to implementing the projects.

A challenge for the G-20 in 2014 is to begin to overcome the reluctance of some G-20 governments to commit the substantial public resources needed to fund their share of any infrastructure, either directly or through international financial institutions. Eurozone governments have essentially outlawed significant new borrowing for any purpose, and ideological issues currently prevent the United States from maintaining, let alone extending, its economic infrastructure.

That reluctance can be corrected over time. Economic theory to explain the potential of a multilateral stimulus to demand for productive investment will build on the work of Lin and Dömeland.[26] The need for a new source of economically sustainable large injections of demand will become increasingly evident, especially if further policy mistakes tip the world into a new financial crisis. In the meantime, Asia can set positive examples of international economic cooperation that lead to a significant upgrading of infrastructure and promote mutually beneficial economic integration of Asian economies.

East Asian Investment in Economic Infrastructure

A 2009 ADBI study details the additional serious shortfall in transport, communications, and energy infrastructure to connect Asian economies. Much of the world's currently excess ex ante savings, which could finance infrastructure investment needs, are being generated in Asia. Due to weaknesses in domestic and regional financial markets in Asia, most of these savings are currently intermediated through London and New York and end up fueling the deficits of advanced economies.[27] Asian governments are becoming increasingly aware of the opportunity cost of financing the growing debts of the rest of the world at negligible rates of return, the risk of accumulating potential capital losses, and the new risk of temporary disruption of debt service payments. Regional organizations, including ASEAN, RCEP, and

26. Lin and Dömeland (2012).
27. Drysdale and Willis (2013). In 2007 the ratio of debt to equity in China's foreign assets was 8.2, India's was 2.6, and Indonesia's was 3.4. The ratio was 0.7 for Australia and 0.9 for New Zealand. See Lane (2012).

APEC, provide vehicles for international cooperation that can enhance the prospects of using more of the region's savings to raise productivity by improving economic infrastructure.

Learning from others can help governments to decide which projects are suitable for PPPs and to maximize the potential contribution from the private sector by sharing the experience of setting financial parameters for these partnerships. Consultations among governments can also help them reach agreement on the contributions from individual governments to projects that connect pairs or groups of economies.

Cooperation can ensure that investments fit into a sound long-term plan for improving connectivity among as well as within economies. Coordinated plans for different forms of transport—road, rail, air, or sea—can lead to efficient interfaces among transport facilities drawn from the state-of-the-art, multimodal ports in some Asian economies, including Korea and Singapore. A coherent set of investments to upgrade or extend infrastructure to connect economies can attract greater interest and potentially better terms for financing, including by widening the scope for pooling the risks of individual investments.

Important cooperative initiatives to improve the depth, breadth, and integration of Asia's financial markets include the ASEAN Infrastructure Fund (AIF), launched in 2012, and the 2013 decision by China to set up the Asian Investment Infrastructure Bank (AIIB). Those initiatives, complemented by policy development work by the G-20, OECD, and MDBs, can be expected to improve the potential for governments, development banks, and institutional investors to invest in filling the gaps in global infrastructure, much of which are in Asia. ASEAN and APEC already are seeking to take advantage of such opportunities and set examples for others in Asia and elsewhere.

The ASEAN Economic Community

Four decades after its creation, ASEAN has become a flexible and durable institution promoting closer cooperation in Southeast Asia. Member countries have expanded the scope of cooperation patiently and carefully, recognizing that nurturing mutual trust and commitment to narrowing development gaps is the most important requirement for building a sense of community and gradually deepening cooperation. Most of ASEAN's cooperative arrangements follow consultations to identify opportunities that are perceived to be mutually beneficial—for example, projects to improve transport and communications links in Southeast Asia. Once such opportunities are identified, there is little need for or reliance on formal, enforceable integration agreements.

The coverage of the ASEAN Free Trade Area (AFTA), launched in 1992, has become quite comprehensive, but it has not had a significant effect on the share of total ASEAN trade accounted for by intra-ASEAN trade, the ease of movement of factors of production, or the ease of doing ASEAN-wide business.[28] This experience is similar to that of Europe, where comprehensive trade liberalization failed to achieve much economic integration and pointed to the need for the European Single Market.[29] In 2003, ASEAN leaders signed the Bali Concord II, creating the ASEAN Economic Community (AEC), with a target date of 2015.

The AEC Blueprint, adopted in 2007, sets out a broad program of economic integration to create a single market and production base and calls for agreements to remove policy obstacles to the free flow of goods, services, investment, and skilled labor and to the freer flow of capital, starting with the 2010 upgrading of AFTA to phase out all tariffs by 2015. This ambition matches the "four freedoms" vision of the EU, which have yet to be fully achieved. Indeed, the AEC aims to do more by investing in the infrastructure and systems needed to take full advantage of liberalization, based on the Master Plan for ASEAN Connectivity (MPAC).

IMPLEMENTING THE ASEAN ECONOMIC COMMUNITY. The AEC is being implemented in an innovative and flexible way. Some agreed policy norms are needed to create efficient transport, communications, and energy networks, but there is no intention to create a massive set of rules to bind the behavior of ASEAN governments. Individual governments are expected to implement the institutional and, where necessary, legal reforms in their economies to realize shared objectives, meeting their AEC commitments in ways that suit their circumstances and capacities.

Luddy provides an insight into the nature of cooperation needed for some dimensions on connectivity—for example, to develop the ASEAN Single Window for customs clearance.[30] Through an iterative process of learning together, members are adapting existing legal frameworks to allow the effective use of information and communications technology to facilitate cross-border electronic exchanges. Officials, drawing on private sector expertise, are helping each government to draft and enforce legislative changes. Because it is in the self-interest of each government to make the systems work successfully, there is no need to rely heavily on any ASEAN-wide authority to enforce compliance.

---

28. Intra-ASEAN trade accounts for close to 25 percent of total ASEAN trade, and the trans-shipment of products through Singapore accounts for a significant part of that share.

29. Checchini (1988).

30. Luddy (2012).

Several negotiations are under way to conclude agreements on services, investments, and mutual recognition of standards and qualifications. These negotiations are taking place in parallel so that problems encountered in one of them do not hold up progress in others. ASEAN is not insisting on negotiating a complex single undertaking on all dimensions of economic integration. Even more important, cooperation to deepen integration does not have to wait for the conclusion of potentially drawn-out trade negotiations.

ASSESSING PROGRESS. According to the AEC Council, ASEAN had realized 67.9 percent of the AEC Blueprint by 2012, including policies for movement of goods across ASEAN countries and the development of the ASEAN Single Window for customs clearance. An independent mid-term review of progress to 2012 by the Economic Research Institute for ASEAN and East Asia (ERIA) also points to significant progress toward all of the targets set for 2015.[31] Some significant components of the AEC, especially for physical connectivity, will not be completed by 2015. Experience confirms that the binding constraints on mutually beneficial cooperation (for example, to improve trade logistics) are limited labor force skills and institutional capacity. Those limits can be eased by time and resources, but they cannot be overcome by negotiations.

Not meeting the very ambitious 2015 target for completing the AEC should not be cause for excessive concern. With the continued commitment of all governments and support from the private sector, many important objectives of the AEC vision will be reached by 2015. By then, ASEAN will be the most integrated group of economies in the world apart from the EU. The substantial progress that has been made already is setting positive examples for accelerating economic integration among the wider group of APEC economies. ASEAN governments, with support from ERIA and others, already are turning their attention to expanding the scope of the AEC beyond 2015, including by taking steps to extend networks and cooperative arrangements to ASEAN's neighbors.

East Asia and the RCEP

The ASEAN Framework for Regional Comprehensive Economic Partnership, endorsed by the heads of ASEAN governments in November 2011, sets out principles for engaging AFTA partners and other external economic partners to establish comprehensive economic partnership agreements. Those principles include transparency, open accession, and consistency with World Trade

31. ERIA (2012).

Organization rules of any agreements on trade and investment and other dimensions of economic integration.[32]

The RCEP could evolve to become a regional economic community, centered on ASEAN, that resembles the AEC. In addition to a negotiated regional trading arrangement, the RCEP could implement a broad-ranging blueprint for harmonizing economic regulations, enhancing connectivity, and improving many other dimensions of economic integration. The RCEP process has begun with an attempt to negotiate a very large regional free trade area by 2015, modeled on the potential Trans-Pacific Partnership, which is being pursued by the United States. The intended coverage is similar: trade in goods and services, investment, intellectual property, competition, dispute settlement, and other issues. Both seek to create trading blocs that include economies accounting for a very significant share of global output and trade—one that currently excludes the United States and another designed in a way that is not likely to accommodate China.

A more positive view of the RCEP negotiations is to see them as a means to rationalize the many trade agreements that already link some or all members of ASEAN to other participants in the RCEP process. Negotiating a single undertaking on a region-wide trade deal will take time, since the fine print of existing agreements reflects the intention to shelter some domestic producers from international competition. Whatever marginal trade liberalization and new rules are eventually agreed, much more will remain to be done.

Rather than waiting for a possible agreement on shallow integration, the governments involved in the RCEP can launch a work program for regulatory convergence and better connectivity with far greater potential all-round economic benefits. That work can begin with drawing up a blueprint for an RCEP-wide economic community whose scope is comparable to that of the AEC.

The APEC Process

During the first twenty-five years of APEC, Asia Pacific governments focused on trade policy. Since 1994 a consistent commitment to the Bogor goal of achieving free and open trade and investment by 2020 has led to significant liberalization of trade and investment.[33] The Asia Pacific region's opening to international trade and investment has been faster and more comprehensive than that in any other region. Average tariffs have fallen from 17 percent to just

32. The current participants in the RCEP are the ten members of ASEAN, Australia, India, and New Zealand.

33. APEC (2010).

over 5 percent. The remaining border barriers are concentrated in a few sensitive sectors, especially agricultural commodities and low-technology manufactures. Most of the products flowing along modern supply chains face negligible or no traditional border barriers to trade. APEC's consistent work to facilitate trade by attention to problems of trade logistics and behind-the-border obstacles is already saving billions of dollars a year and setting examples for the rest of the world.

Open regionalism has maximized the benefits of reducing obstacles to global as well as regional commerce. Without any intergovernment agreement to divert economic activity from the rest of the world, the extent of trade and investment integration among APEC economies compares favorably with that achieved by the European Union and NAFTA.[34] With the region much closer to free and open trade and investment, APEC governments are able to give more attention to the wider objectives that they adopted in Bogor. Along with reducing obstacles to trade and investment, those objectives include

—finding cooperative solutions to global economic challenges

—supporting an open multilateral trading system

—ensuring that all people share the benefits of economic growth, including through access to training and education

—linking Asia Pacific economies through advances in telecommunications and transportation

—using resources sustainably.[35]

Looking ahead, the most serious threats to the future of regional economies are global problems, which require global solutions. Asia Pacific governments need to take the lead in the G-20—most urgently to achieve a robust recovery from the 2008 global financial crisis. Doing so does not require neglecting regional economic integration, but it does call for new priorities and methods to respond to the dramatic changes in the nature of international transactions since the Bogor goals were set, especially the evolution of global production networks.

The most substantial obstacles to deepening economic integration are no longer traditional border barriers but behind-the-border regulatory problems, inadequate transport and telecommunications, limited institutional capacity, shallow capital and bond markets, and weak financial integration. APEC's new focus on improving connectivity among Asia Pacific economies is, therefore,

34. Armstrong and Drysdale (2011).
35. These points are paraphrased from the 1994 Bogor Declaration of APEC leaders, paragraph 2. See APEC (1994).

welcome. Implementing a long-term plan for investment in better connectivity is now the most effective way to promote economic integration as well as a means to boost effective demand and global economic recovery.

Toward a Connected and Seamless Asia Pacific Regional Economy

Thanks to Indonesian leadership in 2013, APEC leaders are now committed to creating a comprehensively connected and integrated Asia Pacific. APEC's Framework on Connectivity (APEC, 2013) looks beyond the 2020 Bogor deadline to a long-term effort to move closer to APEC's agreed vision of a seamless regional economy. Indonesia consulted closely with the next hosts of the APEC process to ensure that the commitment to enhance connectivity is followed up, building on APEC's existing work. A blueprint to be presented to leaders in China in 2014 will elaborate on the scope for reducing transaction costs.

Targets for physical connectivity will include better regional transport and energy networks and universal broadband access. Institutional connectivity will aim for better cross-border financial cooperation and more coherent approaches to economic regulation as well as modernized and harmonized customs procedures. People-to-people links can be enhanced by expanding the coverage of the successful APEC Business Travel Card and by taking advantage of the revolution in higher education toward including innovative use of on-line content.

APEC's Finance Ministers Process has been evaluating policy options to enhance the prospects for long-term investment financing, with the aim of improving regulatory frameworks and planning mechanisms in order to generate a pipeline of bankable infrastructure projects. APEC governments have forged productive links with the business sector through the APEC Business Advisory Council, including

—the Asia Pacific Infrastructure Panel (APIP), which already is working with several governments to boost their capacity to design, finance, and implement economic infrastructure

—the Asia Pacific Financial Forum (APFF), which encourages a convergent approach to managing financial sectors to facilitate regional economic integration.

Visionary leadership by the 2014 G-20 host country, backed by evidence of all-round gains, will be needed to persuade a critical mass of APEC governments to move beyond a blueprint and enthusiastic statements of good intentions by committing the resources needed to launch at least some actual investments. The launch by China of the Asian Infrastructure Investment

Bank provides a new opportunity. Contributions of capital by APEC governments to the AIIB can finance early steps to implement the APEC Framework on Connectivity, avoiding a long debate about whether APEC governments should contribute money to the APEC process and how APEC would manage finance and promote actual investments.

Once some tangible steps are taken, starting with a high-quality APEC master plan on connectivity, the MDBs also can be engaged to enhance Asia Pacific connectivity. They can collaborate with the AIIB to leverage their own financing by mobilizing investment from international capital markets. That can make it possible to launch some significant investments to improve transport and communications links among Asia Pacific economies, for example a coordinated initiative to upgrade the performance of the region's ports and airports. APEC and ASEAN will then be setting an example for the G-20 of how international cooperation can accelerate investment in economic infrastructure.

Toward Global Cooperation on Economic Infrastructure

Almost two decades ago, the late Hadi Soesastro drew attention to the potential for concentric circles of cooperation—first to promote the welfare of ASEAN, then to reach out to others in Asia and across the Pacific, and ultimately to contribute to global welfare.[36] Some economies have already set examples for wider groups on economic integration and can now set positive examples for accelerating investment in infrastructure.

Concentric Circles of Economic Integration

The ASEAN and APEC economies, especially in East Asia, have demonstrated the potential of voluntary cooperation to integrate economies, based on the correct perceptions that

—economies that reduce barriers to trade and investment gain from those reforms

—cooperative arrangements to reduce needless differences in economic regulation or to improve physical, institutional, and people-to-people connectivity among economies lead to mutual benefits.

East Asian governments have acted unilaterally, in their own interest, to eliminate border barriers to almost all trade and investment in order to allow their economies to engage successfully in international production networks.[37]

36. Elek and Soesastro (1997).
37. Baldwin (2012).

In line with the principle of open regionalism, originally adopted by APEC, almost all the liberalization undertaken in the context of the ASEAN Free Trade Agreement was subsequently extended to all economies.[38] The cooperative arrangements to implement the ASEAN Economic Community, such as mutual recognition agreements and technical cooperation to facilitate customs procedures and e-commerce, are open clubs that neighboring economies can join.

The door is certainly open to other APEC economies that wish to participate; in many ways, ASEAN arrangements such as the gradually more efficient single window to facilitate cross-border movement of products are acting as pathways to future APEC-wide arrangements. Any Asia Pacific governments can choose to create the institutions and adopt the policy norms needed to join practical arrangements to reduce transaction costs, such as the APEC Single Window for border clearance or the APEC Travel Card.

In future, arrangements pioneered in ASEAN or APEC will serve as examples for worldwide mutually beneficial economic integration. The positive network effect of additional participants in international transport, communications, and energy grids means that Asia Pacific governments will be keen to help others make the investments needed to link still others to their evolving networks. The fast-accumulating evidence of the very large mutual benefits from joining such cooperative arrangements provides hope of widening the circles of practical cooperative arrangements to improve physical, institutional, and people-to-people connectivity. Doing so is likely to lead to a new, efficient form of global economic integration based on sound perceptions of self-interest. And investments in seizing opportunities to gain from better connectivity will help sustain the momentum of the global economy.

Widening Cooperation to Accelerate Investment in Infrastructure

The opportunity to inject new demand into the global economy by investing in economic infrastructure that increases productivity and does not lead to long-term debt problems is becoming widely recognized. The many constraints on seizing this opportunity can be overcome if some economies produce examples of successful investments, especially those that draw on private sector financing. In recent years, China has been the pathfinder; its investments in infrastructure have helped to prevent world economic production

---

38. Productivity Commission (2010).

from dropping even further below capacity. Much more could be done if other economies also stepped up investment, both to meet their own needs and to improve links to their neighbors.

ASEAN is stepping up investment in economic infrastructure, using new sources of finance, including the AIF and the AIIB. If RCEP governments follow the example set by ASEAN, they can implement their own comprehensive plan to create a wider economic community in East Asia. The combined GDP of RCEP economies account for just over half of that of the APEC group of economies and close to 30 percent of the world economy. Their commitment to making the investments needed to create a well-connected economic community would make a welcome and tangible contribution to global demand. If other APEC economies (accounting for over 55 percent of world GDP) were also willing to commit some of their own resources to mobilize investment to fill gaps in economic infrastructure, they would make an even greater contribution to global welfare as well as to their own economies.

Opposition to increased government spending currently stands in the way of the United States making the investments that are urgently needed to avoid the deterioration of its own stock of economic infrastructure. Therefore, it may not be able to commit funds to coordinated investments in bettering Asia Pacific connectivity for some time. But others in APEC could show the leadership to follow the examples being set in ASEAN and perhaps in the RCEP. At present, the U.S. economic "pivot" to Asia is limited to engaging some economies in negotiations to establish a Trans-Pacific Partnership. Making significant contributions to APEC-wide cooperation to enhance physical, institutional, and people-to-people connectivity would be a more effective way for the United States to demonstrate its future economic commitment to Asia—thereby setting an example for a potentially worldwide deepening of economic integration—as well as its commitment to global economic recovery.

Steering the Global Economy

The G-20 process makes it possible for governments to learn from the examples of others. A review of the extensive opening of Asia Pacific economies to trade and investment demonstrates that most of the "opening to the outside world" by this dynamic group of economies has been by means of unilateral decisions, based on the successful experience of others. Lessons from creating and managing international production networks may persuade G-20 leaders that better physical, institutional, and people-to-people connectivity has become the most effective way to integrate economies. That recognition may lead to a new perception: that trade negotiations, shackled to obsolete mercantilist politics, are not the only way to make progress toward worldwide economic integration.

The 2014 meetings of G-20 finance ministers and leaders afford an opportunity to discuss the efforts of ASEAN and APEC economies to accelerate investment in economic infrastructure, especially investment in better connectivity to integrate their economies more closely. These discussions could help overcome the ideological resistance to boosting public sector investment despite the widening shortfalls in economic infrastructure in most G-20 economies and the evidence of its high multiplier effects on short-term demand combined with higher productivity in years to come.

The G-20 has already initiated cooperative policy development work to help overcome some of the obstacles to steering more of the world's savings into economic infrastructure. In practice, the best way to deal with those obstacles is to learn by example. A strong commitment by G-20 leaders to significant new investment to improve transport and communications links should be sufficient to persuade the MDBs or the new AIIB to assess their huge potential economic returns and use their collective experience to mobilize the expertise and resources to begin to realize some of those gains.

A G-20 commitment to revive the global economy by encouraging productive investment can restore its currently dwindling credibility. If investments in economic infrastructure link more emerging and low-income economies to global markets, that will also shore up the group's legitimacy to be a steering committee for the global economy. And once confidence in a sustained recovery from the 2008 crisis is finally assured, the G-20 may be able to turn its attention to the far greater challenge of scaling up its currently welcome but inadequate commitment to contain global warming.

References

ADBI. 2013. *Connecting South Asia and Southeast Asia: Interim Report.* Asian Development Bank Institute (http://adbi.org/book/2013/05/05/5632.connecting.south.asia.southeast.asia/).

American Society of Civil Engineers. 2013. "2013 Report Card for America's Infrastructure" (www.infrastructurereportcard.org/).

APEC. 1994. "APEC Economic Leaders' Declaration of Common Resolve (Bogor Declaration)," November.

———. 2010. "Progressing towards the APEC Bogor Goals: Perspectives of the APEC Policy Support Unit."

————. 2013. "2013 Leaders' Declaration: Bali Declaration—Resilient Asia-Pacific, Engine of Global Growth," Annex A, October (http://apec.org/Meeting-Papers/Leaders-Declarations/2013/2013_aelm.aspx).

Armstrong, Shiro, and P. Drysdale. 2011. "The Influence of Economics and Politics on the Structure of World Trade and Investment Flows." In *The Politics and Economics of Integration in Asia and the Pacific*, edited by Shiro Armstrong (London: Routledge).

Australian Government. 2013. "G-20 2014: Overview of Australia's Presidency" (www. g20.org/sites/default/files/g20_resources/library/G20Australia2014conceptpaper. pdf).

Baldwin, Richard. 2012. "WTO 2.0: Global Governance of Supply-Chain Trade." *CEPR Policy Insight 64*. Centre for Economic Policy Research. December.

Bhattacharyay, Bishwa Nath. 2010."Estimating Demand for Infrastructure in Energy, Transport, Telecommunications, Water, and Sanitation in Asia and the Pacific: 2010–2020." Working Paper 248. Tokyo: Asian Development Bank Institute.

Checchini, Paolo. 1988. *The European Challenge 1992: The Benefits of a Single Market*. Research study. Aldershot, U.K.: Wildwood House for the Commission of the European Communities.

CSIS (Center for Strategic and International Studies). 2013. *Enhancing India-ASEAN Connectivity*. Lanham, Md.: Rowman and Littlefield (http://csis.org/files/publication/130621_Osius_EnhancingIndiaASEAN_WEB.pdf).

Davies, Robin. 2013. "What Plot? Rationalising the G20's Development Agenda." In *Development and the G20*. Papers and reports. Sydney: Lowy Institute for International Policy.

Drysdale, Peter. 2011. "Re-positioning the G20's Agenda on Development." *East Asia Forum*, October 3 (www.eastasiaforum.org/2011/10/03/re-positioning-the-g20s-agenda-on-development/).

Drysdale, Peter, and D. Simandjuntak. 2013. "Briefing Note on Asia Pacific Economic Cooperation (APEC) 2013." *Indonesian Quarterly* 40, no. 3.

Drysdale, Peter, and S. Willis. 2013. "Asia and the G20." Paper prepared for the Asia and the Pacific Public Policy Society, Crawford School of Public Policy, Australian National University, Canberra, September 7, 2012.

Elek, Andrew. 2011. "How Can Asia Help Fix the Global Economy?" *East Asia Forum*, October 2.

————. 2013. "A New G20 Strategy for Development Cooperation." *East Asia Forum*, July 17.

Elek, Andrew, and H. Soesastro. 1997. "ASEAN, APEC, and ASEM: Concentric Circles and 'Open Clubs.'" Discussion paper. Kuala Lumpur: Institute of Strategic and International Studies.

ERIA (Economic Research Institute for ASEAN and East Asia). 2012. "Mid-Term Review of the Implementation of AEC Blueprint: Executive Summary." October (www. eria.org/publications/key_reports/mid-term-review-of-the-implementation-of-aec-blueprint-executive-summary.html).

G-20. 2011. "High-Level Panel on Infrastructure Recommendations to G-20: Final Report" (www.boell.org/downloads/HPL_Report_on_Infrastructure_10-26-2011.pdf).

G-20/OECD. 2013. "G-20/OECD High-Level Principles of Long-Term Investment Financing by Institutional Investors" (www.oecd.org/finance/private-pensions/G20-OECD-Principles-LTI-Financing.pdf).

Grenville, Stephen. 2013. "Financing for Infrastructure: What Contribution Can the G-20 Make?" In *Tax, Infrastructure, Anti-Corruption, Energy, and the G-20*, Lowy Institute, October (http://lowyinstitute.org/publications/tax-infrastructure-anti-corruption-energy-and-g20).

Lane, Philip 2012. "Cross-Border Financial Integration in Asia and the Macro-Financial Policy Framework." Paper prepared for the 11th BIS annual conference, "The Future of Financial Globalisation." Lucerne, June 21–22.

Lin, Justin, and D. Dömeland. 2012. "Beyond Keynesianism: Global Infrastructure Investments in Times of Crisis." Policy Research Working Paper 5940. Washington: World Bank.

Luddy, William. 2012. "Background Briefing Note on Institutional Connectivity." Paper prepared for the APEC symposium. Jakarta, December.

McKinsey Global Institute. 2013. "Infrastructure Productivity: How to Save $1 Trillion a Year." *Insights and Publications* (January) (www.mckinsey.com/insights/engineering_construction/infrastructure_productivity).

OECD (Organization for Economic Cooperation and Development). 2011. *Pension Funds' Investment in Infrastructure: A Survey*. International Futures Program, Project on Strategic Transport and Infrastructure to 2030.

Productivity Commission (Government of Australia). 2010. "Bilateral and Regional Trade Agreements." Research report. November.

Streeter, William. 2011. "The Quest for Sustainable Infrastructure Finance." In *A Series of Essays*, by William Streeter, prepared for the APEC Finance Minister's Process Workshop. Washington, June 22–23.

Wilson, John S., C. Mann, and T. Otsuki. 2003. "Trade Facilitation and Economic Development: Measuring the Impact." Policy Research Paper 2988. Washington: World Bank.

World Economic Forum. 2013. "Enabling Trade: Valuing Growth Opportunities" (www.weforum.org/reports/enabling-trade-valuing-growth-opportunities).

Contributors

COLIN I. BRADFORD
Nonresident Senior Fellow, Global Economy and Development, Brookings Institution

KEMAL DERVIŞ
Vice President and Director, Global Economy and Development, Brookings Institution

PETER DRYSDALE
Emeritus Professor of Economics, Crawford School of Public Policy, Australian National University; Head of the East Asian Bureau of Economic Research; Coeditor, East Asia Forum

ANDREW ELEK
Research Associate, Crawford School of Public Policy, Australian National University

ROSS GARNAUT
Professorial Research Fellow in Economics, University of Melbourne

HUANG YIPING
Professor of Economics, China Center for Economic Research, Peking University

BRUCE JONES
Senior Fellow and Director, Project on International Order and Strategy, Brookings Institution; Consulting Professor, Stanford University; and Chair, New York University Center on International Cooperation

MUNEESH KAPUR
Adviser to the Executive Director, International Monetary Fund

HOMI KHARAS
Senior Fellow and Deputy Director, Global Economy and Development, Brookings Institution

WONHYUK LIM
Vice President and Director, Department of Competition Policy, Korea Development Institute

RAKESH MOHAN
Executive Director, International Monetary Fund

DAVID NELLOR
Consultant, Jakarta, Indonesia

YOSHIO OKUBO
Vice Chairman, Japan Securities Dealers Association; former Executive Director, World Bank

MARI PANGESTU
Minister of Tourism and Creative Industry, and former Minister of Trade, Republic of Indonesia

CHANGYONG RHEE
Chief Economist, Asian Development Bank

ALOK SHEEL
Secretary, Prime Minister's Economic Advisory Council, Government of India

MAHENDRA SIREGAR
Chairman, Indonesia Investment Coordinating Board; G-20 Sherpa for Indonesia

PAOLA SUBACCHI
Research Director, International Economics, Chatham House, London

CARLOS A. VEGH
Nonresident Senior Fellow, Global Economy and Development, Brookings Institution; Fred H. Sanderson Professor of International Economics, Johns Hopkins University

GUILLERMO VULETIN
Fellow, Global Economy and Development, Brookings Institution

MARIA MONICA WIHARDJA
Economist, World Bank country office, Jakarta, Indonesia; Associate Editor, East Asia Forum

Index

CPSIA information can be obtained at www.ICGtesting.com
Printed in the USA
BVOW04s1128290614

357359BV00002B/7/P

9 780815 725916